THE USA AND THE MIDDLE EAST SINCE WORLD WAR 2

The USA and the Middle East Since World War 2

T. G. Fraser

Head of Department and Senior Lecturer in History
University of Ulster

MACMILLAN

First published 1989

Published by
THE MACMILLAN PRESS LTD
Houndmills, Basingstoke, Hampshire RG21 2XS
and London
Companies and representatives
throughout the world

Typeset by Footnote Graphics
Warminster, Wilts.

Printed in Hong Kong   Essex County Library

British Library Cataloguing in Publication Data
Fraser, T. G. (Thomas G)
The USA and the Middle East since World War 2.
1. Middle East. Foreign relations with United States, 1945–1948.
2. United States. Foreign relations with Middle East, 1948–1983
I. Title
327'.0956
ISBN 0–333–39422–4

For Grace,
Simon and Anna

Contents

Preface

This book charts the progress of American diplomacy in the Middle East from the end of World War 2 to the administration of Ronald Reagan. In order to give some unity to the theme, the Middle East has been taken as the region embracing the Arab world and Israel, and there is an inevitable preoccupation with the Arab–Israeli conflict. The book's origins lie in a public lecture series at Indiana University at South Bend in October 1983 on the theme of 'The United States and the Middle East', occasions which assumed some poignancy as they were accompanied by the tragedy of the marines in Beirut. Chancellor Lester M. Wolfson and his staff did everything possible to ensure a stimulating year at IUSB, when the foundations of this study were laid. Lester and Beth Lamon contributed more than they will ever know.

Further research in the United States was made possible by the British Academy which awarded me a grant to work in the National Archives in Washington, DC, and the Harry S. Truman Library in Independence, Missouri. This was also assisted by the Faculty of Humanities of the University of Ulster and I am glad to acknowledge the help and encouragement of Brian Manning, Keith Jeffery, Peter Roebuck and Richard York. World University Service (Ireland) enabled me to visit Israel, the West Bank, Gaza and the Golan Heights. My stay in Independence was made the more congenial through the hospitality of Mrs Josephine Helm and by the generosity of Alonzo L. Hamby, Wilson Miscamble, Anna Nelson and Gaddis Smith in discussing aspects of the Truman administration and American foreign policy. I am grateful to the staff of the National Archives, especially Sally Marks, and of the Truman Library, especially Niel Johnson. The library staffs of the University of Ulster and Indiana University at South Bend willingly dealt with all my requests for material. David Ross of the University of Ulster carried out invaluable work on the files of the *New York Times* and Felix Agnew, Gillian Coward and Noleen Kennedy of the Faculty of Humanities provided much needed assistance. I am grateful to the staff of the American Israel Public Affairs Committee, Washington, for providing material. I must express general, if inadequate, thanks to all those, American, Arab, British and Israeli, who responded so willingly to my requests for information or comment. My particular thanks must go to Loy W. Henderson and Dean Rusk for their painstaking answers to my enquiries. Responsibility for interpretation is, of course, my own. Thanks are also due to Tim Farmiloe and the staff at Macmillan Press and Susan Kemp.

This book would never have been finished without the help, encouragement and advice of my wife, Grace, who used her historical judgement and analytical skills to criticise and improve my text. This is her book, too.

T. G. Fraser

Introduction

Before her entry into World War 2, the United States of America had few interests, and no obligations, in the Middle East which was then seen as an area dominated by Britain through a subtle network of formal and informal control. Curiosity amongst the public and their representatives was scant. But certain private individuals, and groups, had clearly defined opinions. The most significant groups were Protestant missionary bodies, which had done important educational work in the Levant from the early nineteenth century, and the Zionists, long a minority amongst American Jews, who were working for the creation of a Jewish homeland in Palestine. By 1945, this situation had totally changed. The region had seen both a substantial American military presence and the development of its petroleum resources to help generate the country's war effort. Within a short period after the war's end, the collapse of relations with the Soviet Union meant that the Middle East became an inescapable part of what was seen as a worldwide conflict. Britain's decline dictated America's increasing involvement and though this was played out over a period of years it was irreversible. Strategically, as well as economically, the Middle East had become part of Washington's world commitment and was to remain so.

World War 2 was also responsible for making the future of Palestine the central issue in the Middle East. As news emerged of Hitler's persecution and extermination of European Jewry, any doubts American Jews had about support for Zionism disappeared. The Biltmore Conference in New York in May 1942, which called for Palestine to be made into a Jewish Commonwealth, showed both American Jews' commitment to Zionism and the crucial role they were being called upon to play in realising its aims. Under the leadership of Rabbi Stephen Wise and Rabbi Abba Hillel Silver the American Zionist Emergency Council began to lobby in political circles, which, conscious of what was happening in Europe, felt bound to respond. In January 1943, bi-partisan resolutions were introduced in both houses calling for implementation of the Biltmore Program, the sponsors in the Senate being Robert Wagner (Democrat, New York) and Robert A. Taft (Republican, Ohio). Crucially, in the following year, planks endorsing the Biltmore Program were part of both the Democratic and Republican platforms. On 15

October, President Roosevelt assured Wagner: 'I know how long and ardently the Jewish people have worked and prayed for the establishment of Palestine as a free and democratic Jewish commonwealth. I am convinced that the American people give their support to this aim. If re-elected, I shall help to bring about its earliest realisation.'[1]

In fact, Roosevelt was well aware that the Zionist claim to Palestine was rejected throughout the Arab world, for whom it was an Arab country entitled to be ruled by the Palestinians who formed two-thirds of the population and owned most of the land. Nor were his views on its future as straightforward as his letter to Wagner appeared to suggest. In May 1943, in reply to a letter appealing to him not to adopt the Jewish position on Palestine, he wrote to Ibn Saud of Saudi Arabia, 'it is the view of the Government of the United States that no decision altering the basic position of Palestine should be reached without full consultation with both Arabs and Jews'.[2] In part, his attitude reflected the strongly-held view of the State Department's Division of Near East Affairs that the country's position in the Middle East should not be complicated by pressure for a Jewish state. As the war drew to a close, however, Roosevelt was aware that Palestine would soon become a major issue and was anxious to include it in his thinking for the post-war world. His chance came as he returned from the Yalta Conference in February 1945 by arranging a meeting with Ibn Saud on board the USS *Quincy* in the Great Bitter Lake. The occasion proved to be more picturesque than productive, but the two men did establish a relationship. Any hope Roosevelt might have had of encouraging an Arab–Jewish dialogue over Palestine foundered on Ibn Saud's unyielding opposition to Zionism. For him, it was the responsibility of the Axis countries, not the Arabs, to make restitution to the Jews for what they had suffered. Roosevelt responded by assuring him 'that he would do nothing to assist the Jews against the Arabs and would make no move hostile to the Arab people.'[3]

In his few remaining weeks, he maintained his interest in Palestine. Its 'barren and rocky' terrain, which he had seen from his aircraft on the way to Yalta, had not impressed him but he had clearly been struck by the force of Ibn Saud's views. He was still being pulled in two directions. On 16 March, Stephen Wise, an old and valued ally from the days of the New Deal, visited him and secured a public confirmation of the views he had expressed to Wagner the previous October. The State Department, which was planning for a period of British trusteeship under the new world organisation, immediately

sought to counter what they saw as the ready access to the President
enjoyed by the Zionist leaders. The result was a letter sent in
Roosevelt's name to Ibn Saud confirming what had been said at their
meeting. It proved to be one of his last official acts, for a week later
he was dead.[4] Perhaps he had come close to the position which had
plagued the British throughout their period as League of Nations
Mandatory for Palestine; namely, of being seen to raise the expectations of both sides. That Roosevelt could have resolved this must be a
matter for speculation but it was an uncertain legacy to leave his
inexperienced and unconsulted successor.

By 1945, the principal themes of American involvement in the
Middle East over the next forty years were already present. There
were important strategic and economic interests involving relationships with the Arab world which the State Department felt were its
responsibility to preserve and extend. An extra dimension was the
position of Great Britain, the country's closest ally in the war and an
essential partner in the peace ahead. Specifically, Britain held the
Mandate for Palestine which was already being seen as an urgent and
delicate problem. American legislators had signalled their interest in
its future, partly out of humanitarian concern for the Jews of Europe,
partly prodded by the Zionists. American Jews were stirred as never
before to work for the creation of a Jewish homeland, the more so as
the unimaginable horrors of Hitler's death camps were revealed.
Caught by these competing pressures and emotions, the President
had sought to temporise, if possible to please both sides. Many things
in the Middle East and the United States were to change but these
issues were to recur time and time again.

1 Truman's Search for a Middle East Policy

President Roosevelt died at Warm Springs, Georgia, on 12 April 1945. He was succeeded by Harry S. Truman, a politician of plain Missouri origin who had come through the tough world of Kansas City politics to become the respected chairman of the Senate Special Committee Investigating the National Defense Program in World War 2. Judging Truman to be the kind of man who could see through Congress what would inevitably be controversial plans for post-war reconstruction, Roosevelt adopted him as his running mate in 1944. He had scant experience of foreign affairs, had never ventured abroad apart from his military service in World War 1, and was largely unconsulted by Roosevelt during their brief period together; yet he was fated to be the President who would preside over the era of the atomic bomb, the disintegration of the war-time alliance, the Cold War, the reconstruction of Western Europe, and ultimately war in East Asia. His handling of all these has earned him a notable place amongst American leaders. In Israel he is remembered with affection as a man whose decisive interventions eased the path to Jewish statehood.

Although much has been written about this contribution, his motives and purposes have remained elusive. In the 1970s, both came to be questioned by 'revisionist' historians who saw his Middle Eastern policy as largely shaped by the desire to secure votes for the Democrats, chiefly in New York but also in large and electorally powerful states like Illinois. This interpretation angered former colleagues who countered by emphasising, instead, the essentially humanitarian and idealistic nature of what Truman had done.[1] Truman himself was not much help in resolving this, for his surviving records are hard to interpret. In the years after leaving the presidency in 1953, he understandably took great pride in his role in the creation of the republic which had ended 2000 years of Jewish statelessness, a feeling of achievement reinforced by the way he was fêted by Israeli and American Jewish leaders. At a reception at the Jewish Theological Seminary in 1953, the former President exclaimed that he was Cyrus, a jocular comparison with the Persian credited with the Jews' return to Jerusalem, and in conversation in the early 1960s he could weep at

1

the recollection that the Chief Rabbi of Israel had told him that he had been put in his mother's womb to bring about the re-birth of Israel.[2] By then Truman knew that the decisions he had made had confirmed his place in history, but the contemporary record relates a more complicated series of events than he cared to recollect. While his memoirs describe a relatively uncomplicated progress towards the creation of Israel, his correspondence reveals a more subtle, and hence more interesting, struggle of a leader trying to reach a solution to a problem in which passions were deeply engaged and over which advisers he respected argued for totally opposite policies. His resulting decisions determined the nature of America's involvement in the Middle East.

As Roosevelt had known, the future of Palestine was going to demand urgent decisions once the war ended and the USA would not be able to stand aside. The end of the war in Europe, with its graphic exposure of the Jewish tragedy under Hitler, thrust the Palestine issue before the American public. While the Jews were not the only victims of German rule in Europe, few seriously questioned that the Nazis' particular venom had been reserved for them. With exceptions such as the Danes, the Germans had found willing collaborators throughout Europe. In the city of Hamburg, once noted for its left-wing politics, no one tried to protect the Jews from deportation to the camps of eastern Europe.[3] The Holocaust, as it came to be known, confirmed for most Jews the Zionist message that only through the creation of a state in Palestine could their future be assured. This spurred a campaign of elemental intensity which swept all before it in the next few years. On the military level, this took the form of a co-ordinated campaign by the three Jewish underground groups in Palestine, the Haganah, Etzel and Lehi, to force the British to relinquish their Mandate. War-weary, economically enfeebled, and faced with the country's united Jewish population, the British were soon at their wits' end, their inability to contain the situation revealed to the world by the demolition of their headquarters in a wing of Jerusalem's King David Hotel on 22 July 1946. Anxious to preserve Britain's military and economic stake in the Middle East, Clement Attlee's Labour government tried to favour the Arabs but, lacking the means to defeat the Jewish revolt, it was fast losing control. Taking the initiative on the military front, the Zionists proved to be equally skilled at shaping political events to their advantage. The key to their success proved to be the well-honed campaign which ensured that American politicians and the public were reminded of the Jewish case over Palestine. Convinced that the time for Jewish statehood had come, it was not a time for the faint-hearted either in the military or political arena, though in the latter Zionist enthusiasm came dangerously close to being counter-productive.

Their activities meant that the Zionist message was heard in the White House from the early days of the Truman presidency. 'As far as I am concerned', Truman grumbled in May 1948, 'I don't think there has ever been more lobbying and pulling and hauling than has been carried on by the Jews in this Palestine difficulty with which we have been faced.'[4] But he knew Washington well enough to see lobbying for what it was, and its volume and stridency irritated rather than influenced him. Its point, of course, was to remind him and his political advisers that the strength of feeling amongst American Jews could be used as a political sanction. As the custodian of the Democratic Party's fortunes and a politician to his finger tips, Truman could not ignore this, but it was not the only consideration which weighed with him. In common with most Protestant Americans of rural or small town origins, he knew his Bible and what it said about the Jews' connexions with the Holy Land. Unlike many from such a background, he felt comfortable with Jews. Best known of his Jewish friends was his old army comrade and Kansas City haberdashery partner, Eddie Jacobson. Much less familiar was the important contribution made by Zionist groups in St Louis to his success in the bitterly contested 1940 Democratic primary in Missouri against Lloyd Stark.[5] Finally in the 1930s, dismissed by many as the 'Senator from Prendergast', a creature of the corrupt Kansas City Democrat machine, he had been adopted by the venerable Louis Brandeis who welcomed him into a political and intellectual circle unlike anything he had seen in Missouri.[6] Such friendships and experiences prepared Truman to respond with instinctive sympathy once the scale of the Jewish disaster in Europe had been exposed.

As with most of his countrymen, this empathy with the Jews was not matched by a similar understanding of the Arabs, though Truman was aware that there were two sides to the Palestine problem.[7] In contrast to the skill with which the Zionists pursued their case, Arab handling of affairs after 1945 lacked sureness of touch. This was especially true of the Palestinians who seemed unable to rouse themselves after the effort they had made in the revolt against the British in 1936–39. Their credibility had not been helped by the presence in Germany of Haj Amin al-Husseini, the Mufti of

Jerusalem, and his willingness to recruit Bosnian Muslims into the SS. The image of the Mufti reviewing such units did much to undermine the less well advertised, but highly effective, diplomacy which Ibn Saud of Saudi Arabia and Abdullah of Transjordan had exerted on behalf of the Allies. Arab leaders in Palestine knew how to impress British Colonial Office officials with their courtesy and hospitality but they had scant notion of how to pull the levers of power in Washington and New York. They did not entirely lack a constituency in the United States, for educators, missionaries and former diplomats were willing to argue their case, but they proved no match for the Zionists. In retrospect, it is clear that the Arabs relied too much on the power of their majority in Palestine and what they assumed was the natural justice of their case. While they acknowledged the tragedy that had befallen the Jews, the responsibility for this rested in Europe and they could not admit that part of the Arab birthright should be surrendered to make amends for events in which they had played no part. Their expression of this was not always well calculated to win American sympathy. As the Syrian government expressed it in 1945: 'One injustice cannot be removed by another even more harmful. In this case we will be face to face with the Zionist Nazism against the Arabs instead of a German Nazism against the Jews.'[8] It is hard to avoid the conclusion that as far as influential American circles were concerned, their case went largely by default. Support did come from the State and Defense Departments, but chiefly for strategic and economic reasons. As the international situation worsened, both these factors concerned defence chiefs. In June 1946, the Joint Chiefs of Staff reported their concern that, 'If the peoples of the Middle East turn to Russia, this would have the same impact in many respects as the military conquest of this area by the Soviets.'[9] The belief that a friendly Arab world was essential to Western security meant that when the Palestine question was at its most acute in 1947–48, the head of the newly-created Defense Department, James Forrestal, lobbied strongly against support for a Jewish state.

These views were held even more strongly in the State Department. The three successive Secretaries of State had little impact on the making of policy: Edward Stettinius was a makeweight, James Byrnes became discouraged by the amount of political influence being exerted over Palestine, and George Marshall largely followed the line set by his advisers. The initiation of policy rested largely on the small group of men who formed the Division of Near

Eastern and African Affairs under Loy W. Henderson, who was to become the despair of Truman's White House staff. Henderson had an austere integrity which led him to oppose prevailing orthodoxies which he believed were intellectually flawed. As a specialist in Russian and East European affairs, his deep skepticism about Stalin's purposes had not sat easily with the comfortable notions of the wartime partnership. As a result, he had moved sideways to become Minister to Iraq from November 1943 until returning to head the Division in April 1945. It was in Baghdad that he became aware of the depth of Arab concern over Zionist ambitions. He believed that there were two flaws in the Zionist argument. The best hope for the Jewish survivors in Europe, he felt, would be to settle in the United States, the British Commonwealth and Latin America where they would find greater security than finding fresh problems and uncertainties in a small country in a hostile Middle East. He also sensed that Truman's advisers were misleading him into the belief that a Jewish state could be established in Palestine without violence. Knowing this to be impossible, he felt that it was nothing less than his professional duty to present views totally at odds with what Truman was hearing from other sources. This brought on him the bitter opposition of the Zionist lobbyists and their friends in the White House, even though Henderson retained the respect of Marshall, Under-Secretary Robert Lovett, and of Truman himself.[10] Henderson's Division was not alone in opposing a pro-Zionist policy; it received eloquent support from Dean Rusk, who had particular responsibility for United Nations affairs, and from George Kennan, whose Policy Planning Staff got under way at the height of the Palestine crisis. Henderson, Rusk and Kennan were to form a powerful axis.

If these powerful agencies argued persuasively that support for a Jewish state was against America's interests in the Middle East, they were set against a group of men who felt very differently. Although many influential figures, Jews and non-Jews, were advocating the Zionist case, three in particular profoundly affected the course of events, Truman's old friend Eddie Jacobson, and two of his staff members, Clark M. Clifford and David K. Niles. Jacobson neither initiated nor determined policy. Truman knew perfectly well that his former partner was no expert on Palestine and would not have been influenced by him. Yet from a chronology that Jacobson later compiled, he was evidently in close touch with the White House, if not with the President personally, in the critical months of October and November 1947, and on the eve of the vote on the partition of Palestine he was phoned by Truman's secretary to reassure him of the outcome. Jacobson was never a policymaker but as the events of March 1948 were to show he was a unique channel of communication into the heart of the decision-making process. The State of Israel had every reason to be grateful for his youthful friendship with Harry Truman.[11]

As Special Counsel to the President, Clark Clifford emerged as the key executor of Truman's Middle East policy. Although it was part of his brief to assess political feeling in the country with a view to Truman's re-election, Clifford consistently denied that such factors moulded the President's views, or his own; rather, 'The Jews were entitled to have their own country, and they were entitled to the support of the major powers.'[12] With a lucid legal mind and a fine capacity for rapid negotiation, Clifford proved to be a major asset when Truman decided on a Palestine policy which went against the grain of professional advice.

Clifford did not become a major figure in Middle East affairs until the spring of 1948, but from the start of Truman's presidency David Niles was acknowledged to be the Zionists' key asset in the White House. An intensely private bachelor who died in 1952 before he could begin his projected memoirs, and who made it his practice to destroy office files as a matter of course, Niles has remained an elusive figure, but his pivotal role in the White House makes some analysis of his character and motives unavoidable. Born in Boston, to an orthodox Jewish family called Neyhus, he Americanised his name to Niles, a common enough practice for the time but something his political enemies chose to use against him. Despite their meagre resources, his parents made room for immigrant Jews, a childhood experience which his brother believed led to his later identification with the oppressed. Prevented by family circumstances from proceeding beyond high school, Niles's early employment was in the distribution of motion pictures. Like Truman, he fell victim to post-war circumstances, losing all his savings. Around this time he became active in politics, working in the unsuccessful presidential campaigns of Progressive Robert M. La Follette in 1924 and Democrat Alfred E. Smith four years later. It was with the Roosevelt presidency that he began to make his reputation. As assistant to Harry Hopkins in the Works Progress Administration, he carried much of the work during his chief's illness. By the time the country entered the war, he was publicly identified as a prominent functionary of the New Deal, attracting the enmity of those who denounced Roosevelt's interventionist foreign policy and the 'communistic' measures at home. Much of the attack on Niles was openly anti-Semitic.[13]

Such criticism had no effect on the regard Roosevelt, and then Truman, had for Niles's qualities. As Truman's special assistant for minority affairs, he was well placed to argue the Jewish case. There is no doubt that he felt very deeply the fate of the Jewish survivors in Europe, 'those poor refugees', as he called them.[14] Despite his passion for privacy, there was a romantic streak in Niles which responded to the idea of Jewish statehood, confiding in a young friend in Israel in 1949 that he saw that country's struggles in terms of Lexington, Concord and Bunker Hill.[15] Correspondence from American Zionist leaders which he preserved testify to the contribution which this solitary and self-effacing man made to the creation of Israel. Niles was to die before the Israeli government could fulfil its plan of honouring him in the country he had done so much to assist.

But Truman was always his own man, proud of his ability to take decisions and, above all, resentful whenever he felt he was being pushed too far, whether by the 'experts' of the State Department or by the 'pressure boys' of New York Zionism. The tone was set from the start by a letter Stettinius was moved to send him six days into his presidency. Warning him that he would soon be lobbied by Zionist leaders, the Secretary offered the patronising advice that he should handle the question of Palestine 'with the greatest care and with a view to the long-range interests of the country'. As the matter was 'highly complex', Truman would wish to 'call for full and detailed information before taking any particular position'.[16] This was not the tone best calculated to win the new President's sympathy, but the Department was clearly anxious to pre-empt any Zionist moves by ensuring that Truman was committed to his predecessor's 'full consultation' formula. With the war in Europe ending, he had many other preoccupations and in the course of May letters over his name were sent to Amman and Cairo reassuring them that there would be no retreat from this formula.[17] The State Department had apparently succeeded in using these early days to set down a marker preventing Truman from making any hasty gestures towards the Zionists, but as Evan Wilson of Near Eastern Affairs later complained, it was 'the last time that the Department exercised a dominant role in our Palestine policy'.[18]

Stettinius had correctly judged that the Zionists would not long delay bringing their case before the new administration. At a meeting on 20 June with Henderson and his staff, Dr Nahum Goldmann of the world Jewish Congress warned of the rising temper among Jews who 'had seen millions of their fellow Jews ruthlessly murdered, their homes destroyed, and their culture completely stamped out, in certain parts of Europe'. If the British and American governments failed to make an imminent move over Palestine, then moderate leaders like Chaim Weizmann and himself could not hold the line against those who were prepared to resort to violence. In a further meeting a week later, Goldmann was joined by David Ben-Gurion in what turned out to be a revealing exchange. When asked by Henderson if their immediate aim was to assist immigration into Palestine, Ben-Gurion naturally agreed, but added that it was not enough: 'they had come to the point where they could no longer accept anything less than the granting of all their demands including the immediate establishment of a Jewish State'.[19] The Zionist leadership was already working along these lines, lobbying both at the United Nations Conference on International Organisation at San Francisco and for Truman to raise the issue with Churchill and Stalin at their forthcoming meeting in Potsdam. Although the subject was not on the agenda at Potsdam, Truman did raise it with Churchill, asking that the 1939 White Paper restrictions on Jewish immigration be eased and for some statement of British intentions on Palestine. But this proved badly timed as Churchill lost the election in the course of the conference and his Labour successor Clement Attlee had to be non-committal.[20]

But the exchange showed how Truman's attention had been engaged. His views were still forming and he had still a long way to go before adopting the full Zionist programme of a Jewish state; interestingly, a survey reported to Niles in early April that 59 per cent of Americans favoured the idea while 42 per cent would welcome the United States exerting its influence to bring it about.[21] Despite the fact that by the end of May Senator Wagner and others were lobbying in Congress for such a programme, Truman confined his efforts to trying to find a home for the Jewish displaced persons in the European camps. Even so, his efforts to help them were not entirely focused on Palestine. In June he told Jacobson that he was trying to get large numbers of them admitted to the United States but was being thwarted in Congress.[22] In an attempt to find out more about the condition and wishes of the displaced persons, he sent Earl G. Harrison, Dean of the University of Pennsylvania Law School, to

Europe. Deeply affected by what he saw there, Harrison reported that for many of the survivors the only acceptable solution was emigration to Palestine and he accepted the Jewish Agency's suggestion that 100 000 immigration certificates be issued. Harrison was seeing the displaced persons at their lowest and the details in his report touched Truman's sympathies: 'The misery it depicted could not be allowed to continue', was how he later described his reaction.[23] Moreover, if the Jewish displaced persons wished to go to Palestine, he could avoid the politically sensitive issue of a mass relaxation of immigration quotas into the United States of America. Harrison's adoption of the 100 000 figure came to be engraved on the record of Truman's diplomacy.

Even before Harrison had reported, Truman made a public commitment linking the displaced persons with Palestine. Asked to define his Palestine policy at his press conference on 16 August, he replied that it was to get as many Jews into the country as possible, an answer which triggered an immediate alarm in Arab capitals. On 31 August, armed with Harrison's report, he entered the debate over Palestine with a long letter to Attlee. Taking the figure of 100 000, he asked the British to issue that number of immigration certificates: 'I concur in the belief that no other single matter is so important for those who have known the horrors of concentration camps for over a decade as is the future of immigration possibilities into Palestine'. Attlee's reply was not encouraging. Arguing that the camps held people of all nationalities who had suffered under Hitler, he said it would do the Jews no service to put them 'at the head of the queue', an insensitive phrase, which was to cause great offence when later published. As far as Palestine was concerned. Britain still was responsible for its affairs and 'had the Arabs to consider as well as the Jews'. Attlee concluded by reminding Truman of the American commitment to full consultation with the Arabs before reaching any decision.[24] Two things were clear. Truman's campaign for the 100 000 had stalled at the start and the British were not going to take kindly to Washington's interference in an area they regarded as their own, however vexatious its problems might be. The pattern of relations between the two countries had been set and was fated not to improve as the Palestine problem grew increasingly embittered.

These early moves showed that the President was already mapping out a course of action independent of, and unwelcome to, his officials in the State Department. Uneasy that his sympathy with the victims of Nazism and exposure to political pressure were leading him into policies which they believed would harm the national interest, by mid-August Henderson and his staff were preparing a counter-offensive. Their fears were not eased when they learned of Truman's letter to Attlee which had by-passed usual State Department channels. From early September 1945, they had an important ally in the new Under-Secretary, Dean Acheson, who 'had learned to understand, but not to share, the mystical emotion of the Jews to return to Palestine and end the Diaspora'.[25] Highly articulate men, Acheson and Henderson provided a counter to the established pro-Zionist forces in Congress and, increasingly, in the White House.

Alarmed at the tone of Truman's press conference, on 24 August Henderson presented the Secretary of State with his division's analysis of the possible solutions for Palestine. Four possibilities were considered. The first was the adoption of the Biltmore Program, making Palestine into a Jewish Commonwealth, which would fulfil the promises made by both parties in the 1944 elections and the wishes of the American Zionists. Because of the strong support this enjoyed, Henderson was anxious to point out that:

... in our considered opinion the active support by the Government of the United States of a policy favoring the setting up of a Jewish state in Palestine would be contrary to the policy which the United States has always followed of respecting the wishes of a large majority of the local inhabitants with respect to their form of government. Furthermore, it would have a strongly adverse effect upon American interests throughout the Near and Middle East.

Support for Palestinian independence as an Arab State was also judged to be unacceptable, not just for the obvious domestic political reasons but also because 'it would fail to give to the large Jewish minority in Palestine the just and equitable treatment to which that minority is entitled'. Partition was acknowledged to be gaining support among sections of the Jewish leadership, but on the evidence of the 1938 British Woodhead Commission it was believed to be impracticable. This led to the division's preferred way forward; namely, that Palestine should be retained under British trusteeship as a land sacred to the three religious groups. In such an arrangement, Arabs and Jews would 'be recognized as national communities having jurisdiction over all those rural districts, villages, towns and cities where the Arabs and Jews respectively are in the majority, with the exception of Haifa, Jerusalem, and the undeveloped areas of the Jordan Valley and the Negeb.'[26] While they knew that this idea fell far short of Arab or Jewish aspirations, Henderson and his staff saw it as the only option which might be politically viable while doing the least damage to American interests. It totally underestimated Zionist determination and the tide of emotion running in their favour, but it became orthodoxy in the State Department which pursued it with remarkable tenacity down to the day that the State of Israel was proclaimed.[27]

With Acheson's support, the division tried to ensure that the administration held to the State Department line on Palestine. At his press conference on 26 September, the President appeared to dismiss the terms of Roosevelt's letter to Ibn Saud. Acheson felt he should be reminded of the nature of his predecessor's commitment, arguing that Truman's request to the British to admit 100 000 Jews into Palestine would run counter to what had been pledged. His stricture that 'The disposition on our part to fail to carry out our promises would constitute the severest kind of blow to American prestige not only in the Near East but elsewhere' was not calculated to win over the President.[28] Henderson had also been building up a case to show the extent to which a pro-Zionist policy would damage national interest, not just in the region. In October he presented Byrnes with an analysis he had secured from the War Department examining the military implications of the expected Arab reaction if immigration restrictions on Jews were relaxed. It was not reassuring, for the military estimated that as the British could no longer contain the situation, an indefinite American commitment of between 200 000 and 300 000 would be needed. Such a burden would seriously impair the two countries' ability to sustain the occupation of Germany and Japan, while involving 'an indefinite delay in demobilization of U.S. Army forces', a matter of the greatest political sensitivity.[29] Acheson and Henderson might have been allowed to congratulate themselves in undermining the Zionist case, their success seemingly confirmed on 12 October when Byrnes reassured the Egyptian, Iraqi, Syrian and Lebanese Ministers that his government had not wavered from the 'full consultation' formula.[30] Seeking to underline its position, the following week the State Department secured publication of Roosevelt's letter promising Ibn Saud that he would take no action hostile to the Arabs.[31]

Henderson and his officials needed to look to their corner, for other factors were at work which were confirming that the State Department was only one part of the decision-making process. In fact, they had already lost the initiative, clearly indicated in mid-December when Byrnes told his officers in the Middle East that 'full consultation' with Arabs and Jews did not imply 'agreement' with them, a significant qualification. In the previous two months, pressure had again built up in political circles for some positive move over Palestine, a growing aspect of which was political manoeuvring between the two parties. On 19 October, Byrnes confessed to Lord Halifax, the British Ambassador, how he and the President needed to keep a watchful eye on the New York mayoral election where Paul O'Dwyer was being opposed by Jewish Republican Jonah Goldstein.[32] New York politics were to accompany the Palestine question as it unfolded. Equally, there was the possibility that the Republicans might steal the initiative over Palestine, for the leadership of American Zionism was passing to Abba Hillel Silver whose antipathy to Roosevelt's policies had made him cordially disliked by Truman and Niles. At the end of October, the White House received disquieting intelligence that the previous bi-partisan approach might be about to collapse. An alarmed Wagner learned of the Republican intention to introduce a pro-Zionist resolution on their own and requested a 'rather vital politically' meeting with the President.[33] The Democrats could not ignore these developments, not least because the opening of the Nuremberg trials on 20 November reminded the world in the most graphic way of the fate of some 6 000 000 Jews. The Republican threat never developed, possibly because of Taft's known opposition and, on 17 and 19 December, Senate and the House adopted a joint motion demanding the free entry of Jews into Palestine 'so that they may freely proceed with the upbuilding of Palestine as the Jewish national home'. Such was the political consensus, that there was little debate in either chamber. As 1945 ended, the gap between the State Department and the legislature over the Middle East could not have been wider; equally, the Democrats now faced the possibility of their flank being turned.

Truman still hesitated. He knew what the political position was but he had been sufficiently impressed by professional advice to fret over the resolution. 'I told the Jews', he wrote, 'that if they were willing to furnish me with five hundred thousand men to carry on a war with the Arabs, we could do what they are suggesting in the Resolution – otherwise we will have to negotiate awhile. What I am trying to do is make the whole world safe for the Jews. Therefore, I don't feel like going to war for Palestine.'[34] This reference to negotiation referred to the way that the British had conveniently rescued him from having to make any immediate commitments. His intervention over the

100 000 certificates had touched a raw nerve with the British who rather uncharitably viewed it as the gratuitous interference of a man who had his eye to domestic politics but who had no responsibility for the complex realities of Palestine. Although opinion in London was divided on the wisdom of the move, Foreign Secretary Ernest Bevin was determined that if the Americans chose to interfere then they should be made to face these realities. On 4 October, he convinced his colleagues that the Americans should be invited to participate in an Anglo–American committee to examine at first hand the problems of Palestine and the displaced persons.

As conveyed to Washington, however, Palestine did not feature in the proposed terms of reference for the committee, which, it was suggested, would 'examine the position of the Jews in British and American occupied Europe', and as a result find out the extent to which the Jews who did not wish to be settled there could be found homes in 'other countries outside Europe'.[35] Truman and Byrnes wanted a clearer emphasis on Palestine. Thus when the agreed terms of reference were announced on 13 November, the Anglo–American Committee of Inquiry was charged with examining the 'political, economic and social conditions in Palestine as they bear upon the problem of Jewish immigration and settlement therein and the well-being of the people now living therein'.[36] Opinion has varied on whether this alteration in the terms of reference represented a victory for the Zionists. Certainly, opinion amongst the Jewish Agency thought not, but it is difficult not to catch the significance of the fact that the administration had deliberately brought Palestine to the top of the committee's agenda.[37]

This is confirmed by the importance the White House attached to having men on the committee who were known to sympathise with the Zionist position. The two governments had agreed that there would be no members of Arab or Jewish extraction, but Truman's initial list included Walter Clay Lowdermilk, whose enthusiasm for Jewish colonisation was well known, Frank W. Buxton, James G. McDonald and Bartley C. Crum. In the event, Lowdermilk did not serve, but McDonald, Crum and, to a lesser extent, Buxton, became leading advocates of the Zionist position when the committee began its work. McDonald's warm support for the Jews resulted from his time as League of Nations High Commissioner for Refugees from Germany in the 1930s. Crum was a liberal lawyer from San Francisco who was close to Niles. Although dismissed as a lightweight by the other committee members, he provided a direct link between its work and Niles's office. His membership was to ensure that the White House had its man at the heart of the committee's work.[38] Conscious of the accusation in Congress that such committees were merely a cover for procrastination, the administration insisted that it report within 120 days. Even so, the immediate effect of its work was to take the linked issues of Palestine and the displaced persons out of the Washington political spotlight for much of the winter of 1945–46.

Innocent of the nuances of the Palestine problem though they might be, the committee members were soon brought up against its passions. The Soviet government barred them from pursuing their investigations in its zones of Germany and Austria or in Bulgaria, Rumania and Hungary. The Jewish Agency made it known that its executive had only agreed to co-operate by a narrow margin, while the Arab League announced that it did not recognise the committee's right 'to decide the Palestine issue'.[39] Nonetheless, as a rare, and in the event unique, example of Anglo–American co-operation over Palestine, it worked surprisingly well. It proved a taxing experience. Evidence was heard in Washington and London, after which the committee split into sub-groups to visit the camps in Germany, Austria, Poland and Czechoslovakia. A similar pattern was followed in the Middle East. After hearing the Arab case in Cairo, groups of committee members visited Baghdad, Amman, Damascus, Beirut and Riyadh. Finally, the committee went to Palestine for extensive hearings with the Jewish Agency, the Arab Higher Committee and the Mandatory government. By the time they retired to Lausanne to consider what they had seen and heard, the members possessed a formidable body of evidence on the post-war state of Palestine and of the Jews of Europe. Perhaps because of this weight of material, they did not feel sufficiently confident to draft a detailed plan for the country's future.[40]

As might have been expected among twelve men from two national jurisdictions, unanimity proved elusive. While there was reasonable agreement on acceding to the Jewish Agency's demand for the admission of 100 000 Jews into Palestine, there was much less on the country's political future. The pro-Zionist members, Crum and McDonald, pressed for a form of partition which would allow a Jewish state in part of Palestine, but they could not convert their colleagues who 'felt partition was the solution only if the two sides could agree, but without agreement it seemed likely to aggravate the situation and lead to conflict'.[41] As they could agree that Palestine should become neither an exclusively Arab nor Jewish state, three obvious lines of recommendation were thus ruled out. The principles which governed the committee's findings on Palestine, then, were defined as follows: '(1) That Jew shall not dominate Arab and Arab shall not dominate Jew in Palestine. (2) That Palestine shall be neither a Jewish state nor an Arab state.' The reasoning behind these principles was nothing if not exalted: 'the fact that it is the Holy Land sets Palestine completely apart from other lands and dedicates it to the precepts and practices of the brotherhood of man, not of narrow nationalism'.[42] How this ideal state was to be brought about was less than clear, though the committee's recommendation that 'a long period of trusteeship' would be necessary was close to the thinking of the State Department.[43]

Rejection of the Zionist case was a clear setback for their hopes, but they could take satisfaction from, and make good use of, the committee's one clear-cut recommendation; namely, 'that 100 000 certificates be authorised immediately for the admission into Palestine of Jews who have been the victims of Nazi and Fascist persecution'. In presenting these recommendations, the committee took it for granted that their report would be accepted, or presumably rejected, by the two governments in its entirety. They saw their report as a judicious one in which they had balanced the claims of the two sides. 'The last thing the members anticipated', Evan Wilson later observed, 'was that one or two of their recommendations would be accepted and not the entire report.'[44] But that was to be its fate.

The committee's proceedings had been watched with keen interest and no little apprehension by the parties involved, not least in the White House. Truman kept in touch with its work through Crum and Niles and in February intervened at least twice in its deliberations, once to head off Crum's threatened resignation. As the committee was supposed to be independent this had to be done with consider-able delicacy. 'I am trying to play down my talks with the President', Niles confided in Henderson, while to Crum he wrote, 'Yesterday we sent word to the Commission our advice that there be no interim report. Nothing is to be construed as any attempt on the part of any one over here to suggest how the Committee should conduct itself.'[45] While Crum's was not a decisive voice in the committee's affairs, Niles's correspondence reveals the deep concern felt in the White House over what might be proposed. Henderson certainly believed that it was through Crum and Niles that the American Zionist leadership kept itself informed of how the committee was proceeding.[46]

Conceding the substance of neither the Arab nor the Jewish claim, the report's reception on 1 May 1946 was less than rapturous. Incensed that their hopes of independence had once again been relegated to a distant future and that the Jews had been given their 100 000 immigrants, the Arab Higher Committee called a general strike. The Jewish Agency Executive, though pleased with the latter recommendation, were equally bitter at the rejection of their claim to statehood, feeling that the aim of Zionism had 'been sacrificed to philanthropy', and confirming the fears of those who had felt uneasy at the linking of the issues of Palestine and the displaced persons.[47] The British reaction was tepid and mixed. Not without serious misgivings, Bevin saw the committee's proposals as the way to involve the Americans directly with Palestine. Attlee's initial statement to the House of Commons was very cautious but indicated that his government would need to know the degree of possible American commitment before proceeding to admit 100 000 Jews. Privately, Bevin told the Americans what he wanted from them. To admit this number would, he argued, put the British in an unacceptable military position, both because of the expected Arab reaction and the increased fighting potential of the Jewish underground. The two and a half divisions in Palestine could barely contain the situation as it was; the increased military burden would involve another two divisions which the British did not have. 'It would be necessary', Bevin argued, 'for American forces of the required strength to be immediately available before the policy recommended could be endorsed by the British Government.' He also questioned how the additional 100 000 were to be paid for and indicated that his government 'would be glad to know to what extent it can count on American financial assistance should it be decided to put these measures into operation'.[48] By accepting equal partnership in the Anglo–American Committee, the United States had become involved in the search for a solution in Palestine; Bevin was simply pointing out that participation might also entail responsibility.

Truman did see the report as a positive way forward. In February 1948, he informed Senator Carl A. Hatch: 'It has been a most difficult problem. I thought we had it all settled once after the report of the British American Commission on Palestine but the settlement was upset.'[49] Three days after he had recognised the State of Israel he told a correspondent in New York that: 'In 1946 when the British–American Commission on Palestine was appointed and Mr. Bevin had made an agreement with me that he would accept the findings of that Commission I thought we had the problem solved but the emotional Jews of the United States and the equally emotional Arabs in Egypt and Syria prevented that settlement from taking place, principally because of the immigration clause in that settlement.'[50] Although a simplified view of why the committee's proposals failed to achieve any momentum, as an indication of the President's views, this has the ring of truth. On 11 May 1946, he wrote to Edmund J. Kaufmann of the United Jewish Appeal: 'I hope the Palestine situation will work out as suggested in the report of the British American Commission.'[51]

This was in response to Kaufmann's appeal to the President to proceed with the 100 000 proposal and, significantly, congratulating him on the influence he had brought to bear in having this accepted, something he had learned from Niles. The report's publication signalled the start of an intensive lobbying campaign on behalf of the 100 000 immigrants, though not for the acceptance of those parts which dismissed Zionist claims to statehood. On 2 May, Silver, Wise, Goldmann and other leaders of the Jewish Agency wrote to Truman promising their organisation's assistance with the immediate implementation of this provision. Pressure was intense. Realising that the British would put obstacles in the way of the immigration provision, Zionist leaders and their friends in Congress urged immediate action.[52]

An indication of the degree of pressure Truman was under at this time, and of his resentment, came in late June when the tireless Representative Emanuel Celler put together a bi-partisan delegation of both Senators and thirty Representatives from New York to lobby him. Determined not to receive them, Truman resorted to having his staff phone Celler's office at a time when he was known to be out of town! But his stalling tactics had no effect. Celler continued to press Niles and Matt Connolly, Truman's appointments secretary, reminding them that New York was facing a crucial election and that it would be 'bad politics' for the President not to meet them.[53] However much Truman might like the report, its practical effect was to push him in two directions he did not especially want to go: the British demand for his military and financial assistance and the insistence of American Zionists that he move quickly to implement that part of its recommendations which suited them. The hard realities of Palestine were making themselves felt.

The first was never a serious possibility. On 7 June, the State Department asked the Joint Chiefs of Staff to consider the British request for military assistance and the strategic consequences of a joint trusteeship for Palestine. Military involvement in the Middle East was the last thing defence chiefs wanted. At a time when Churchill's Fulton speech had sounded the alarm many were feeling over Stalin's intentions in Europe, the country was implementing the most dramatic demobilisation in history. American forces, which had numbered 12 123 455 at the end of hostilities, were now some 3 030 088 and falling fast. By 1947, they were down to 1 582 999, with the army's strength no more than 685 458. Faced with such figures, which reflected the nation's desire to return to normal civilian life, there was not the slightest chance of the Joint Chiefs contemplating a military role in Palestine: 'We urge that no U.S. armed forces be involved in carrying out the Committee's recommendations. We recommend that in implementing the report, the guiding principle be that no action should be taken which will cause repercussions in Palestine which are beyond the capacities of British troops to control.'[54] Their reply, which was seen by Truman at the end of June, was a weighty reminder to him of the complexity of the situation. Aware of this, yet sensitive to the aspirations of Celler and American Zionism, he spent the following months groping toward an acceptable Middle Eastern policy.

In doing so, he had to balance the conflicting advice being offered by his professional and political advisers, the latter acutely conscious of the strength of American Jewish feeling over the 100 000 Displaced Persons. Realising this, but relieved that the committee's recommendations fell far short of Jewish statehood, the State Department tried to chart a way forward which would be politically acceptable, while sensitive to the country's Middle Eastern interests. Henderson drafted a telegram in which Truman would impress upon the British the urgency over the 100 000 immigration certificates and proposing a machinery for the two governments to consult both parties in Palestine, as well as the Arab states and American groups. In forwarding this, Acheson made it clear that a possible outcome might be to place Palestine under United Nations trusteeship.[55] In advising Truman on this, Niles tried to find a way round the apparent blocking mechanism of Roosevelt's 'full consultation' formula by drawing a distinction between a change of policy over Palestine and the transfer of '100 000 human beings'. His suggestion appealed, for the 100 000 figure had dominated the President's thinking over the past year: 'The late President made a commitment to the King of Arabia in a famous letter which later I confirmed. We have to consult both sides.

I doubt if the 100 000 necessarily means any change of policy – but the whole report does.'[56] On this occasion at least, Niles and Henderson seemed to agree on the way forward.

But to emphasise the 100 000 immigrants was the wrong way to attract the British. Interestingly, on the same day that Niles was considering the State Department's draft telegram, Crum informed him that he believed that the British would not implement the report. From what he had heard from senior British figures in Palestine, he told Niles that the request for military assistance was a blind.[57] The British response seemed to confirm this, for Attlee's reply to Truman's telegram was non-committal. Far from acknowledging any urgency over the 100 000, it did not mention them. The British were still insisting that any hope of implementing the report would depend on financial and military assistance from Washington.[58] While these issues were being debated, it fell to Niles to fight off the inevitable frustration building up amongst the Zionists and their supporters.

The Zionists had long known that Britain could be vulnerable to American pressure. Financially devastated by the war but committed to ambitious schemes of social welfare, in September 1945 the British government opened negotiations for an American loan. Isolationism was not dead and this could not be taken for granted. American Zionists were divided about the opportunity this presented. Loyal to his Rooseveltian traditions, Stephen Wise supported the loan, while Silver and others saw it as the chance to lobby effectively against the British.[59] Niles was well aware of these moves and his papers offer some fascinating insights into the nature of the campaign. In February 1946, Dr Edward Acheson of George Washington University was approached by Rabbi Baruch Korff with a view to writing articles opposing the loan. As he was Dean Acheson's brother, any such action would have had considerable impact. Acheson learned that $240 000 had been raised to finance the campaign and he was assured that any articles would be placed in the Hearst press and the New York papers. Such backing was assured because the American Zionist Emergency Committee and the American Committee for a Free Palestine were behind the campaign. Korff confided that they did not expect to defeat the loan but that by forcing delays they could extract important concessions from the British.[60] Niles did not approve of this, especially if Silver were involved. Hence, when Silver publicly attacked the loan, he lobbied to ensure that other Jewish leaders, including Wise, supported it. His activities helped ensure that the House approved the loan on 13 July 1946, but once again the White House had been made aware of the intense emotions with which they were dealing and how these related to the political balance.[61] As the summer passed with increasing tension in Palestine and scant agreement between Washington and London, these pressures could only increase.

Important as the events in Washington had become, the pace of events was being forced in Palestine, where the Anglo–American Committee's findings had not been well received by the Jewish leadership. Convinced that nothing short of statehood could ensure their future, the three underground groups intensified their campaign. On 17 June, the Haganah destroyed the main bridges out of Palestine. On the 29th, the British responded with a two-week systematic search of Jewish areas, detaining leading officials of the Jewish Agency. As Jewish resentment grew, the attack on the King David Hotel followed. Equally effective was the Haganah campaign to organise the shipping of illegal immigrants from the Displaced Person camps in Europe. These ships were invariably intercepted off the Palestine coast and their passengers interned in Cyprus. But their appearance in the newsreels of America served to reinforce the image of floundering British heartlessness and the need to remedy Jewish homelessness.

The administration could not ignore a situation which touched the emotions of so many Americans. At Henderson's suggestion, on 11 June it was announced that Palestine would be handled by a special Cabinet Committee of the Secretaries of State, War and Treasury. The real work was done by their deputies under the chairmanship of Henry F. Grady to whom Truman turned when faced with the furious Zionist reaction to the British military actions of 29 June. On 2 July, in response to a protest visit from Wise, Silver, Goldmann and Louis Lipsky, he issued a statement requesting the release of the Jewish leaders and expressing his 'regret at these developments in Palestine'. More tangibly, Grady and his colleagues were flown to London in Truman's personal plane to try to secure some movement on the 100 000 immigrants.[62] In joint meetings with the British minister Herbert Morrison, Grady agreed to a solution which the Colonial Office had favoured for some time but which the Anglo–American Committee had rejected. The 'Morrison–Grady Plan', as it came to be known, provided for continued trusteeship, but with autonomy for Arab and Jewish provinces, with Jerusalem and the Negev retained by the British. In reporting this to Washington, Ambassador Averell

Harriman concluded that 'this plan seems to offer the only means now apparent of moving the 100 000 into Palestine in the near future'. From Paris, where he was attending the Peace Conference, Byrnes also telegraphed his approval.[63]

But the scheme fell far short of Jewish hopes and expectations and quickly collapsed once details were leaked by members of Grady's staff. Despite Byrnes's efforts to launch it, the plan failed to survive the concentrated assault which was now made upon it. Disillusioned, he later castigated Niles for intervening decisively against it on political grounds, but his was not the only voice.[64] As hastily as he had been sent, Grady was recalled. At a meeting with the American members of the Anglo–American Committee his plan was denounced as incompatible with their recommendations. Such was the depth of feeling that Acheson, the unfortunate chairman of the meeting, later noted that the 'Archangel Gabriel would have declined the assignment'.[65] As telegrams of protest once again flooded into the White House, Truman at last bowed to Celler's request to meet the New York congressional delegation – but not with a good grace. A curt note of thanks from Celler merely acknowledged the differences between them.[66] A meeting with James McDonald and New York Senators Wagner and Mead proved equally fiery. 'It has been a most difficult problem', he told McDonald, 'and I have about come to the conclusion that there is no solution, but we will keep trying.'[67] The campaign worked. Although he had liked the Morrison–Grady plan, on 7 August he telegraphed his rejection to Attlee.[68]

The plan's quick death marked an important step in the development of American policy. At one level, it put an end to hopes for Anglo–American co-operation over Palestine, confirming for the British their view that American Middle East policy would turn at the beckoning of domestic pressures. They could be forgiven for thinking so. Byrnes was particularly galled by what had happened and took little further interest in Palestine. Truman's letters suggest that he was open to any well-constructed plan for Palestine's future, provided it contained provision for the 100 000 immigrants. They also show his growing irritation at the amount of lobbying which was being directed at him, particularly as it showed signs of being successful.

Rejection of the Morrison–Grady proposals now meant that the Americans could not have much hope of influencing the discussions which the British convened in London in September. It was never a very promising affair, for neither the Arabs nor Jews of Palestine would attend, though their positions were well enough known. The Arabs had not abated their demand that Palestine should become independent as a unitary state, with minority rights for the Jews. For its part, however, the Jewish Agency had considerably modified the Biltmore Program. At a meeting in Paris, its Executive had secretly agreed to negotiate for a partition scheme which would allow a Jewish state in an acceptable part of Palestine, and an American endorsement of this would clearly strengthen their hand in negotiating with the British. What then took place has become a matter of controversy, for not only was the London conference under way but the USA was heading towards congressional and gubernatorial elections in which the Democrats were known to be fighting from behind. Not only were people chafing against wartime controls, but, on 20 September, Truman dismissed from his cabinet former Vice-President Henry A. Wallace, the last important link with the New Deal. In these circumstances, it is not surprising that leading American Zionists would wish to use their political muscle at a time when their compatriots in Palestine needed it most. In fact, they were not unanimous that this should be done, with Wise and Silver as usual on opposite sides.[69] Truman's intervention was finally prompted by the news on 2 October that the London conference was being adjourned until mid-December; in short, that the Democrats would face the elections with no movement on the 100 000 immigrants. To the fury of the British government, which was engaging in sensitive negotiations with the Zionist leadership, Truman chose the festival of Yom Kippur on 4 October to issue a lengthy disavowal of the postponement and a definition of the administration's position which went much further than any before. It was obvious that the statement would recount his efforts on behalf of the 100 000 and plead for some movement before another winter settled on the camps in Europe. But it went beyond that by identifying the Jewish Agency's move towards partition as the best way forward. 'To such a solution', the statement went, 'our Government could give its support.'[70]

The President was well aware of the domestic political context in which this was being said. To Celler, who wrote to reassure him of the very desirable political effect upon their chances in New York, he replied that it was 'merely a reiteration of the policy I have been urging since August 1945, but it was necessary to make it at this time'.[71] This was only true as far as the 100 000 immigrants were concerned. Support for partition was the start of a new phase in his policy, though that could hardly have been discerned at the time. Once a course of action registered with Truman he tended to stay with it; the dogged way he had pursued the 100 000 immigration certificates had shown that. As partition became settled as the Jewish Agency's aim, his commitment to it in the Yom Kippur statement assumed a fundamental importance in his own Middle East policy. Nothing more was heard of Roosevelt's commitments to 'full consultation'; Truman had moved toward support for Jewish statehood. Upset by the degree of pressure which had been put upon him to reach that position and still uncertain as to the way forward, he lamented on 22 October:

> That solution is insoluble in my opinion. I have spent a year and a month trying to get some concrete action on it. Not only are the British highly successful in muddling the situation as completely as it could possibly be muddled, but the Jews themselves are making it almost impossible to do anything for them. They seem to have the same attitude toward the 'underdog' when they are on top as they have been treated as 'underdogs' themselves. I suppose that is human frailty.[72]

2 The USA and the Birth of Israel

The years 1947 and 1948 saw America's decisive entry into Middle East affairs when Truman first ensured that the resolution for the partition of Palestine found the necessary two-thirds majority in the United Nations General Assembly and then extended *de facto* recognition to the State of Israel within minutes of its proclamation. These actions were the logical sequel to the Yom Kippur statement but they only became possible as the result of a chain of events which could not have been foreseen and after keen in-fighting in the Washington bureaucracy. At the end of 1946, Henderson and his staff tried to undo the damage which they believed the President's statement had dealt to American interests. Although acknowledging that 'the almost world-wide feeling of insecurity felt by Jews, results in something like a cosmic urge with respect to Palestine', they argued that Zionist lobbying had led the administration to adopt an ill-defined policy of support for a Jewish state through partition. Unconvinced of the wisdom of this, they returned yet again to their proposal for a continuing form of British trusteeship under the United Nations, pending a satisfactory formula for Palestinian independence.[1] This stood no chance of satisfying the Zionists whose stance was, if anything, hardening. When their Congress met in Basle in December 1946, Weizmann and Wise, figures of semi-legendary reputation, found themselves thrust aside, and Silver became head of the Jewish Agency's work in the United States. At issue was whether they would accept the partition of Palestine, or, as Silver wished, hold out for the full Biltmore Program. It did not bode well for an accommodation with the British who were about to re-convene the London conference in a final attempt to negotiate a settlement acceptable to both Arabs and Jews.

Few in the United States appreciated the degree of weariness felt by British ministers and their officials. The post-war years had been grim and the country was passing through a winter of particular severity, with fuel shortages and their attendant hardships. Tough decisions were being taken about a world role which had ceased to be remotely congruent with the nation's reduced resources; a date was set for Indian independence and the Americans were informed that the British were about to end their assistance to Greece and Turkey. The London conference produced a similar policy for Palestine. British and Zionist definitions of what might constitute an acceptable part of Palestine were far apart, while the Arabs remained steadfastly opposed to any idea of partition. On 14 February 1947, the cabinet agreed that the future of Palestine would be referred to the United Nations, without any recommendation of a preferred way forward.

There was no clear strategy behind the British move, beyond the knowledge that for the time being the situation might be 'held', starting a lengthy process of discussion which might result in some continuing form of British trusteeship.[2] That the British could see no way forward reflected not just their frustration over the Arab and Jewish positions but also a mounting resentment that Truman's ready advice was not matched with any tangible assistance. The State Department viewed the British action with deep alarm as something likely 'to lead to much confusion and violence in Palestine and elsewhere in the Near East'.[3] The idea that a congregation of over fifty states might agree on a successful strategy for the impassioned Palestine problem seemed implausible at best.[4]

Anxious though they were, State Department officials took an active part in advising the course of action which was to lead to the appointment of the United Nations Special Committee on Palestine (UNSCOP). In consultation with their British colleagues, it was decided that a Special Session of the General Assembly would set up UNSCOP to report back in September. Its composition was to avoid the permanent members of the Security Council and countries felt to have a special interest in Palestine. On Henderson's admission, the Americans largely failed to have their nominees on the comittee, something he attributed to the Zionists' superior lobbying power on the floor of the Assembly. Only two American-sponsored states, Canada and Sweden, were elected, the others being Guatemala, Uruguay, Peru, Australia, the Netherlands, Czechoslovakia, Yugoslavia, Iran and India. Believing it to be a white man's committee weighted against them, the Palestinian Arabs made the historic error of boycotting its proceedings. The Zionists made no such misjudgement. Their strategy was twofold: to convince the committee members that British rule was so discredited as to preclude any recommendation for continued trusteeship, and to point them in the direction of partition as the preferred solution. The first was brilliantly achieved when the former Chesapeake Bay ferry, *President Warfield,* renamed *Exodus 1947*, was intercepted by the Royal

Navy and its illegal immigrants brought ashore at Haifa while the UNSCOP members were in the country. Britain's propaganda defeat was compounded by Bevin's irritated decision to return them to Germany rather than place them in the internment camps in Cyprus.

To convince UNSCOP of partition took careful lobbying by the Zionist liaison officers, David Horowitz and Abba Eban, and testimony in Jerusalem whereby Weizmann 'unofficially' made the case for such a solution and Ben-Gurion acknowledged that the Jewish Agency would acquiesce in it. Even so, when it came to report on 1 September 1947, UNSCOP was divided. Conscious of Muslim sentiment, India, Iran and Yugoslavia favoured a unitary bi-national state, while the Australian member preferred not to support any scheme. The majority reported in favour of partition. Palestine was to be divided into an Arab and a Jewish state. Because of its unique religious position, and partly as the result of lobbying from the Vatican, Jerusalem was to be a *corpus separatum* with an international regime. Finally, there was to be an economic union of the whole country. It was a complex scheme open to many criticisms, not least that the proposed Arab state was to be in three segments, the Galilee, the mountainous interior, and the coastal area around Gaza, and that the borders of the Jewish state seemed indefensible. Nevertheless, UNSCOP believed, 'Only by means of partition can these conflicting national aspirations find substantial expression.'[5]

These were crucial deliberations from which the Americans consciously stood aside. As UNSCOP started its work, intensive consultations took place inside the State Department, involving Acheson, Henderson, Rusk, and Warren Austin, representative at the United Nations, over what role, if any, the country should take. The consensus of their views, with which the new Secretary of State George C. Marshall seems to have agreed, was that 'Palestine should become neither an Arab nor a Jewish State but a single independent Palestine State in which all its people, of whatever religion or blood, may dwell together in concord'. This was to be achieved through their now-familiar preference for continued trusteeship.[6] Nevertheless, there was a conscious decision that this scheme should not be thrust upon UNSCOP. Behind this lay a sincere view that the United Nations should not be interfered with in its first major task and that whatever solution emerged should not be American, but international.[7] Truman agreed. On 5 June, he issued a statement urging that while UNSCOP was working Americans should refrain 'from engaging in, or facilitating, any activities which tend further to inflame the passions of the inhabitants of Palestine, to undermine law and order in Palestine, or to promote violence in that country.'[8]

His appeal for restraint was largely a reaction against the renewed flood of telegrams into the White House urging an active role in the working of UNSCOP. This reached a peak during the *Exodus* affair during which an American, William Bernstein, was killed, stoking emotions amongst American Jews. The Jewish community was alarmed by the President's silence, fearing that Henderson and the State Department were now in the ascendant, and the scale of lobbying reflected that feeling. Had they sensed the effect this was having on Truman they might have reined back. He had recently confided in Niles that: 'We could have settled this Palestine thing if US politics had been kept out of it ... I surely wish God Almighty would give the Children of Israel an Isiah [sic], Christians a St Paul and the Sons of Ishmeal [sic] a peep at the Golden Rule. Maybe he will decide to do that.'[9] By August, he was writing to Wise, who had joined in the call to action: 'I read your telegram of the first with a great deal of interest and appreciate your viewpoint but there seems to be two sides to this question. I am finding it rather difficult to decide which one is right and a great many people in the country are beginning to feel just as I do.'[10] Balancing the lobbying, which was becoming dangerously counter-productive, was the steadying influence of Niles. Truman trusted Niles's judgement and knew that he shared a deep antipathy towards Silver and his associates. Niles was also aware of the political realities they would have to face once UNSCOP's recommendations reached the General Assembly and hence he was concerned to head off a situation which 'might become very damaging in these areas that gave us trouble last November', a reference to the poor showing of the Democrats in the mid-term elections. He was particularly alarmed at the influence which Henderson and George Wadsworth, the former ambassador to Syria, would have on the delegation at the United Nations, 'Because both are widely regarded as unsympathetic to the Jewish viewpoint.' To counteract them, he recommended to Truman that General John H. Hilldring, who knew the problem of the Jewish Displaced Persons in Europe at first hand, be added to the delegation.[11] Truman took the point and Hilldring was to prove the conduit between the White House and the workings of the delegation in New York.

His appointment showed considerable prescience on Niles's part, for the delegation was initially hesitant towards the UNSCOP recommendations and was always subject to the State Department's continued penchant for trusteeship. The tensions emerged clearly when Marshall and Henderson met them to prepare the American response. Henderson and Under-Secretary Robert Lovett had drafted a low-key address for Marshall to give before the General Assembly which would avoid any commitment to partition. Henderson believed that partition was unworkable unless it were to be implemented by force, which none of the major parties seemed prepared to do. The head of the delegation, Warren Austin, apparently shared these reservations, fearing for the viability of what was being proposed: he '. . . did not see how it was possible to carve out of an area already too small for a state a still smaller state. He thought it was certain that such a state would have to defend itself with bayonets forever, until extinguished in blood'. John Foster Dulles, his eye to the Republican interest, was non-committal, while Eleanor Roosevelt was prepared to support the UNSCOP plan as that 'would strengthen the United Nations in the minds of the American people'. Sensing that the time was not ready for a definitive statement, Hilldring reminded the others that this 'would certainly be a disappointment to American Jews and Jews everywhere'. Reflecting these uncertainties, when Marshall addressed the Assembly two days later his speech seemed to lean towards partition, if only just: 'The Government of the United States gives great weight not only to the recommendations which have met with the unanimous approval of the Special Committee, but also to those which have been approved by the majority of that Committee'.[12]

This tepid endorsement seemed to indicate that the balance was tilting in the direction favoured by Henderson and his colleagues. Vexed that his presentation had been less effective than he would have liked, because he had just returned from an overseas trip, Henderson now prepared a lengthy memorandum designed to confirm Marshall's doubts. Striking at the UNSCOP plan's weakest link, the proposed economic union of the two states, he argued:

If complete partition would be unsuccessful unless acceptable to Jews and Arabs, how much chance in the face of fierce Arab opposition has the UNSCOP majority plan which provides for an economic union of the two states – a union which cannot possibly succeed without Arab–Jewish friendship and cooperation? Irrigation ditches, railways, roads, telephones and telegraph lines, etc. must pass through both states. These facilities cannot function if the population of one state is hostile to that of the other.[13]

He had gained a powerful ally in the administration, James Forrestal, newly confirmed as the first Secretary of Defense. Aware that the war had accelerated the consumption of oil, matched by the depletion of domestic reserves, Forrestal was opposed to any policy which might antagonise the oil-producing states of the Middle East.[14] But despite such strongly argued positions, it was increasingly clear that the United States would endorse the partition plan. At a meeting in New York on 24 September, at which Marshall met Hilldring, Eleanor Roosevelt, Rusk, Charles Bohlen and Charles Fahy, the strategy for the forthcoming *Ad Hoc* Committee on the Palestinian Question was mapped out. The Americans would indicate no early commitment but once the other major participants, notably the British, the Arab Higher Committee and the Jewish Agency, had declared their policy, the delegation would announce that they supported a workable plan of partition. Should this fail to mobilise the necessary two-thirds majority, they would then have to decide whether to negotiate for an alternative policy or to force a vote which would expose the absence of support for the UNSCOP plan. Marshall insisted that this strategy was to be held in the 'utmost secrecy'.[15] While this showed a continuing uneasiness with the plan's chances of success, his decision to endorse partition would clearly have enormous impact.

The Zionist leaders were well aware that with the prospect of a Jewish state so close they dared not falter. Knowing the historic opportunity before them but aware that the weight of expert opinion in the State Department would be marshalled against them, they unleashed a sustained lobbying campaign to ensure clear-cut support for partition, only a taste of which can be given here. It involved such veteran partisans as Wagner and Celler and non-political figures as Jacobson.[16] In response to hundreds of letters, telegrams and personal calls from their constituents, forty-seven members of the Illinois State Legislature telegraphed Truman, as did the Governors of twenty-three states, all urging support for the UNSCOP plan. The leaders of organised labour, Philip Murray of the Congress of Industrial Organizations and William Green of the American Federation of Labor, did the same.[17] As before, the political dimension was central. On 6 October, Paul Fitzpatrick, Chairman of the powerful Democratic State Committee of New York, informed Truman that In the past few weeks he had been pressed by numerous groups, as well as by party leaders, for a statement of their position on this 'important question'.[18] The same day, Democratic National Chairman Robert Hannegan raised the same issue at a cabinet lunch, describing the pressure coming from people who had contributed to the party's 1944 campaign fund.[19] Such representations, orchestrated from so many levels of his party, could not be ignored, but Truman strongly resented them. 'The Jews are doing everything they possibly can to upset the applecart just as they did before when we had the thing almost settled', he told Fitzpatrick. 'I would suggest that you advise them to keep still – they will be in a lot better position under these circumstances.'[20] To Wagner, who had wired advising him not to yield to pressure over the UNSCOP proposals, he was even more testy: 'I know of no pressure except the pressure of the Jews, which has always been extensive and continuous.'[21]

Niles kept the situation under close review. His papers show that from the time the *Ad Hoc* Committee opened its proceedings down to the final General Assembly vote of 29 November, he was in constant contact with such key figures as Hilldring and Jacobson. His main contact with the Jewish Agency appears to have been the economist Robert Nathan who was working tirelessly for it at the United Nations. On 7 October, Nathan sent Niles a lengthy memorandum on how the delegation should proceed. Despite Marshall's plea for secrecy, he was well aware on the highest authority that the administration had decided to support the partition plan; as a result, it was necessary to go beyond Marshall's 'great weight' initial statement to a clear and emphatic espousal of partition. Anything less, Nathan predicted, would have an atomic impact in the country. Reminding Niles of the degree to which Truman had already been subjected to pressure over Palestine, he predicted a spontaneous torrent if the administration failed to support partition, with obvious political consequences. The Republicans, he concluded, would have a heyday.[22] The impact of this memorandum may only be surmised, but two days later its substance was embodied in instructions Truman sent to the State Department to support the UNSCOP plan. In his memoirs, he placed this move in the context of Arab League belligerency towards partition.[23]

On 10 October, then, Herschel Johnson announced that the United States would support partition, though not without qualifications. Discussions had revealed another flaw in the partition scheme; namely, that while the proposed Arab state was virtually homogeneous, the same could not be said of its Jewish equivalent. Johnson's speech promised to seek modifications to the plan, such as the port of Jaffa, which would reduce the number of Arabs in the Jewish state. It was not a particularly popular stance, as the Arabs and the British remained opposed to the very principle of partition, while the Jews were portraying it as a sacrifice on their part. On 21 October, the *Ad Hoc* Committee appointed subcommittees to make detailed recommendations on the UNSCOP majority and minority reports. Subcommittee 1, charged with the majority report, was dominated by the United States of America and the Soviet Union and as the latter had already gone on record as favouring partition, on this occasion at least the two powers could work together.

The Americans had two aims in the subcommittee, one of which Johnson had already announced. But the population of coastal Palestine was so intermingled as to prevent any easy way of reducing the number of Arabs in the Jewish state. Jaffa apart, the only obvious possibility was the Negev desert with its Arab Bedouin population. By 17 November, the Jewish Agency was aware that it would be asked to cede substantial areas around Aqaba in the south and Beersheba in the north. Despite its Bedouin population, the Negev had excited the Zionists' imagination, for its possession would allow access through the Gulf of Aqaba to the east and it seemed to hold out the possibility of agricultural and mineral developments which would help the new state absorb its immigrants. Weizmann had long been intrigued by its potential and it was to him that the Zionists turned to intervene with Truman. It was to prove an inspired choice, for Weizmann's charm and powers of persuasion were exactly what were needed to appeal to a President who was becoming weary and irritated by the Zionists' lobbying campaign. On 19 November, he met Truman at the White House, convincing him of the Negev's importance for the Jewish state. The immediate consequence was a telephone call to New York instructing the delegation that the Negev was not to be transferred. The long-term significance of the interview proved much greater, for, like many a statesman before him, Truman had been captivated by the force of Weizmann's personality.[24]

The second aim of the delegation was to ensure that there would be a proper scheme for the implementation of partition, without which it stood no chance of success. The British government had declared that as it believed that the UNSCOP scheme was 'so manifestly unfair to the Arabs', their administration would take no part in implementing the scheme, should it be adopted. The alternative seemed to be the unwelcome one of establishing a United Nations force drawn from members of the Security Council, which opened up the possibility of Soviet troops appearing in the Middle East. A meeting between the delegation and Britain's Sir Alexander Cadogan yielded nothing of substance on implementation beyond his personal belief that Britain would not actually hinder a peaceful transfer of power.[25] On this unsatisfactory basis, Subcommittee 1 presented a plan which allowed for the Mandate to end on 1 August 1948. At the Americans' suggestion, the British were to transfer power to a five-man Palestine Commission which would set up provisional councils of government for the two states as well as delineate their frontiers and those of the Jerusalem enclave. But the British were in no mood to acquiesce in this. When Cadogan responded to the subcommittee's report on 20 November, he made it plain that Britain would neither co-operate with the proposed Commission nor permit the formation of provisional governments.[26] Faced with this clear defiance of what the United Nations might recommend, the most the Americans could do was redraft the resolution of Subcommittee 1 in an attempt to reinforce its implementation provisions. Britain's adamant refusal to co-operate with the partition plan threatened to destroy any hopes for its success and as they prepared for the vote on Subcommittee 1's work, the Americans could hope for little more than a change of heart. It was to prove unrealistic.

When the resolution was presented to the full *Ad Hoc* Committee on 25 November, it passed, by twenty-five votes to thirteen with seventeen abstentions and two absentees, but this fell significantly short of the two-thirds majority which would be necessary to make it a recommendation of the General Assembly. With that vote due in a few days, and the British and the Arabs unyielding in their opposition, urgent and decisive action was needed to safeguard the Zionist position. In the lightning campaign which followed, the Jewish Agency used to the fullest both its own resources and those of its American supporters. Weizmann, for example, telegraphed his old friend, the former socialist premier Leon Blum, to use his influence to change French voting intentions. On the floor of the Assembly, the Zionist representatives worked unremittingly on the delegations of key states.

But the decisive moves came from the United States, directly inspired by the President. Because much of what happened in the hectic days before the vote was never written down, the record is incomplete, but enough has survived for the broad shape of events to emerge. Immediately after the event, Truman vigorously condemned much of what had been done and in his autobiography he took pains to distance himself from events. Nevertheless, the records show that the members of his staff were hard at work, and that the orders to the delegation in New York to secure the partition vote came directly from the President, though exactly when is less easy to determine.[27] Throughout, the Jewish Agency had a line of communication which ran from Nathan, to Hilldring, and thence through Niles and Matthew Connolly to Truman.

On 22 November, Truman was informed by Connolly that Nathan had called passing on Hilldring's complaints about Henderson's negative influence. As a result, Robert Lovett talked to Hilldring, instructing him 'that he and Herschel Johnson are to operate independently and without restraint insofar as the end result agreed upon will be obtained'.[28] Connolly kept in close touch with Jacobson, who had been promised by Truman that he would do everything to ensure the resolution's success, twice telephoning Kansas City to reassure him that events were proceeding satisfactorily.[29] Niles, too, was predictably active, as an alarmed Henderson discovered when he phoned Johnson to find out what was happening in New York. Apparently in tears from the strain of events, Johnson recounted a phone call from Niles threatening 'hell' if the President's campaign to secure the necessary votes were to fail.[30] Despite his subsequent disclaimers, Truman's personal involvement cannot be doubted. A week after the vote, he proudly told Jacobson and another old Kansas City friend, A. J. Granoff, how he had been solely responsible for securing the votes of several delegations.[31]

Of necessity, the methods used were controversial. On 25 November Lovett assured Connolly that, in contrast to the 'high pressure' coming from the Zionists, the American campaign was being conducted 'with good taste and courtesy'.[32] With the situation so urgent, that was not what the Zionists wanted. The following day, Celler telegraphed Truman demanding that the delegation throw off its restraint in trying to persuade Greece, Haiti, China, Ecuador, Liberia, Honduras and Paraguay. On the 27th, Joseph Proskauer sent a similar wire, adding the Philippines to the list and asking that instructions be sent for more energetic action. Truman's draft reply after the vote noted 'that the facts didn't justify your feeling uneasy as to what would happen'; in fact, it seems certain that clear instructions were sent out from the White House that day.[33]

American officials and politicians worked hard at several levels. An Arab attempt to adjourn the Assembly was thwarted when the American delegates realised that their floor leader, Camille Chamoun, had made a procedural error.[34] In addition to the lobbying in New York, interventions were made in a number of foreign capitals; interestingly, some observers felt that this proved the more effective tactic.[35] With its large Muslim population, the Philippines did not wish to support the resolution. According to Truman's Assistant Press Secretary, Eben Ayers, a direct approach was made to the Philippine ambassador who passed on the information to President Roxas; Roxas was separately approached by a group of ten senators who warned him of the 'adverse effect on United States–Philippine relations' if the country voted against partition. In Haiti, the President was told by the American consul, claiming Truman's authority, that 'for his own good' he should change his country's vote.[36] When the roll-call of states was taken on 29 November, the historic resolution recommending the partition of Palestine passed by thirty-three votes to thirteen, with ten abstentions.

Jewish reaction, both in Palestine and the United States, where Weizmann was wildly received at a rally in New York, was ecstatic, and Truman drew his fair share of plaudits. They were not accepted with particularly good grace, for the entire episode had left a bitter taste. He did not think, he later recorded, He ever had as much 'pressure and propaganda aimed at the White House' as he had in this affair.[37] This sentence in his memoirs was culled from a letter he drafted, but did not send, to Weizmann on 1 December, in which his real feelings emerge with characteristic pungency:

> I don't think I ever had as much pressure and propaganda unnecessarily aimed at the White House as I have had in this instance and it didn't please me a great deal but showed that evidently the people for whom we had done the most had no confidence in the integrity of the White House. I am certainly sorry for this viewpoint.[38]

In similar vein, he wrote to Celler that 'The pressure boys almost beat themselves. I didn't like it.'[39] The episode had evidently left him confused and somewhat embarrassed, for when Marshall raised with him the way that certain states had been interfered with, he replied that he was conscious that such pressure threatened the very existence of the United Nations and should be stopped.[40] When the events of the past few days were raised at a staff meeting on 2 December, Truman maintained that he had merely been carrying out the 1944 Democratic platform on Palestine. It seems he did not even have particularly high expectations of Jewish support in the elections: commenting that when the election came round they would say he had done nothing for them.[41] In contrast with his chief's ambivalent response, David Niles was able to derive satisfaction from the messages which acknowledged his crucial contribution to the course of events in New York. Some day, one correspondent assured him, the Jews of the world would know how much he had done.[42]

It would be difficult to overestimate the significance of what Truman and his aides did in these hectic days. Resolutions of the General Assembly, being recommendations, are not normally binding. But because the United Nations had inherited the ultimate authority over Palestine from the League of Nations, American officials involved with UN affairs believed that on this occasion the General Assembly was legislating.[43] Although the partition plan was to fall apart in the months ahead, the resolution provided the basis in international law for the establishment of the Jewish state and was so acknowledged when the State of Israel proclaimed its independence. But the road to that independence was still far from assured, for the Arabs and the British refused to acknowledge the legitimacy of the partition resolution and, in the resulting confusion, Truman's policy was to come within measurable distance of being reversed.

If American policy satisfied Jewish hopes for statehood, in almost every other respect it was based upon illusion. In his final speech before the General Assembly, Johnson had expressed the belief that the boundary between the two states would 'be as friendly as the boundary which runs for three thousand miles between Canada and the United States'. The statements of every Arab speaker belied such optimism; for them, it would be a line of 'blood and fire'. Johnson also anticipated 'co-operation on the part of the Members of the United Nations'. Sir Alexander Cadogan had just repeated that no such co-operation could be expected from the Mandatory. Events soon confirmed the emptiness of Johnson's rhetoric. On 3 December, the British authorities set a date for their departure, confirming that they would 'make every effort' to prevent the Palestine Commission 'trying to set up its authority until we are ready to hand over'.[44] In short, unless the British could be coerced, no mechanism to implement the partition resolution existed. The previous day, the Palestinian Arabs had proclaimed a general strike in protest against the General Assembly's decision. As had been the case in 1936, this proved to be the prelude to violence. Boisterous Jewish celebrations in Jerusalem provoked rioting in the city. The situation fast deteriorated. British military commanders, having no desire to see more men killed in a cause that was now lost, did little as Palestine increasingly became a battleground between its two communities. British policy had become one of leaving the two sides to fight it out to see which side would win.[45] They thought this preferable to a partition plan which they believed to be unrealistic and unworkable. If this was more in tune with the realities of Palestine, it did nothing to enhance the dignity and authority of the United Nations, and these had been matters of real importance for many Americans, not least the President.

Events in Palestine shocked many Americans, but merely confirmed Henderson, Rusk and others in the State Department in the soundness of their judgement. They believed that Truman's political advisers had too easily convinced him that a Jewish state could be brought about without violence, neglecting to point out that there was more to the Palestinian situation, and the Middle East, than the pressures of domestic politics and humanitarian concern for the Displaced Persons in Europe.[46] Truman was well aware that there were two sides to the Palestinian question, as he indicated in reminding Henry Morgenthau on 2 December that 'the Jews must now display tolerance and consideration for the other people in Palestine with whom they will necessarily have to be neighbors'.[47] When developments in Palestine failed to conform to his expectations, his responses became confused and hesitant.[48] Clearly, what he wanted was that the United Nations' settlement should run its course, allowing him to disengage from the problem, as he had been able to do for a period after the Yom Kippur statement. It was important that he should do so, for the international situation was fast demanding that he turn his full attention to Europe and relations with the Soviet Union. Beginning with a curt 'no' to a request from New York Congressman Arthur Klein for a meeting to congratulate him on his role in the United Nations, he issued orders that he would not see any more 'extreme' Zionist leaders.[49]

In the circumstances, the State Department felt justified in preparing a well-coordinated campaign aimed at reversing support for the partition resolution. Basic to their strategy was the belief that the escalating violence in Palestine had nullified a fundamental assumption behind previous policy; namely, the idea that partition could be accomplished without violence. Henderson was joined by George F. Kennan, Director of the newly-established Policy Planning Staff, and one of the keenest minds in the State Department. On 20 January, he submitted an analysis of the current situation in the Middle East aimed at shattering any comfortable illusions. 'The US

Government should face the fact that the partition of Palestine cannot be implemented without the use of force', Kennan warned, 'and that the US would inevitably be called upon to supply a substantial portion of the money, troops and arms for this purpose.' Arguing that their standing in the region had already been seriously impaired by the measures adopted to secure passage of the partition resolution, he concluded that any such role in implementation 'would result in deep-seated antagonism for the US in many sections of the Moslem world over a period of many years'. Any Arab reaction would hazard Western military bases and oil concessions which were vital to the reconstruction of Europe. Furthermore, to commit American troops could only encourage the Russians to do the same. Kennan was adamant that America should take no action in implementing, or even aiding, partition. Rather, he recommended that once 'the march of events has conclusively demonstrated that effort to carry out the partition plan as prescribed by the UN General Assembly offers no reasonable prospect for success without the use of outside force', they should work towards an alternative in the form of a federal state or trusteeship.[50]

It was Kennan's analysis that set in train the series of events which not only led to one of the most serious embarrassments of the Truman administration but almost succeeded in overturning the United Nations' decision. His initiative had the full support of Henderson and Henry Grady, rather less so that of Rusk. In January, Rusk's office was renamed that of United Nations Affairs and as its Director he was anxious to ensure that any reversal of the partition policy did not involve a fatal undermining of the world body. Castigating British policy as 'irresponsible', Rusk argued that merely to reiterate the State Department's familiar objections to the UNSCOP plan would no longer do, but that neither the United States nor the United Nations should regard the plan 'as sacrosanct, to be pursued at all costs despite new or unforeseen conditions'. Such a 'new situation', as he termed it, would be brought about if the Mandatory refused its co-operation or if a condition of civil war were to develop within Palestine. Then, he argued, they ought to seek a fresh solution based upon trusteeship. Whatever the ultimate solution, however, Rusk strongly believed that the United States could not, short of forfeiting her credibility, 'shirk our responsibility'.[51] From a rather different angle, Rusk was pointing to the same end as Kennan and Henderson; namely, a new initiative in which the United States would abandon partition for trusteeship.

Their campaign was powerfully reinforced by James Forrestal, who was galvanised into action by the partition vote. Forrestal continued to be deeply concerned about his country's future vulnerability over oil supplies. His information made him uncomfortably aware of how increasing petroleum consumption was not being matched by corresponding increases in domestic production. Skeptical about Latin America's capacity to provide an alternative, he could only point to the Middle East. His belief that this crucial dimension to Western strength had been placed in jeopardy by American actions over the partition vote was confirmed at a meeting with a leading oil executive who informed him that the main petroleum companies had suspended work on their Saudi Arabian developments because of the situation over Palestine. Convinced that domestic pressures held the key to the problem, he approached the Republicans with a view to taking Palestine out of politics. But Thomas Dewey, the leading contender for the 1948 nomination, could not conceive that the Democrats would surrender the advantages they had gained among Jewish voters and hence was not interested in such a bi-partisan approach. Democratic Party Chairman Senator Howard McGrath, who informed him that they stood to lose the pivotal states of New York, Pennsylvania and California if they forfeited Zionist support, was no more encouraging. At a cabinet meeting on 16 January 1948, Forrestal argued that if Middle East oil supplies were imperilled it would destroy the Marshall Plan for Europe, dislocate the domestic economy and make it impossible to wage war. Failing to strike a responsive chord, he wrote a paper for the State Department outlining his fears which he then discussed with Lovett. The Under-Secretary, who had just received Kennan's paper, thus gained telling confirmation of how sections of the Washington bureaucracy felt about the administration's Middle East policy. But Forrestal's intervention was not sustained. On 3 February, he lunched with Bernard Baruch who advised him that he had become identified with opposition to the partition scheme to a degree that was not in his own interests, and reminded him of the question's importance for the Democratic Party.[52]

These various pressures were brought to a head by the imminent meeting of the Security Council on 24 February 1948. The Palestine Commission had been unable to make the slightest move towards implementing the partition resolution and, on the advice of Secretary-General Trygve Lie and his officials, they had requested that the Security Council furnish armed assistance. State and defense officials were as one in opposing this, not least because any such move by the Security Council would give the Soviets a reason for deploying their troops in the region. Hence, on 17 February, the Policy Planning Staff recommended that the United States should continue its support for the partition plan 'by all measures short of the use of outside armed force'; its military members, echoing Forrestal, urged that the 'United States should alter its previous policy of support for partition and seek another solution to the problem.'[53] Four days later, the State Department presented its views to Truman. While the Security Council should continue to work for a solution along the lines of the General Assembly resolution, the UN Charter did not empower it to sanction the use of force to give effect to General Assembly resolutions. Military force could only be justified in the event of external aggression against Palestine, and even then only to the extent of repulsing such an attack. In short, the State Department had decided that the United States could not support the Palestine Commission's plea for armed assistance to enable its work to go ahead. This was to be the substance of Warren Austin's subsequent speech to the Council. Not to form part of the speech, but submitted 'for the President's consideration and approval', were the State Department's proposals for the next stage. If the Security Council could not effect implementation of the resolution, the whole question should be referred back to the General Assembly. 'The Department of State', the message concluded, 'considers that it would then be clear that Palestine is not yet ready for self-government and that some form of United Nations trusteeship for an additional period of time will be necessary.'[54]

The recommendation was nothing short of a reversal of existing policy and because of Truman's bitter response to what developed, it is only fair to note his reply: 'I approve in principle this basic position. I want to make it clear, however, that nothing should be presented to Security Council that could be interpreted as a recession on our part from the position we took in the General Assembly. Send final draft of Austin's speech for my consideration.' His approval 'in principle' of the State Department position was to discomfit all concerned. Austin's speech to the Security Council on 24 February, which Truman approved, made clear the American belief that the 'Charter of the United Nations does not empower the Security Council to enforce a political settlement'.[55] With British intransigence over the Palestine Commission's work undiminished, Austin's statement meant that the partition plan was dead in the water. To dismayed officials of the United Nations, it was clear that their organisation had been thwarted in the first real test of its authority. To the ever-vigilant Zionists, the change of tone in American policy was unmistakable.

It confirmed a growing belief that the administration had cooled towards them. Conscious of the fact that they would have to fight to establish and defend their state, they had been looking to Truman to end the arms embargo which had been placed on Palestine, especially as the British were assumed to be arming the Arabs. As the violence grew, so did their concern. The issue was raised, rather delicately, by Weizmann as early as 9 December 1947 in his letter thanking Truman for his role in the United Nations.[56] But as the embargo remained in force, and Truman was clearly avoiding Zionist leaders, the campaign to mobilise Jewish opinion was revived through the familiar means of congressional action, the despatch of thousands of telegrams, and a mass petition in New York. Signs of a split between the Zionists and leading Democrats did appear to be showing, for in early February Senator McGrath resigned from the Congressional Advisory Board of the Political Action Committee for Palestine, much to the consternation of its leaders who were lobbying on Capitol Hill.[57] The Zionists now had a rival to play off against the Democrats, for Henry Wallace had recently formed his left-wing American Labor Party which was bound to strike a chord with New York's traditionally liberal Jews. The point was not lost on the city's Democrats. On 12 February, New York Congressman Andrew L. Somers requested that he present a petition on Palestine signed by 35 000 Jews, stating 'that they are the principals from which the Wallace group gained their strength and he thinks it would be wise, politically, for the President to receive them'.[58] Five days later, the point was driven home when a Wallace candidate, Leo Isacson, won a congressional seat from the Democrats in a strongly Jewish area of the Bronx.

Coming at a low point in the party's general popularity, this upset seems to have stung Truman, confirming his already cynical view of Jewish voting intentions. It was evidently a major factor behind his authorisation of Austin's speech to the Security Council on the 24th.[59] It might well have contributed to a total reassessment of his position. Already resentful over what he felt were unnecessary Zionist tactics, he had become, as Jacobson conceded, 'very bitter', against the New York Jewish leadership.[60] That bitterness expressed itself in a refusal to see Weizmann, whom he had come to respect. On 23 February, Weizmann was reduced to complaining that he had not had so much as a telephone call from Niles.[61] Relations between the White House and the Zionists had touched their nadir.

With Truman in this mood and the State Department in full cry, a radical shift in policy was not impossible, with all that this held for the future of the Middle East. Their actions were partly the culmination of Henderson's long campaign, but they should also be seen in the context of the alarming reports of Russian intentions in Europe; if there were to be a war with Stalin, the Middle East and its oil resources would be of critical importance. By early March, Henderson and his colleagues, together with Rusk's staff, prepared what was in effect a 'breakdown' speech to be made to the Security Council once it was clear that the partition plan had collapsed. It would call for the suspension of efforts to implement the plan as well as for a special session of the General Assembly to put into effect a policy of temporary trusteeship, which would be without prejudice to the nature of an eventual settlement. Henderson gave the draft speech to Lovett but what then happened aroused a storm of major proportions and historic consequences.

On 19 March, Austin spoke before the Security Council using Henderson's speech. It amounted to a clear repudiation of partition and threw the whole issue of a Jewish state, which had seemed tantalisingly close, into doubt. Truman was inevitably denounced for this *volte face*. It was a stunning reversal for Zionist diplomacy, albeit one they had been increasingly sensitive toward for some weeks. But those who criticised Truman could not have been aware of his incensed reaction. 'This morning', he confided in his diary, 'I find that the State Department has reversed my Palestine policy. The first I know about it is what I see in the papers! Isn't that hell? I'm now in the position of a liar and a double crosser. I've never felt so in my life.'[62] At his staff meeting that morning, 'shocked and depressed', he claimed that he had been unaware of Austin's move and ordered an enquiry as to how it happened.[63] Already, the volume of protest testified to the Zionist reaction. This reached a peak on 4 April when the Jewish War Veterans organised a parade of 40000 to protest against the betrayal of the Jews in Palestine. The marchers were applauded by a crowd estimated at a quarter of a million – an impressive display of the depth of emotion felt in the Jewish community.

But Zionist protest was something Truman had grown used to and that in itself would not have accounted for the strength of his reaction. The real source of his embarrassment was the assurance he had given to Weizmann the day before Austin's speech. The importance of that meeting can hardly be overstated but it only took place as the result of tortuous negotiations. Weizmann's depression at being excluded from the White House at such a critical time in Zionist fortunes has already been noted. The idea of using Jacobson to break this barrier originated with the Boston Zionist, Dewey Stone, and Frank Goldmann, the National President of B'nai B'rith, who had recently met Jacobson in Kansas City.[64] On 13 March, Jacobson went to the White House. Knowing that he was no expert on Palestine, Truman's reception was frosty, but Jacobson won him over by comparing his own feelings for Weizmann with the President's hero-worship for Andrew Jackson. The subsequent meeting with Weizmann was treated with great discretion but it renewed the warm feeling generated in November. Although the discussions were 'off the record', and no minutes were kept, Truman confirmed that he still supported partition; hence his embarrassment the next day.[65] Truman's respect for Weizmann increased as the veteran statesman made no move to join in the clamour of denunciation. His reliance on Truman's good faith was justified and rewarded.

For the time being, Truman was mortified by appearing to be a 'liar and a double crosser'. Faced with his sulphurous reaction, his staff tried to piece together what had happened. According to the record, the extent of presidential approval did not appear to extend beyond the letter of 22 February in which Truman had approved the Lovett–Henderson draft but cautioned that there was to be no retreat from partition.[66] It was an interpretation which left his reputation, and those of his aides, conveniently intact. But there is strong evidence that he had approved Austin's controversial speech. Stung by the President's response, Lovett sought to defend his reputation and those of his officials, maintaining that he had discussed the draft with Truman and Marshall on the 8th. In weighing up the relative merits of partition and trusteeship, Truman had come to the following conclusion: 'The President said we were to go through and attempt to get approval for implementation of the GA resolution but that if we did not get it we could take the alternative step. That was perfectly clear. He said it to General Marshall and me ... There is absolutely no question but that the President approved it.'[67] Handwritten notes by Clark Clifford, who had been directed to conduct the investigation into the affair, seem to confirm his account, for they indicate that on 8 March Truman had approved proposals for further action and that Marshall had communicated this to Austin. They also show that

Austin had not been directed to give Truman prior information about the date of his speech and that although the actual text had not been submitted to Truman it was substantially the same as the draft he had seen.[68] The real problem seems to have been the result of timing, as Austin's speech the day after Weizmann's visit, which the State Department knew nothing of, appeared to show American policy in disarray. He more or less confessed as much to Marshall: '. . . he said that the reason he was so much exercised in the matter was the fact that Austin made his statement without the President having been advised that he was going to make it at that particular time. He had agreed to the statement but said that if he had known when it was going to be made he could have taken certain measures to have avoided the political blast of the press.'[69]

Truman's rage, then, takes on the appearance of something of an act, though his discomfiture was real enough. But such is the role of chance, or perhaps of a keen sense for the drift of events, that the Stone–Goldmann–Jacobson–Weizmann initiative, which had nothing to do with the Austin statement, succeeded in thwarting a fundamental change in policy. The wrath which Truman had been directing against the Zionist pressure groups now turned against the officials of the State Department, who, he felt, had always wanted to cut his throat.[70] The State Department's influence now waned and he listened instead to his staff members who reminded him that the foreign policy professionals did not have to take into account domestic political realities.[71] By 24 March Truman had recovered his good spirits and the next day held a press conference in which he made it clear that trusteeship would be a temporary expedient not a substitute for the partition plan. This was done against State Department advice, a clear indication of how the initiative was slipping away from them.

Marshall, Lovett, Rusk and Henderson were all involved in discussions in the six weeks that remained of the British Mandate, but the decisive views were those heard in the White House. Clifford increasingly took the key role of facilitator of the President's wishes over Palestine, with a clear-sighted view of what Truman and the USA stood to gain. Trusteeship could not be abandoned, short of confirming Washington's confusion. On 1 April, the Security Council acted on the American suggestion that a special session of the General Assembly be convened. On 16 April, nearly a month after Austin's speech, delegates assembled to consider the plan for temporary trusteeship. But no firm leadership was given and a sense of resigned weariness descended over the proceedings which bogged down in sterile debate.

The pace of events was being forced not in New York or Washington but in the towns, villages and hillsides of Palestine, as Arabs and Jews fought an increasingly bitter battle in advance of the British withdrawal. It was a struggle in which the Jews increasingly held the initiative. Jewish statehood was too close, and the threat of an American offensive against partition too real, to admit any hesitation. While the Jewish forces were divided amongst Haganah, Etzel and Lehi members, the Arabs proved to be even more fragmented, with the Liberation Army of Fawzi al-Qawukji in the north frequently at odds with the forces of Abd al-Qadr al-Husseini around Jerusalem. Once the Haganah succeeded in flying in arms from Czechoslovakia, they steadily asserted their dominance, with areas vital to the future of the Jewish state falling into their hands. On 22 April, Haifa, the country's only significant port, was taken as the British garrison withdrew. On 14 May, Jaffa, with its potential threat to the security of Tel Aviv, also fell. In each case, the Arab inhabitants left or were driven out. The bitterest battles of all were for the lines of communication through the Judean hills from Tel Aviv to Jerusalemn, whose extensive Jewish western suburbs were isolated in Arab territory. In the course of this fighting Abd al-Qadr al-Husseini was killed, but the affair most vividly remembered was the massacre at Deir Yassin on 9 April when Etzel and Lehi members slaughtered 200 Arab villagers. Three days later, a Jewish medical convoy travelling through Jerusalem's Sheikh Jarrah to Mount Scopus was ambushed with the death of seventy-seven doctors and nurses. It was in such circumstances, which bore no resemblance to the General Assembly's partition plan, that the shape of a Jewish state began to emerge. With its well-tried organisation, the Jewish Agency had long been a shadow government, but with the progressive collapse of the British administration, its officials were fast becoming the *de facto* government of Jewish Palestine. Under the tough-minded direction of David Ben-Gurion, its Council of Government prepared for the imminent British departure.

Sensing that little momentum was gathering behind their trusteeship plan, the State Department searched for an alternative which might at least 'hold' the situation, preventing full-scale war in the Middle East. The only possibility was to try to arrange a truce, something which Rusk explored with Truman on 30 April. Agreeing that war had to be averted, the President gave his backing to the truce negotiations, counselling Rusk to remind the Arabs of his 'difficult political situation within this country' and authorising him to warn the Jews of the likely consequences of their refusal to co-operate.[72] But Rusk's well-intentioned initiative proved barren, for the Jews did not trust any proposal which might postpone their drive for statehood and the Arabs were bent on avenging Deir Yassin.

Faced with a diplomatic impasse and unable to lay any restraining hand on events in Palestine, Truman was being nudged ever closer to the inevitability of recognising Jewish statehood. This was already implicit in the promise he had made to Weizmann, who was far too wise and experienced in the art of diplomacy to join in the clamour of denunciation after Austin's speech. Instead, he waited until 9 April to write an elegant letter to Truman, distinguished by an absence of rancour, thanking him for his assurance of support for partition at their meeting and setting out the reasons why he had supported this since 1937.[73] Although no reply was sent, such a gesture of trust in his good faith was finely calculated to appeal to Truman.

Perhaps Truman needed to be reminded of the intellectual arguments for partition at this stage, for, as he had indicated to Rusk, he could not ignore the domestic political situation. With the Democratic convention in sight, his party's position appeared increasingly depressing. To add to the Wallace secession, his stand on civil rights had resulted in revolt in the party's southern heartland, setting in train the events which were to rob him of four 'Dixiecrat' states in the November election. With Austin's speech provoking what his advisers were calling the 'Brooklyn revolt', Truman had good reason to fear for his political fortunes. At a staff meeting on 24 March, he ruefully speculated on the future if he managed to alienate the farmers and distillers as well as the south and 'Brooklyn'.[74] His Press Secretary, Charles Ross, and Senator McGrath were corresponding anxiously about Republican lobbying amongst the Zionists in an attempt to turn Truman's embarrassment to their advantage.[75] Truman's own correspondence shows his concern over the political situation. On 5 May, Dean Alfange, leader of the New York Liberal Party and Chairman of the American Christian Palestine Committee of New York, sent a bleak analysis of Truman's prospects in the state to his military aide, General Harry Vaughan. Alfange reported that the President could not carry the state because of the overwhelming Jewish vote against him. The only possible way to remedy this would be for Truman to make a move which would 'electrify' the Jews by recognising the Jewish state when it was proclaimed in ten days' time and appointing an American minister to it. Truman read Alfange's letter and on 18 May was able to reply: 'It looks as if things have turned out as you anticipated in your letter'.[76]

He continued to be irritated by the intensity of Zionist lobbying, complaining on 5 May to Representative Arthur G. Klein that he had 'no objection to their lobbying – neither have I any objection to the Arabs doing so if they feel like it but, in neither case, does it affect my decisions or judgement'.[77] It was a candid answer, for his decisions were being influenced by his respect for Weizmann, his sense of political reality, his resentment at the 'career people' at the State Department, an attempt to anticipate how the country should react to the imminent reality of a Jewish state, and a desire to try to prevent a war in the Middle East.

Clifford was now the key player, though Niles continued to attend important meetings. A keen advocate, Clifford was aided in preparing his case by Max Lowenthal. In addition, Robert Nathan and Eliahu Epstein kept in close touch with the White House, ensuring that officials were accurately briefed on the Jewish Agency's intentions. Their information was of great importance if Clifford were to provide an effective riposte to the foreign policy professionals with their wealth of experience and reports from throughout the Middle East. With the British departure only days away, Truman told Clifford that he intended to hold a conference. As Marshall would be hostile to recognition of a Jewish state, Clifford was directed to prepare and present the case for the other side.[78]

Together with Lowenthal and George Elsey of the White House staff, he prepared his position with great care. The purpose of the exercise was to have Truman issue a statement before the end of the Mandate, announcing 'his intention to recognise the new Jewish State in Palestine as soon as it comes into existence'. The arguments for such a course were developed in a lengthy memorandum of 9 May. This argued persuasively that the Jewish Agency had already succeeded in making partition an 'accomplished fact'. From this premise, it naturally followed that the country, and the administration, should not throw away such advantages as might be gained. An immediate recognition by Truman of the Jewish state would restore the somewhat battered reputation of the United Nations and American prestige, which had become associated with a series of floundering initiatives. Even more important was the need to pre-empt a similar move by the Soviet Union: it is clear that the desire not to be second in the field weighed heavily with Truman and his associates. Finally, there were the inevitable domestic political considerations, with the elections now on the immediate horizon. It hardly needed emphasising that 'the Republicans are making their bid too'. This all argued for decisive action in support of what was an established reality in Palestine, the practical result of which would be that the President would no longer be subjected to 'unjust and unjustified losses and sacrifices'.[79]

These arguments were the basis of a statement Clifford, Elsey and Lowenthal drafted to be read by the President at his press conference on 13 May. As promised, Truman held his conference the day before. He was assisted by Clifford, Niles and Connolly, while Marshall and Lovett brought Fraser Wilkins of Near Eastern Affairs and Robert McClintock of United Nations Affairs. It was an ill-tempered affair. Marshall and Lovett reviewed their recent negotiations with Epstein and Moshe Shertok of the Jewish Agency, whom they had warned not to expect an American response 'if they came running to us for help'. Clifford then developed his case for the President to announce his intention of recognising the Jewish state. His notes show that he emphasised how this would be consistent with American policy on Palestine and that it was necessary to forestall the Russians. Above all, not only was the Jewish state's proclamation inevitable but so was American recognition. 'Why not now?', Clifford asked. His forensic talents provoked Marshall into asking why he was there at all, to which Truman replied that it was at the President's request. Lovett could not accept the argument that it was necessary to move before the Russians and tried to undermine confidence in the nature of the Jewish state by producing intelligence reports on the movement of Jewish communists from the Soviet Union to Palestine. But it was left to Marshall to express the pent-up frustration felt in his Department over how Middle Eastern issues had been handled:

> The transparent dodge to win a few votes would not in fact achieve this purpose. The great dignity of the office of President would be seriously diminished. The counsel offered by Mr. Clifford was based on domestic political considerations, while the problems that confronted us were international. I said bluntly that if the President were to follow Mr. Clifford's advice and if in the elections I were to vote, I would vote against the President.[80]

Faced with this massive rebuke from a man he greatly admired, Truman retreated. With the observation 'that he was fully aware of the difficulties and dangers in the situation, to say nothing of the political risks involved which he, himself, would run', he ended the meeting. As Clifford collected his papers, he was consoled by the President. There seemed no possibility that the United States would recognise the Jewish state in just three days' time. But Clifford knew that this was not the result his chief had wanted.

Although the evidence for the next two days is fragmentary, and somewhat contradictory, it is possible to reconstruct the major moves. Truman's press conference on 13 May, when he had to turn aside the question of the recognition of the Jewish state, fell flat, threatening to unleash another storm of protest. But his intentions had not changed and Clifford was working hard to bring them about. On the evening of the 12th, there was the first sign of weakening on the side of the State Department, when Lovett phoned Clifford about his uneasiness over what had happened at the conference. Clifford advised him to convince Marshall of the need for recognition and, according to his account, by the 14th, Marshall had 'come around' to the idea.

On that day, the hopes, once wildly improbable, of Zionism were realised. The High Commissioner, Sir Alan Cunningham, left Jerusalem and that evening sailed from Haifa. As he did so, the leaders of the Jewish Agency assembled in Tel Aviv where Ben-Gurion read the proclamation establishing the State of Israel from midnight. Jubilation that centuries of Jewish statelessness had ended was tempered with the knowledge that the state's survival would soon be tested in war. Events in Washington, if less dramatic, were exciting and hectic, with Clifford, Lovett, Niles, Lowenthal, Nathan and Epstein all closely involved in the day's events. Truman's decision was not in doubt: 'Now that the Jews were ready to proclaim the State of Israel, however, I decided to move at once and give American recognition to the new nation.' He instructed a member of staff to communicate his decision to the State Department and prepare it for transmission to Ambassador Austin at the United Nations in New York.[81] This account does scant justice to the fast-moving events of the day.

Clifford met Lovett for lunch, informing him 'that the President was under unbearable pressure to recognize the Jewish state promptly', that at 6 o'clock Washington time title 'would be lying about for anybody to seize', and that Truman had decided to recognise the new state once the request for this had been received. Lovett argued for delay until the situation was clearer but Clifford responded 'that the timing of the recognition was "of the greatest possible importance to the President from a domestic point of view" '. 'My protests', Lovett recorded, 'against the precipitate action and warning as to consequences with the Arab world appear to have been outweighed by considerations unknown to me, but I can only conclude that the President's political advisers, having failed last Wednesday afternoon to make the President a father of the new state, have determined at least to make him a midwife.' As the decision had been made, the two men prepared the text of the American recognition. To ensure that there was such a request, Clifford contacted Epstein. He now needed two pieces of information: when the proclamation would become effective and whether it was to be a provisional government. Epstein's request was delivered to the White House and the State Department with little time to spare. The proclamation came into effect at 6 o'clock Washington time. Truman's *de facto* recognition of the State of Israel came eleven minutes later.[82]

These events caught many off-guard, not least the hapless delegation in New York. At 5.45, Clifford called Rusk directing him to tell them what was about to happen. Rusk protested that recognition would undermine all they had been trying to do at the United Nations but was told that the President had decided. When the information reached Austin, he went home rather than let it appear that he had been deceiving the General Assembly. In an atmosphere of confusion, it fell to Philip Jessup to confirm to the Assembly that his government had extended *de facto* recognition to the provisional government of the State of Israel.[83] For Arabs, it confirmed what they had always feared would be the culmination of American policy. Israelis could take comfort from the knowledge that Truman's recognition held the key to the international community's acceptance of their venture in statehood; few knew of the in-fighting within the bureaucracy which had preceded his action or what a 'close run thing' it had been.

3 Policy in the Cold War Era

In the spring of 1948, Czechoslovakia's precarious democracy fell to a Soviet-backed *coup*. In June, the Soviets began their blockade of the western sectors of Berlin, setting in motion the events which resulted in the formation of the North Atlantic Treaty Organisation the following April. America's isolation was formally at an end. Suspicion of the Soviet Union and fear of Communist expansion became the prevailing national emotions, fuelled by the collapse of Kuomintang China in the autumn of 1949, and given expression in the Korean War which began the following year. While the Middle East was peripheral to these events, its strategic and economic importance, which the State Department and the Pentagon had been emphasising with modest success since the end of the war, could not now be overlooked. Fully committed in Europe and Asia, American planners were content that the British should continue to have the main Western military presence in the region. It was an assumption seemingly justified by Britain's extensive network of bases, colonial possessions and intricate network of treaty obligations, but flawed by a failure to appreciate the nature and extent of the country's post-war decline. The hollowness of her position in the Middle East had been cruelly exposed by the Jewish underground. Humiliated by the Jews and regarded by the Arabs as having 'let them down', Britain was presiding over a military and diplomatic illusion and, as this was systematically exposed in the 1950s, the United States was drawn into the affairs of the region in her stead.[1]

On 15 May 1948, the old Arab–Jewish dispute over Palestine became the Arab–Israeli conflict, involving all the major states of the region. In offering prompt recognition to the State of Israel, Truman probably hoped that he might help forestall a war in the Middle East. If so, he was disappointed, for on that day the armies of the Arab League began hostilities. Faced with the disintegration of all its hopes for a peaceful resolution of the Palestine problem, the United Nations appointed as its Mediator Sweden's Count Folke Bernadotte who had used his position in the Red Cross to try to rescue Jews from Himmler in the latter stages of the war. Bernadotte succeeded in arranging a truce on 11 June but when this collapsed a month later and the war resumed with the two sides now reinforced with foreign arms supplies, he tried to negotiate for a wider settlement. By early August, he confided in the American *Chargé* in Egypt that the Secretary General of the Arab League and the leaders of Trans-jordan and Lebanon were ready to acquiesce in Israel's existence. His proposed solution was the return of Arab refugees to their homes and the consolidation of Israel's territory, taking into account what had happened in the fighting.[2] When he completed his recommendations on 16 September, he proposed that Israel retain Galilee, which she had conquered, but that the Negev should be Arab territory. Haifa would be retained by Israel but as a free port, and Lydda, returned to the Arabs, would be a free airport. Jerusalem was to be placed under the United Nations and the Arab refugees were to be allowed to return to their homes in Israeli territory. The following day, he was assassinated in Jerusalem by members of Lehi.

These events were followed with interest in the State Department and alarm by Israel's supporters. Truman had ensured that relations between the two states began as warmly as possible. On 25 May, Weizmann, now President of the State of Israel, was received at the White House prior to his departure, starting negotiations for a loan from the Export–Import Bank to meet the country's urgent financial needs and raising with Truman the possibility of appointing an American Minister.[3] This was quickly done. Anxious to pre-empt the appointment of a career officer, Truman chose James G. McDonald over the protests of the State Department. McDonald's ready sympathy with the Jews and informal manner helped foster a spirit of goodwill between the two countries, even though his uncritical support of Israeli government policies reinforced the State Department's view of his unsuitability for such a delicate post.[4] Once again, tensions between the White House and the State Department were coming to the surface, heightened by the successful campaign to have Henderson removed from Washington. Despite Zionist attempts to see him dismissed from the service, Truman appointed him ambassador to India, an honour he appreciated but which meant the departure of the sternest critic of the administration's policy.[5] The scene was set for yet another test of strength, this time over the Bernadotte proposals which were viewed with great apprehension in Israel.

In one of his first despatches on arrival, McDonald reported to Clifford that Bernadotte was 'completely discredited'. In fact, the Mediator's views were close to those of the State Department, which had concluded as early as June that the most realistic solution would be for Israel to exchange western Galilee for the Negev, that Jerusalem should be under the United Nations, and that Transjordan should take over Arab Palestine, with the area forming a customs union.[6] As with the trusteeship controversy in the spring, officials believed that the President was aware of, and had personally approved, this line of policy. With this apparent reassurance, on 21 September Marshall, who was attending the United Nations in Paris, issued a statement that the United States accepted the Bernadotte plan 'in its entirety'.[7] The result was a virtual repeat of the March fiasco. The American Zionist Emergency Council ran adverts denouncing Marshall's statement as contrary to the Democratic Party's position. With Truman engaged in his famous 'whistle stop' campaign for re-election and about to campaign in New York, the lesson was obvious; Clifford informed Lovett that 'the pressure from the Jewish groups on the President was mounting and that it was as bad as the time of the trusteeship suggestion'. Eliahu Epstein, now officially the Israeli government representative in Washington, turned to Jacobson, who flew to Oklahoma City on 27 September for a meeting with Truman and his staff on board the campaign train. Jacobson argued that the President was trying to summon a few votes in Oklahoma while the State Department was losing him millions in New York and Pennsylvania. Clifford, Connolly and the others impressed on Truman that he must stand by the Democrats' commitments on Israel. As a result, Clifford phoned the hapless Lovett instructing him to telegraph Marshall 'completely disavowing' the statement he had made. As in March and May, American policy would have been exposed as inconsistent and Marshall deeply embarrassed. A lengthy telephone wrangle between Lovett and Clifford prevented this with the compromise of a telegram to Stephen Wise promising *de jure* recognition of Israel once elections had been held. Nevertheless, on 17 October Truman felt it necessary to wire Marshall 'that no statement be made on the subject of Palestine by any member of our delegation in Paris without obtaining specific authority from me and clearing the text of any statement'.[8] Once again, the Jewish community, and particularly Eddie Jacobson, had been mobilised with telling effect, for in the absence of American support the Bernadotte plan atrophied. On 3 November, Truman was re-elected in one of the most unexpected victories in presidential history. Defying conventional wisdom, he did so without New York and Pennsylvania which were carried by Thomas Dewey.

When asked, Truman had consistently maintained that his Palestine policy had always been governed by the 1944 Democratic platform. A week after his election he confirmed to Lovett that his administration would abide by the principles of the 1948 platform, which looked forward to full recognition of Israel, her admission to the United Nations, the provision of appropriate aid, the modification of the arms embargo in her favour, her right to the boundaries of the 29 November 1947 resolution with modifications 'only if fully acceptable to the State of Israel', and the internationalisation of Jerusalem. With the election now safely behind him, Truman authorised Lovett to inform Marshall that as events had rendered the 29 November partition line redundant, he was to work for a solution which would allow Israel to retain Galilee and Jaffa in return for giving the Arabs most of the Negev south of a line from Gaza through Beersheba to the Dead Sea.[9] But once again there was no clear line to follow. In writing to congratulate him on his election victory, Weizmann had raised the subject of the Negev and in his reply Truman had responded that he 'would deplore any attempt to take it away from Israel'.[10] It was an important issue, for the final battles of the war were being waged over the Negev, which Israelis saw as the key to providing for their immigrants. This reached a pitch of international delicacy in early January 1949 when Israeli aircraft shot down five Royal Air Force Spitfires over Egyptian territory south of Rafah. As ceasefire negotiations were currently being conducted in Rhodes under United Nations' auspices, the Americans were upset by what they saw as aggressive Israeli tactics and, in discussions with Epstein, Lovett thought fit to warn that 'the British would take no action if the Israeli forces stayed where they were but that if the Israelis crossed any of the Arab frontiers, Israel would have to realize that it might be getting into a war which would be very different from that which they had been waging against the Arabs'. This reminder that Britain had treaty obligations towards a number of Arab states was acknowledged by Epstein. Faced with American disapproval and the threat of British retaliation, Ben-Gurion ordered his reluctant commanders to halt their operations in the Rafah area which had been intended to secure the entire Gaza coastal region.[11]

In January 1949, Lovett set out the administration's basic policy for Mark Ethridge, the Louisville newspaperman who was about to assume the thankless post of American representative on the Palestine Conciliation Commission convening at Lausanne, repeating that 'Israel is not entitled to keep both the Negev and western Galilee and Jaffa'. But he also instructed Ethridge to work within the terms of the General Assembly resolution of 11 December 1948, which the United States had helped to draft and which brought together current thinking on the problems of Jerusalem and the Arab refugees. On the latter, this had set out that 'the refugees wishing to return to their homes and live in peace with their neighbours should be permitted to do so at the earliest practicable date and that compensation should be paid for the property of those choosing not to return'. Jerusalem was to be considered a separate entity under the United Nations and Lovett did not consider that Israel was entitled to claim a land corridor to the city. [12] These, then, formed the agenda of the new Truman administration: Israel's border, especially in relation to the Negev, the status of Jerusalem, the future of the refugees, financial assistance to the Israelis and full recognition of the state.

True to the Zionist tradition of creating realities on the ground, the Israeli army settled the question of the Negev without interference from the Americans or anyone else. In the Rhodes negotiations, conducted by Dr Ralph Bunche, armistice agreements were reached between Israel and her main antagonists which set the pattern of that area of the Middle East for the next eighteen years. Faced with the possibility of pressure to trade it against Galilee and Jaffa, the Israelis' priority in the final phase of the war had been to secure the Negev, which they did despite their frustration in the Rafah–Gaza coastal area. Although the armistice agreements laid down that the 'Armistice Demarcation Line is not to be construed in any sense as a political or territorial boundary', it came to be accepted as Israel's border and little more was heard of the American idea that the Negev should be transferred to the Arabs. The effective ending of hostilities in January enabled the administration to move quickly on two of its 1948 election pledges. On 19 January, the negotiations with the Export–Import Bank were at last completed, with a loan of $35 million to cover agricultural work and $55 million to assist communications, transportation, manufacturing, housing and public works. It proved to be the start of the financial connexion between the two countries which was to become a vital part of Israel's security and prosperity. The Israeli general election also allowed Truman to grant *de jure* recognition to the state. This was done at a ceremony at which he insisted that Eddie Jacobson be present. Jacobson also received one of the pens used to sign the announcement, as did David Niles. [13] It was no less than they deserved.

Jerusalem lay at the heart of Zionism, just as it had been the focus of Jewish yearning throughout the centuries in the Diaspora. To achieve the aim of Zionism without making Zion the capital of the Jewish state was 'unthinkable'. Although the state was proclaimed in Tel Aviv, in December 1949 the Knesset and most ministries moved to Jerusalem.[14] It was not formally proclaimed to be the capital; Ben-Gurion took the view that it had never ceased to be the capital of the Jews since the time of King David. Although it was an inevitable decision, it ran counter to the stated policy of the American government and was the beginning of a source of continuing irritation. From the time of UNSCOP, the Vatican had been concerned to prevent the Christian Holy Places coming under exclusively Jewish control. In the summer of 1948, American Catholics had responded to this with a mass lobby of the White House, in which New York's Cardinal Spellman was well to the fore. The administration's policy was relatively straightforward: it supported the 29 November partition resolution which had defined Jerusalem as a *corpus separatum* and when discussing the nature of diplomatic relations between the two states on 27 May 1948, Lovett had assumed 'that Tel Aviv or a suburb of that city will be selected as the capital by the Provisional Government of Israel'.[15] That assumption was carried through to the General Assembly resolution of 11 December which recommended a United Nations' administration for Jerusalem. The move of the Knesset and government departments from Tel Aviv threatened the good relations which the two countries were enjoying, especially as it was not a matter on which Israel was likely to compromise.

The opening encounter on the subject came in February 1949 when the Israelis announced that they would open their first Knesset in Jerusalem and invited all diplomatic and consular representatives to attend. McDonald argued that to refuse would be to 'wound Jewish sensibilities', but Ethridge believed that the action was the prelude to the incorporation of west Jerusalem into Israel and advised non-attendance. Their views were discussed by Truman and his new Secretary of State, Dean Acheson, on 10 February, resulting in instructions that no American officials were to attend. As if to emphasise the point, the Israelis were to be informed that McDonald would attend the first Knesset session held in Tel Aviv.[16] This heralded the dispute later in the year, once the formal move to Jerusalem was made. At the suggestion of the British, a joint Anglo–American response was made, informing the Israelis that as their sovereignty over Jerusalem was not recognised, all business would be conducted in Tel Aviv. American embassy staff were instructed to keep any unofficial visits to Jerusalem 'to absolute minimum'.[17] As the Foreign Ministry had not been transferred from Tel Aviv, there was no immediate problem, beyond the Israelis' sense of *amour propre*, but in January 1950 its Director-General, Walter Eytan, asked the Americans to indicate what office and residential space they needed in Jerusalem. Acheson refused.[18] Ben-Gurion and his colleagues clearly hoped that the United States would come to terms with the reality that west Jerusalem was firmly in Israel and east Jerusalem had become part of Jordan. Moreover, they resented pressure on them for internationalisation, pointing to the fact that most of the Christian Holy Places were in the Jordanian sector. They also contrasted their own policy of open access for pilgrims in areas such as Nazareth with Jordanian desecration of ancient Jewish sites and refusal to allow Jews to pray at the Western Wall.[19] Evidence that they were not going to compromise came in the summer of 1952 with indications that they were about to transfer the Foreign Ministry to Jerusalem. The United States, Britain, France and Turkey lodged protests, which drew the reply that the move would be made the following May when the offices were ready.[20] In short, if the United States was remaining true to the principle of the international status of Jerusalem, it was in the teeth of Israeli determination to show that the Jews had returned to their ancient capital, or at least part of it.

The Truman administration also had to confront the problem of the dispossessed Palestinians. By 1949, Arab Palestine had ceased to exist. What remained of it, the so-called West Bank and the Gaza strip, had been severed from their traditional economic connexions in what was now Israel, and their populations were swollen with destitute refugees. The annexation of the West Bank by Transjordan in 1950 seemed a sensible arrangement to the State Department but no one had any easy solutions for Gaza, beyond a brief flirtation with the idea that it might be returned to the British. Administered by Egypt and with a population suddenly thrust from 60 000 to 270 000, the bleak refugee camps of this small area, much of it sand dunes, symbolised, for those who cared to visit them, the tragedy of the Palestinians. The plight of the refugees had been identified by Bernadotte in the summer of 1948 and on 17 October, McDonald, a veteran in this field, reported to Truman that the 'Arab refugee tragedy is rapidly reaching catastrophic proportions and should be treated as a disaster ... Of approximately 400,000 refugees [the] approaching winter with cold heavy rains will, it is estimated, kill more than 100 000 old men, women and children who are shelterless and have no food.'[21] Although 400 000 was a widely-quoted figure, it proved to be an underestimate; the following year the Palestine Conciliation Commission calculated the total refugee number to be 774 000.[22] Their hope lay in the General Assembly resolution of 11 December 1948.

American strategy took two directions: measures to secure immediate relief for the refugees and pressure on Israel and the Arab states to face up to the more permanent problem of their future. On 19 November 1948, the United States jointly sponsored a resolution setting up the United Nations Relief for Palestine Refugees. Stanton Griffis, ambassador to Egypt, was appointed director and Truman recommended to Congress that they meet half the cost, $16 000 000. In announcing approval of this on 3 April 1949, Truman expressed the hope that 'before this relief program is ended means will be devised for the permanent solution of the refugee problem'.[23] The men charged with devising this were Ethridge, through his work on the Conciliation Commission, and George McGhee, who had been in charge of the aid programme to Greece and Turkey and who was approached by Rusk to assume special responsibility for the refugees.[24] McGhee's initial conclusions were pessimistic. On 15 March, he reported that it was clear that most of the refugees wished to return to their homes but that this was an 'illusion'. 'Israeli authorities', he observed, 'have followed a systematic program of destroying Arab houses in such cities as Haifa and in village communities in order to rebuild modern habitations for the influx of Jewish immigrants from DP camps in Europe. There are thus, in many instances, literally no houses for the refugees to return to.' In these circumstances, he recommended that Israel repatriate an 'agreed number' of refugees and provide compensation to those whose property had been expropriated. The bulk of the refugees would have to be resettled in 'Arab Palestine', failing which, in other areas of the Middle East.[25]

Acheson tried to follow through these ideas in discussions when the Israeli Foreign Minister, Moshe Sharett, visited Washington a week later. With Truman's approval, he pressed Sharett to allow the return of a quarter of the refugees, especially those from the parts of Israel which had not been allocated to her in the partition resolution. But Sharett would offer no concessions, stating 'that Israel could not give up the minimum security which it had won with so much blood and expenditure by reintroducing large numbers of refugees into the very areas from which Israel had been so seriously threatened'.[26] Truman also took up the matter during Weizmann's visit to Washington but was told that the solution lay 'not in repatriation but in resettlement'.[27] Faced with this impasse, the State Department recommended that Truman make a direct appeal to the Israeli government. If this failed, he should withhold the $49 million still to be transferred under the Export–Import Bank loan. Truman agreed and on 28 May a stern note was sent to the Israeli government which brought together American disquiet on the issues of territory and the refugees; if the Israelis would not honour the resolution of 11 December 1948 and the Americans' 'friendly advice', then 'the US Govt will regretfully be forced to the conclusion that a revision of its attitude toward Israel has become unavoidable'.[28] Although the tone of this message caused considerable alarm to the Israeli government, their reply offered no concessions. They had already indicated to American officials in Tel Aviv that any pressure over the refugees would be countered by a political campaign in Washington. This was swiftly done. McGhee met the Israeli ambassador to inform him that the $49 million would be delayed; Epstein was unimpressed and within an hour McGhee was informed from the White House that the President did not wish to be associated with such a move.[29] There is little reason to doubt that once again David Niles had acted. He took an active interest in anything to do with financial assistance to Israel and, later in the summer, intervened with Truman over moves to delay on a second application to the Export–Import Bank.[30] Although Epstein was prepared to indicate the possibility of allowing the return of 100 000 refugees, the threat of American pressure for large-scale repatriation had been headed off. Convinced that no leverage was going to be put on the Israelis for concessions, Ethridge resigned from the Conciliation Commission.[31]

The encounter had important consequences. For the refugees, it marked the failure of the one serious attempt to force the Israelis to accept a substantial, though far from total, measure of repatriation. American officials, who had already accepted that most of the refugees would have to be resettled outside Israel, now turned to measures of relief and possible rehabilitation. On American suggestion, the Conciliation Commission set up the Economic Survey Mission headed by Gordon Clapp of the Tennessee Valley Authority. Convinced that the political obstacles in the way of repatriation or resettlement were too great, the Mission recommended the establishment of an international agency to be responsible for relief and the provision of works. As a result, in December 1949, the General Assembly set up the United Nations Relief and Works Agency for

Palestine Refugees.[32] Originally created for eighteen months, four decades later UNWRA remained the sole means of sustenance, shelter, education and medical provision for hundreds of thousands of refugees in Gaza, the West Bank, Jordan, Lebanon and Syria, its dedicated workers daily confronting the hopelessness surrounding them.[33] It was not a situation that the American public, or their legislators, knew very much about. In March 1949, McGhee observed that with the exception of the *New York Times* and the *Herald Tribune*, the matter had been ignored in the press and radio. At the end of 1953, a Californian Congressman who had become aware of the refugees during an official visit to Beirut, wrote in some bewilderment to the State Department that within the boundaries the United Nations had intended for Israel 'there must have been some Moslems.'[34]

But in fending off the American challenge the Israeli government could work toward international acceptance; even Britain was becoming reconciled to the reality of the Jewish state. Western leaders were anxious that, with its large east European population, Israel should not incline to the Soviet bloc, especially as they were well aware of the essential role of Czechoslovakia, Bulgaria and Yugoslavia in supplying Israel during the war, obviously with Soviet encouragement.[35] Interests of Western solidarity also argued against a situation whereby the Arab states were armed by the British and Israel by the Americans, particularly if an arms race developed in the region. By the spring of 1950, State Department thinking favoured a joint declaration, presenting a draft to the conference of Western foreign ministers in London at the end of April.

The resulting Tripartite Declaration, issued by the United States, Britain and France on 25 May, ended the Western embargo on arms, so that the states of the region could 'play their part in the defense of the area as a whole'. 'The Three Governments', it added, 'should they find that any of these states was preparing to violate frontiers or armistice lines, would, consistently with their obligations as members of the UN, immediately take action, both within and outside the UN, to prevent such violation.' In part, this was intended to reassure the Arab states that the supply of arms to Israel would not lead to the conquest of the remainder of Arab Palestine, but for the Israelis it carried the clear message that their 1949 frontiers were hardening into reality.[36]

A month after the Tripartite Declaration, the Korean War began. The attention of the Truman administration, already engaged by the 'fall' of China, turned to East Asia. In the global confrontation with communism, the Middle East was a gap between the emergent NATO alliance in Europe and the United Nations' war effort in Korea. American officials were becoming aware of the limitations in Britain's position and began looking for political and military means to help sustain it. In October 1951, proposals were put forward for a Middle East Command to include the United States, Britain, France, Turkey and Egypt. If accepted, it would allow British troops to remain in the network of bases along the Suez Canal, which were considered vital to Western defence, with Egyptian agreement. But the idea died a quick death, as it ignored the strength of Egyptian nationalism which had grown up during seventy years of British presence and which saw the bases as a standing affront to national dignity. Resentment, too, had been stoked by the humiliation of defeat at the hands of Israel which Egyptian officers blamed, with some justice, on the poverty of the training and arms the British had given them. On 23 July 1952, the incompetent and venal regime of King Farouk was overthrown in a military *coup* by the Free Officers. Their titular head was General Mohammed Neguib; the real force came from a group of younger officers of whom Gamal Abdul Nasser and Anwar al-Sadat were to dominate Egyptian affairs for almost thirty years, becoming pivotal figures in the history of American foreign policy.

Despite Truman's association with the creation of Israel, the United States had assets of goodwill in the Arab world. 'The whole picture of the United States at that time was a glamorous one', wrote Nasser's friend and the doyen of Egyptian journalists, Mohamed Heikal, 'Britain and France were fading, hated empires. Russia was five thousand miles away and the ideology of Communism was anathema to the Moslem religion. But America had emerged from the Second World War richer, more powerful and more appealing than ever.'[37] The United States had no cause to be upset at the turn of events in Egypt. On 20 August, their experienced ambassador, Jefferson Caffery, dined with Neguib and his principal officers, reporting that 'they are well-intentioned, patriotic and filled with desire to do something for Egypt. On other hand, they are woefully ignorant of matters economic, financial, political, and international.' For their part, the officers 'emphasized their desire to be particularly friendly with US; they affirmed again they hope in due course to receive "help" from US.'[38] Moves were already in hand for Acheson to issue a statement wishing the new regime well and, despite British misgivings, this was done on 3 September.[39] The State Department was not the only body taking a constructive interest in the Egyptian revolution. The Central Intelligence Agency's Kermit Roosevelt had taken a keen interest in the Free Officers from an early stage, meeting their representatives in Cyprus. The CIA was to foster close links with the new Egyptian leadership, which it saw as a strong counter to communism in the Middle East.[40] While everything seemed set for a productive relationship, the potential for disaster was already there, for a power struggle soon developed between Neguib and Nasser. Two separate government agencies operating in Cairo did not assist the American response; nor did the British and Israelis who soon came to dislike the new regime.

But the nature of that response was to be set by the new administration of Dwight D. Eisenhower. Although an outsider to politics, the new President was not unfamiliar with the Middle East and its problems. As allied commander in North Africa, he had seen something of the Arab world for himself and, as Commander-in-Chief in Europe, had been confronted by the fate of the Jews. But he had no close associates like Niles or Clifford who had a strong sense of commitment to Israel and, in the view of his biographer, he 'was uncomfortable with Jews'.[41] His election in 1952 owed little to their support. His Secretary of State, John Foster Dulles, knew a great deal about the politics of the Arab–Israeli conflict, having been both foreign policy adviser to Dewey and a member of the delegation to the United Nations during the critical days of the Palestine question. He believed, in the view of the leading Jewish Republican, Jacob Javits, 'that Israel was lucky to exist at all and that it should be content to remain as it was.'[42] The communist threat inevitably governed their view of foreign policy. Not content with Truman's policy of containment, the Republicans promised in 1952 that they would 'roll back' communism, a pledge well calculated to engage the emotions of voters of East European origin but which they did nothing about. It meant that the Middle East was seen primarily in the context of Western defence. To Eisenhower's old friend Winston Churchill, since 1951 once again Britain's leader, there was nothing constructive about what was happening in Egypt; Nasser was the 'Egyptian Dictator', threatening positions British troops had defended so tenaciously against the Afrika Korps.

In May 1953, Dulles undertook an extensive tour of the region, visiting Egypt, Israel, Jordan, Lebanon, Syria, Iraq and Saudi Arabia, and meeting spokesmen for the refugees. Its purpose was to try to cultivate better relations with the Arabs, in the obvious hope of involving them more directly in Western defence arrangements. In Egypt he met separately with Neguib and Nasser, seeking to impress the latter with America's goodwill, even assuring him 'that the Republican Administration does not owe the same degree of political debt as did the Democrats to Jewish groups'. But the two men could not agree on the future of the British bases, with Dulles anxious that Britain retain depot facilities to be activated in the event of war. Nasser, for whom the British sixty miles away on the canal were a more obvious threat to national integrity than the Russians at 5000 miles, would concede nothing.[43] Ben-Gurion sought to impress Dulles with the advantages of a defence arrangement with Israel rather than the Arabs, but would offer no concessions on frontiers or the repatriation of refugees: 'what was done cannot now be undone'. Dulles was clearly concerned that America's standing in the Middle East had suffered as 'Arabs feel Roosevelt and Truman administration so subject to Jewish influence that Arab viewpoint ignored'. The main thrust of the discussions with the premier was that Israel could no longer expect to divert American intentions through the exercise of political power in Washington: 'Decisions often taken under pressure United States Jewish groups which felt they had right exercise influence because of contributions to election victory. New administration, Secretary pointed out, was elected by overwhelming vote of American people as a whole and neither owes that type of political debt to any segment nor believes in building power by cultivating particular segments of populations.'[44] It was an unwelcome signal to Ben-Gurion that a test of strength might come.

It came quickly. The previous year, the Israelis had announced that the transfer of their Foreign Minstry would take place in May. This was not done in deference to Dulles's visit but, as the offices were about to close for the weekend on 10 July, the Americans were informed that the move would be made in two days' time. Angered by the decision and the timing of its delivery, there was nothing they could do. Eisenhower ordered Dulles to contact Silver in an attempt to put pressure on the Israelis to reconsider but the Rabbi could not be reached over the Sabbath.[45] Dulles's response was to announce that the embassy would not be transferred to Jerusalem. Embassy staff were instructed to refuse invitations to official functions in the city and only to conduct business with the Foreign Ministry through a liaison office it had left behind in Tel Aviv. Despite an Israeli protest that it was 'inconceivable' that the Americans should regard Jerusalem as 'out of bounds', the State Department considered that Dulles's action would 'help to impress upon Israel Government that it cannot act on matters of area of world concern without regard to legitimate interests of other countries and free world as a whole.'[46]

Serious though it was, the quarrel was merely the prelude to the most bitter episode yet to develop between the two countries. From Roosevelt's time, the idea had lingered in Washington that a possible way forward in the Middle East was the development of its water resources with a view to fostering development and encouraging co-operation. It was not a good idea but it was well intentioned and, as such, taken up by the new administration. A study was undertaken by the TVA and Eric Johnston was appointed Personal Representative of the President to work out a plan. But as water was the key resource in the region, the Israelis wanted as much of it as possible to sustain their own rising population and irrigation schemes. Not only was the issue one of the utmost sensitivity, but on 2 September the Israelis began cutting a canal at Banat Yacoub in the demilitarised zone with Syria to divert the Jordan waters. This was a highly sensitive area where the United Nations Truce Supervision Organisation had responsibility for seeing to the observance of the armistice agreement. The organisation's head, Major-General Vagn Bennike, investigated the work and ordered it stopped. Not only was Israel's action seen to be in violation of the United Nations, but the embassy in Tel Aviv reported that it was an attempt to undermine the TVA study and gain control of all the Jordan waters.[47] Coming so soon after the Foreign Ministry move, Dulles was deeply angered at the turn of events. In a frigid interview with Abba Eban, he taxed the ambassador with his government's recent actions: 'The Israeli Foreign Minister had said, "What we have, we hold." This makes for a situation here that it is Israeli government policy to create situations and then say "Here I am, unless thrown out by force." It would be much easier if Israel had more regard for UN action and legal processes.' Dulles ended the interview by threatening to withhold American aid.[48]

This, of course, was a possibility that had first been raised in 1950. The Americans had long known how vulnerable Israel was to the possibility of financial sanctions. Under her Law of Return the state had pressed ahead with the absorption of hundreds of thousands of European and Middle Eastern Jews without the money to do so and, in the American view, 'regardless of the exiles' capabilities, as individuals or as groups, to contribute to the productivity of the nation'. Moreover, contributions through the United Jewish Appeal in the United States were falling dramatically from a peak of $148 million in 1948, to $85 million in 1951 and $39 million in the first five months of 1952. In June 1952, with the country unable to meet its financial obligations, Sharett had to come to Washington to arrange for a re-funding of Israel's short-term debts, having to accept the services of an American expert to sort out the financial confusion.[49] In such circumstances, it was not surprising that the State Department advised Dulles in May 1953 that 'Israel is not a viable state and requires outside financial assistance. It has been largely sustained by United States contributions, private and public.'[50] Faced with Israel's refusal to follow Bennike's orders on Banat Yacoub canal, Dulles ordered the suspension of $26 million in aid provision, this at a time when Israel was already appealing to Jews for funds to avoid having to default on debt repayments.[51]

But the crisis deepened. On 13 October, an attack on a house at the Israeli settlement of Tirat Yehuda killed a mother and her two children. Although the Jordanians offered to help capture the killers, the following day Israeli forces retaliated against the Jordanian village of Qibya, demolishing some 39 houses and killing 69 villagers, many of them women and children. At first, Ben-Gurion tried to claim the action as the work of civilians incensed at the Tirat Yehuda attack, but the American government knew better.[52] On 18 October, the administration issued a statement condemning the 'shocking' events at Qibya and two days later Dulles revealed at his news conference that Israel's aid allocation had been deferred.[53] As in 1950, political forces were activated in Washington to counter Dulles's move. It was co-ordinated by I. L. Kenen, a veteran of the 1947–1948 campaign, who had registered as a lobbyist on behalf of the American Zionist Council in 1951. As well as letters from Congressmen, Kenen put together a group of influential Jews, including Jacob Javits, Senator Irving M. Ives, Philip M. Klutznick, President of B'nai B'rith, and Louis Lipsky, Chairman of the American Zionist Council, to meet Dulles. Faced with the complaint that he was treating the Israelis and Arabs with different standards, the Secretary went on the offensive: 'He suggested that the group might spend some time working with representatives of the Israeli Government to try to change their policy of presenting the world with *faits accomplis*. Cooperation seemed to be a one-way street as far as Israel was concerned. He said that we had been working very hard with the Arabs but no one in the group seemed interested in that.'[54] The following day, 27 October, the Israeli government announced the suspension of work on the canal; Dulles released the $26 million.[55]

This was the first serious rift between the two governments, but the undercurrent of tension continued throughout much of 1954. Dulles was principally concerned during that time with the Geneva Conference, which brought to an end the French war in Indo-China, and was content to leave the Middle East to his Assistant Secretary of State for Near Eastern, South Asian and African Affairs, Henry A. Byroade. Byroade shared the State Department's irritation with the Israelis over a number of issues. In particular, they contrasted the reparations agreement which Konrad Adenauer's Germany had made with Israel in 1952, partly at America's urging, with Jerusalem's refusal to compensate the Palestinian refugees for the loss of their property or to release their blocked bank accounts. Although they were alarmed over violations of the ceasefire line, they were inclined to believe that those from the Arab side were the work of isolated individuals and compared them unfavourably with the large-scale retaliation of the Israeli state.[56] In addition, the idea of some kind of Middle East Defense Organisation had never gone away, and in February it was decided that military aid would be extended to Iraq. When added to the problems which had arisen the previous year, this did not foster a climate of goodwill. The Israelis were annoyed by the tone of American policy and stung by charges they felt took inadequate account of their security concerns, which they believed were being further threatened by Western moves to bring certain Arab states into their defence network and by Britain's impending departure from the Suez Canal. The tensions between these separate perceptions were becoming palpable, the frustration felt by many American officials being expressed forcefully by Roger S. Tyler, Consul in Jerusalem: 'If Israel from her sense of chosen destiny, arrogance and terrible subjectivity cannot be made to realize the consequences of her acts she may perish and not impossibly the world with her. She must be patient and know that we will support her if she does and that because we disapprove certain of her acts does not mean we are deserting her. But there is a limit.'[57]

On 19 April 1954, Dulles confided to the President his fears over Israeli attitudes, who 'agreed that we should continue our present policy of impartiality and should not be deterred by political pressures which might generate in connection with the forthcoming elections'. Their discussion was almost certainly the result of the storm of diplomatic and political protest provoked by a speech

Byroade had made in Dayton on 9 April. Here, Byroade had indulged in serious public criticism of Israel in a manner so far unique to an American official:

> To the Israelis I say that you should come to truly look upon yourselves as a Middle Eastern State and see your future in that context rather than as a headquarters, or nucleus, so to speak, of worldwide groupings of peoples of a particular religious faith who must have special rights within and obligations to the Israeli state. You should drop the attitude of the conqueror and the conviction that force and a policy of retaliatory killings is the only policy that your neighbors will understand. You should make your deeds correspond to your frequent utterance of the desire for peace.

Despite the storm such a hard-hitting attack on Israel's policies and the attitudes of her American supporters inevitably aroused, Byroade maintained his offensive in a second speech on 1 May, pointedly to the anti-Zionist American Council for Judaism. In this, he took up the issue of the refugees, the need for some to be repatriated inside Israel and for all of them to be compensated for the loss of property. This was a familiar theme in Israeli–American relations, but he went further in pointing to Israel's Law of Return as a basic element of instability in the Middle East, as Arab 'fears are enhanced by the knowledge that the only limitation imposed by statute on immigration into Israel is, in fact, the total number of those of the Jewish faith in the entire world. The Arabs know the capacity of the territory of Israel is limited. They see only one result – future attempt at territorial expansion – and hence warfare of serious proportions.'[58] To say this was to question the essence of the State of Israel, as her diplomats pointed out in their pained reaction to Byroade's speech.

Despite the controversy generated by Byroade's speeches, they were not to mark any major new departure in American policy. By the autumn, relations between the two countries were beginning to improve and were not seriously marred by the tragically mismanaged Israeli secret mission inside Egypt which began to unfold in July. Fearful of the effects of the planned British departure from Egypt, Israeli intelligence officers set up an operation designed to discredit Nasser's regime in Western eyes. Amongst other places, the United States Information Service offices in Cairo and Alexandria were bombed before the agents were arrested. Within days of the network's discovery and interrogation, the Egyptian police showed an official of the Cairo embassy their evidence that the bombing of

American property had been the work of Israeli intelligence agents.[59] It is not known what use the Americans made of this inconvenient knowledge but, when thirteen members of the network were put on trial at the end of the year, delicate approaches that Washington might intervene to reduce their sentences were politely declined.[60] Two were hanged and the rest given long prison terms.

The affair shook the Israeli political establishment. Ben-Gurion, who had retired from office, returned to the cabinet in February as Defence Minister, subsequently resuming the premiership. Within days of his taking office, the Israeli army invaded the Gaza Strip in force. Frontier violations had for months irritated Egyptian–Israeli relations, each side inevitably casting blame on the other. They formed the ostensible reason for the Israeli action, which was really concerned with reassuring a public opinion rattled by the intelligence disaster, and demonstrating to the Egyptians and the West that Israel was an effective military power. But, with thirty-eight of his soldiers dead, it presented Nasser with a challenge which, as a newly-established revolutionary military leader, he could not afford to ignore. Faced with the necessity of improving the quality of his armed forces, he grew increasingly frustrated at the slow progress of his negotiations with the United States and Britain. Attracted by the idea of neutralism coming from India's Prime Minister Jawaharlal Nehru, he accepted an invitation to attend the non-aligned conference in Bandoeng in March, contrary to American advice. Not only did this mark the beginning of tensions between his government and the Americans, he also took the opportunity to sound out China's Chou En-lai about the possibility of military supplies from the Soviet Union.[61] By the summer, encouraging noises were coming from the Soviet leaders, and another massive Israeli raid on the Gaza Strip on 31 August convinced Nasser that he should accept what they had to offer. He had confided in Henry Byroade, now ambassador to Cairo, something of what was happening, but despite America's interventions in the course of September, including an attempt by the CIA's Kermit Roosevelt to impress on the Egyptians how seriously Washington would regard such a move, on 30 September Nasser announced his acceptance of an arms deal with 'Czechoslovakia'. Although the CIA saw his action as successfully playing off East against West rather than an as a straightforward anti-Western move, it gave the Soviet Union her first foothold in the Middle East and, as such, could not but strike a hostile chord with Dulles and the administration.[62]

Although the Americans tried hard to maintain a relationship with him, Nasser's action set the scene for the Middle East crisis of 1956. Evidence that Washington had not given up on the Egyptian leader came in December with the start of discussions for Anglo–American financial assistance for the construction of the Aswan Dam through the agency of the World Bank. As the dam was believed to hold the key to Egypt's economic progress, it sat well with the American belief that such projects would help bring peace and stability to the region. The same month, Eisenhower sent Robert Anderson as his special envoy to probe what common ground existed between Nasser and Ben-Gurion. But the Egyptians found him naive and uninformed and in any case Nasser knew that his position as hero of the 'Arab revolution' could not stand direct negotiations with the Israeli leader.[63] Anderson's failure did not encourage the administration to push ahead with the Aswan project, which it knew would meet with congressional resistance, and in the meantime Nasser's standing in the West continued to decline. Feelings against him ran strongest amongst the French who believed him to be the inspiration behind the rebellion in Algeria which was increasingly tying down their resources. Britain's new Prime Minister, Anthony Eden, vulnerable to Conservative criticism that he had abandoned the Suez Canal bases, increasingly saw him as a threat to the imperial posture in the Middle East. This was apparently confirmed when on 1 March 1956, Sir John Glubb and other senior British officers were dismissed from command of Jordan's Arab Legion, the incident seen by many as the start of the 'Suez crisis'. From then on, Eden saw Nasser through the prism of his experience in the 1930s when Britain and France had failed to stand up to the dictators until it was too late.

These views of Nasser's anti-Western posture were confirmed for the administration in May when Nasser recognised the People's Republic of China, always a sensitive issue with Americans but particularly so in view of the crisis over the Formosa Strait the previous year. 'By the middle of June', Eisenhower recorded, 'my associates and I were becoming doubtful of the wisdom of United States participation in the Aswan Dam project', not least because they doubted Egypt's ability to pay. With congressional opposition growing in an election year, on 19 July Dulles informed the Egyptian ambassador that American aid was no longer on offer.[64] Although he had not consulted the British, they, too, withdrew. Nasser's riposte, announced in a speech at Alexandria on 26 July, was the national-isation of the Suez Canal Company, an international concern with its headquarters in Paris which ran the canal. The British and French saw his actions as a direct challenge for control of the Middle East, which they could not afford to shirk. Military preparations using the British bases in Malta and Cyprus were soon under way. 'Failure to keep the canal international', Eden recorded, 'would inevitably lead to the loss one by one of all our interests and assets in the Middle East, and even if Her Majesty's Government had to act alone they could not stop short of using force to protect their position.'[65]

From the start, Eisenhower and Dulles kept cooler heads than their British and French counterparts. This was not easy, for these were the country's closest allies, bound by personal ties extending back to World War 2. But the American view was that the canal fell clearly within Egyptian sovereignty and that to resort to action without fully exploring the possibility of an acceptable settlement, ideally through the United Nations, would be a breach of international legality. On 31 July, Dulles flew to London bearing a letter from the President warning Eden of his 'own personal conviction as well as that of my associates, as to the unwisdom even of contemplating the use of military force at this moment'. Even if the situation were to deteriorate, he reminded Eden of the constitutional obstacles in the way of using American forces.[66] Faced with the massive Anglo–French military build-up in the Mediterranean, the Americans hoped that by sending such warnings against action they could allow diplomacy to work and, as the summer passed with Nasser operating the canal normally, they had grounds for believing that this would happen. Negotiations at the London Conference in August, in which Dulles took a leading part, produced a scheme for a form of international control for the canal. Diplomacy appeared to be working as Australia's Robert Menzies and diplomats from the United States, Ethiopia, Iran and Sweden took the proposal to Cairo.

But, as Dulles was not convinced that Britain and France were really committed to the plan, or that Nasser would accept it, an even stronger message to the British on the use of force was judged necessary. Eisenhower's letter, sent on 2 September, shocked Eden. 'I must tell you frankly', it said, 'that American public opinion flatly rejects the thought of using force, particularly when it does not seem that every possible means of protecting our vital interests has been exhausted without result. Moreover, I gravely doubt we could here secure Congressional authority even for the lesser support measures for which you might have to look to us. I really do not see how a successful result could be achieved by forcible means.' Eden's reply showed how far apart the two countries were in their appreciation of the situation. Drawing on the parallel of the failure to stop Hitler in the Rhineland, the British leader ended with an emotional appeal that it would be an 'ignoble end' to his country's history to submit to Nasser's blackmail. Eisenhower's reply, more prosaic but recognising the essential point that an impoverished Middle Eastern country could hardly be equated with Nazi Germany, told Eden that he was making of Nasser a much more important figure than he was.[67] The administration could not be accused of sending weak signals to London.

But any hope that the Americans could hold the line against hostilities was fated by approaches being made between the French and Israelis and by the growing distaste, verging on contempt, Eden felt for Dulles. By the end of September, the British Prime Minister had become convinced that Dulles's diplomatic moves were simply designed as delaying tactics and was anxious that Britain and France should take their own action.[68] The opportunity to do so was presented to him by the French and Israelis. As the Middle East crisis developed, Ben-Gurion and his government had sensed that it could be used to advantage in their own quarrel with Egypt. Israel, of course, had been even more apprehensive over Nasser's military links with the Soviet bloc than the Americans and British; in particular, they feared the threat posed to the civilian populations of Tel Aviv, Haifa and Jerusalem by his Ilyushin-28 jet bombers. When the French suggested in early September that Israel might take part in an Anglo–French military action, Ben-Gurion and his defence chiefs responded eagerly. For the Israeli military commanders the irresistible prospect had opened up of conducting an operation against the Egyptians with their cities protected by the French air force.[69] But neither party could move without the British, bound by treaty to a number of Arab states and not notably partial towards Israel, for the French air force needed their bases in Cyprus and only the Royal Air Force had the long-range bombers needed to destroy the Ilyushins' airfields. By 14 October, discussions were sufficiently advanced for a French military mission to put to Eden the essence of a plan whereby the Israelis would attack in the Sinai desert, allowing the British and French to present ultimata to Israel and Egypt to stop fighting. On this being refused, an Anglo–French landing on the canal would be launched to 'separate the combatants'. This was the essence of the plan agreed at a secret meeting at Sèvres on 22–24 October attended by representatives of the three governments, including Ben-Gurion and his Chief of Staff, Moshe Dayan, the French Prime Minister, as well as a rather reluctant British Foreign Secretary.[70]

On 29 October, Israeli paratroops dropped at the Mitla pass, armoured columns advanced into Sinai secure in the knowledge that French aircraft were protecting Tel Aviv and Haifa, and the plan unfolded. The Anglo–French ultimata issued the following day were rejected and the Royal Air Force began bombing Egyptian airfields preparatory to a landing on the canal. As all of these moves had been prepared in the utmost secrecy, the Americans were left to respond as best they could. The first indication to Eisenhower of a possible new dimension to the crisis came on 15 October when Dulles presented him with intelligence reports of Israeli mobilisation; their interpretation at this stage was that Ben-Gurion might seize the opportunity presented by the canal controversy and the imminent presidential election to attack Jordan, and an appropriate warning was issued. The Americans fell victim to a skilled and highly effective disinformation campaign by the Israeli intelligence services that Jordan was the target of their military preparations; as a result Eisenhower's warnings were irrelevant. As his attack began, Dayan confided in his diary that the position with the Americans was 'complicated, and not at all agreeable'.[71] He was identifying, rather belatedly, the fatal flaw in the tripartite plan, the American response.

The various accounts of the Anglo–French–Israeli moves give little indication that the American response was adequately considered. The British attitude appears to have been that Eisenhower would only have been embarrassed if he were informed in advance and that the Americans had never ruled out the use of force as a last resort. The French held that Dulles would not raise serious objections to what they were contemplating. The Israelis, relying on the close friendship between London and Washington, did not expect the Americans to adopt an anti-British position.[72] In the event, these were false assumptions which proved fatal to their plans. From the start of the crisis, Eisenhower, while making clear his distaste for Nasser's actions and possible intentions, had urged against the use of force. Despite his advice, the Middle East was at war at a time of maximum embarrassment to him. On 19 October, the first signs of trouble appeared in Poland which by the 22nd had led to confrontation with the Soviet leadership and demonstrations in many cities. By the 23rd, revolution had broken out in Budapest. The new leader, Imre Nagy, informed the Russians that Hungary was withdrawing from the Warsaw Pact. Unable to tolerate such a fracturing of their authority in Eastern Europe, on 4 November the Soviet leaders responded with overwhelming force and in bitter street fighting the Hungarian rising was suppressed. With the presidential election due on 6 November, an administration which had once promised to 'roll back' communism was forced to contemplate the hollowness of its rhetoric.

In the Middle East, America's allies were threatening to expose what had been another element in Eisenhower's successful appeal in 1952, namely that he would be the President of peace. Both from an international and a domestic point of view, their action was unfortunate and ill-timed, the more so when he learned on 2 November about the nature of the 'collusion' amongst the three countries.[73] On 5 November, the Anglo–French airborne assault on Port Said began, followed on the 6th, polling day, by their amphibious forces. As the battle raged around Port Said and the Soviet leadership issued threats against Britain, France and Israel, the pressures on Eden, whose health had become precarious, became intolerable. Hostilities between Israel and Egypt, the ostensible reason for the expedition, had stopped. But the ultimate sanctions came from Washington. The crisis had triggered a run on British reserves, particularly serious since sterling was a reserve currency and much of the speculation against it was the work of the United States Treasury. Moves by Britain's Chancellor of the Exchequer, Harold Macmillan, to draw on British funds from the International Monetary Fund were obstructed by Treasury Secretary George Humphrey. As the British cabinet met on the evening of 6 November, Macmillan told the Foreign Secretary that 'in view of the financial and economic pressures we must stop'.[74] In a decision much resented by the French, the military operations were halted from midnight. Eisenhower said nothing in his memoirs about the pressure which had been exerted; nor did Eden, beyond an admission that the 'course of the Suez Canal crisis was decided by the American attitude to it'.[75]

Nor did American pressure relent in the days ahead. A mechanism for defusing the crisis had been provided by the Canadians through a United Nations Emergency Force (UNEF) which could supervise the situation until the British, French and Israeli troops had been evacuated from Egypt. But the British and French wished to retain their troops in the Port Said bridgehead as a 'gauge' which would force Nasser to negotiate a settlement of the Arab–Israeli conflict and internationalisation of the canal. Even more pronounced was Ben-Gurion's reluctance to relinquish his gains in the Sinai, especially

Sharm al-Sheikh at the entrance to the Strait of Tiran which guaranteed freedom of navigation to the port of Eilat. None of this proved possible. Negotiations by the British to use their bridgehead as a bargaining counter with Nasser drew a stony response: nothing short of unconditional withdrawal would satisfy the administration. When it became clear at the end of November that the Anglo–French force was being withdrawn from Port Said, Eisenhower was satisfied. 'We now began financial help to the British', he later commented.[76] His disobedient European allies had at last been brought to heel.

The withdrawal of Israeli troops from Sinai was likely to prove more obstinate, for not only was Ben-Gurion a tougher character than Eden but Nasser's Egypt was his country's main antagonist. Before tackling this problem, Eisenhower turned to what he saw as the most immediate danger likely to arise out of the recent debacle: Soviet aggrandisement in the Middle East. On 1 January 1957, he and Dulles met leading congressmen to persuade them that the vacuum in the region 'must be filled by the United States before it is filled by Russia'. So important did he judge it that Eisenhower felt it necessary to deliver a major speech to Congress four days later, the theme of which was 'Russia's desire to dominate the Middle East'. In outlining the threat, he asked Congress to authorise programmes of economic and military assistance for the countries of the region. More importantly, he asked for the power to use armed force to maintain the independence of any country 'requesting such aid, against overt armed aggression from any nation controlled by International Communism'.[77] Despite reservations on the part of many congressmen, not just those sympathetic to Israel, these proposals, now known as the 'Eisenhower Doctrine', passed into law on 9 March. It was an act of real symbolism. Just as the Truman Doctrine in regard to Greece and Turkey in 1947 had marked the transfer of world power from Britain to the United States, this confirmed that Western interests in the Middle East from now on would be the prime responsibility of the Americans.

As if to confirm their new pre-eminence, Eisenhower and Dulles turned their attention to the Israelis. Although in the initial elation at his military victory, Ben-Gurion indicated that Israel was in Sinai to stay, it soon became clear that what he really intended was to use his occupation to bargain for secure navigation through the Strait of Tiran and Israeli administration of the Gaza Strip. The American view was that Israel's withdrawal had to be 'prompt and unconditional' but that the functions of UNEF should be expanded to include Sharm al-Sheikh and the Gaza Strip. When Israel refused to accept this on 15 February, confrontation was in the air. Dulles's argument was simple. If they failed to secure Israeli compliance, then the states of the Middle East would conclude that their policy was controlled by Jewish influence in the United States and would see no alternative but to turn to the Soviet Union, destroying the Eisenhower Doctrine at birth. Agreeing with this analysis, Eisenhower began to prepare sanctions which would include the suspension not just of official aid but of private Israeli fund-raising in the country.[78]

Faced with a threat which would undermine their financial stability, the Israelis could mobilise the legendary stubbornness of their leader, the diplomatic skills of their ambassador, Abba Eban, and sympathetic politicians. Political support was rallied in Congress, with Senator Lyndon B. Johnson prominent, a matter of some importance when he had to preside over a similar situation a decade later. But the timing was out: with the election safely behind them the administration could ignore congressional opposition. On 20 February, Eisenhower went on television and radio. While he did not make public the nature of the sanctions he was contemplating against Israel, his tone was stern and unyielding. 'I would, I feel', he said, 'be untrue to the standards of the high office to which you have chosen me if I were to lend the influence of the United States to the proposition that a nation which invades another should be permitted to exact conditions for withdrawal.' He indicated that they should not assume that Egypt would interfere with Israeli shipping. This probably referred to a secret assurance given by Nasser as part of the conditions for an Israeli withdrawal that he would maintain the Strait of Tiran as an international waterway.[79]

In view of the speech and the prospect of United Nations sanctions, Ben-Gurion held an extraordinary cabinet meeting as a result of which he informed Eisenhower of his desire to co-operate. In detailed discussions involving Dulles, Eban and UN Secretary-General Dag Hammarskjold, the terms of Israel's evacuation were worked out. In return for total withdrawal, UNEF was to be stationed in Sinai, including the Gaza Strip and Sharm al-Sheikh. It took up position in March and worked well for ten years. Ultimately no more than 1400 strong, its presence could be nothing more than symbolic but it allowed the peace to be kept. On 1 March, Foreign Minister Golda Meir announced to the General Assembly that Israel would withdraw from the Sinai, instancing Eisenhower's statement on Egyptian intentions towards Israeli shipping as an important consideration with her government but also warning that any future interference with that traffic would be regarded as a *casus belli*. American pressure had succeeded but it was an acrimonious affair for all concerned. Mrs Meir considered Dulles a 'cold, grey man' with whom she could not communicate her country's fears. As the Israelis withdrew from Sinai they destroyed installations and left uncleared and uncharted minefields. Most worrying of all was Nasser's breach of an assurance he had given not to reoccupy Gaza by sending in administrators.[80] It was a predictably rancorous end to an unsatisfactory affair.

The policies pursued by Eisenhower and Dulles have been bitterly criticised. Their punitive attitude towards Israel in Sinai was inevitably contrasted with their acquiescence in the Soviet repression of the Hungarian rising. Following Eden's logic, if they had supported their two principal allies Nasser would have been destroyed, or at best curbed, avoiding the growth of pan-Arab radicalism in the late 1950s to which the pro-British monarchy in Iraq fell victim. Their policy had not been without its ambiguities which deluded the British into the belief that they would not oppose the use of force, but ultimately they saw the undertaking as unjustified, ill-conceived and in defiance of the accepted standard of international morality. Many of these assumptions were soon to be tested in the final Middle East crisis of the administration, the landings in Lebanon in July 1958.

As a consequence of the events at Suez, anti-imperialist sentiments, inspired by Nasser, caught the imagination of much of the Middle East. At the beginning of 1958, the Syrians joined Nasser in forming the United Arab Republic. The fragile unity of Lebanon was threatened by the growing restiveness of 'Nasserist', mostly Muslim, groups hostile to the pro-Western government of President Camille Chamoun. American fears for the West's interests in the region were brought into sharp focus on 14 July when the Iraqi army overthrew the monarchy, killing Nuri as-Said, a long-standing ally of the British. Fears grew for the fellow Hashemite monarchy in Jordan, which was known to inspire limited loyalty from its Palestinian majority. Faced with the possible collapse of the Western position in the region, the administration had to respond to appeals from Chamoun and King Hussein for Anglo–American military intervention to sustain their regimes, in short the Eisenhower Doctrine was under test. There were obvious objections to intervention: the reaction of the Soviet Union had to be considered, as did the inevitable comparison which would be made with the Anglo–French landing at Suez. Nevertheless, the decision was taken and with the Sixth Fleet already in a position to respond, on 15 July marines began landing near Beirut. Two days later, with Israeli concurrence, British paratroopers arrived at Amman. On 25 October, with a pro-Western successor to Chamoun safely in office, the American forces withdrew. As a limited operation, efficiently conducted and with a finite purpose, it had been a success. Later policymakers might have profited better from it.

The Lebanese intervention proved to be the last major American initiative for nearly a decade. Other foreign policy issues dominated the agenda at the end of the Eisenhower period and into the 1960s. The relative quiet in the Middle East was partly the result of the settlement of the 1956–57 crisis in which the United States had taken the leading part. It may be said that Eisenhower and Dulles had fulfilled their aim of preventing Soviet domination of the Middle East, but whether that was because of or, as their critics claimed, despite, their policies is less clear. They had certainly broken with the strong support for Israel which had continued to mark the Truman administration's perspective of the region. Even so, many of the criticisms of Israel, especially over Jerusalem and the repatriation of refugees, were already coming through strongly under Acheson and perhaps only really matured under his successor. Only once, however, prior to 1956 was Dulles's displeasure translated into any kind of sanction, and then only briefly. The public criticisms of Byroade never formed the basis of a new policy. By the late 1950s, the Palestinians had largely ceased to feature in policy statements and even contributions to UNWRA became an area of controversy. Yet the eight years of the Eisenhower administration were the low point of the American–Israeli relationship and Israelis never forgot the pressure which had forced them out of Sinai. On the other side, the Americans had tried to develop, but ultimately failed to sustain, a relationship with the forces of Arab revolution. As the Eisenhower period ended, the British had been eliminated as the dominant Western power in the region, their place taken by the Americans. However fraught it might have been, the relationship with the United States had become, as Abba Eban conceded, the 'central truth' for those in charge of Israel's foreign policy.[81] The history of American policy in the Middle East was to become in no small measure the story of that simple fact.

4 The Transformation of America's Middle East Policy

The years between John F. Kennedy's inauguration in January 1961 and the end of the October war of 1973 saw the Middle East develop from an area where the United States had interests but no deep commitments into one of Washington's main priorities in foreign policy. By the end of this period, the United States had become Israel's chief friend and protector, was fostering a new relationship with Egypt, had been deeply involved in conflict regulation, and was engaged in the search for peace in the Middle East. These were developments which it would have been difficult to predict in the early 1960s. Kennedy took office at a time when the Middle East was relatively quiet. Israel was making rapid advances toward achieving a European standard of living and Nasser showed no interest in provoking another conflict with her, sheltering behind the convenient fiction of UNEF's 1400 soldiers. Kennedy's Secretary of State, Dean Rusk, had a close knowledge of the Arab–Israeli conflict but that only served to confirm the official view of its intractable nature. As neither man could see any promise of negotiating a final settlement between the parties, the best policy seemed to be to let well alone. A major dimension of Kennedy's foreign policy was to try to improve relations with the leaders of the non-aligned movement of which Nasser's Egypt was an important part. As a result, a major food programme was started which resulted in the United States feeding some 40 per cent of the Egyptian population but when Nasser's capacity for rhetoric led him to denounce this, it was discontinued.[1] Under Kennedy and Lyndon Johnson the country's interests were elsewhere, in Berlin, over Cuba, and then increasingly the involvement which was to overshadow all other aspects of foreign policy and threaten to tear the country apart, Vietnam.

But the peace which seemed to have settled over the Middle East was an illusion, for the old distrust and hatred remained. These found particular focus on the familiar issues of the Syrian demilitarised zone, the Palestinian refugees and that most precious Middle Eastern resource, water. The Israeli Jordan Waters Scheme of the early 1960s aroused a furious, but impotent, reaction in surrounding Arab countries. It was out of the Cairo conference held in January 1964 to consider the Arab response to this that the Palestine Liberation Organisation was born, though it was kept under firm control by the Egyptians. The ambiguous nature of the arrangements in the demilitarised zone, which had plagued Dulles, led to what the Syrians believed were systematic Israeli encroachments on Arab farmland. The resulting Syrian bombardments of Israeli settlements in the Chula valley from the Golan Heights measurably increased the sense of tension. It took over a decade for members of the Palestinian elite to recover from the shattering events of 1948–49. But as hundreds of thousands of Palestinians endured the sterile existence of the refugee camps, their hopes for a return to homes and land unrealised year after year, groups began to form, the most notable of which was The Movement for the Liberation of Palestine, Al Fateh, led by Yasir Arafat. On 1 January 1965, having had the benefit of Syrian training and arms, Fateh began its policy of raids into Israel which it was able to sustain to the increasing irritation of the Israelis. By November 1966, when the Israeli army mounted a large-scale retaliatory raid on the West Bank village of Samu, the precarious nature of 'peace' in the Middle East ought to have been apparent, but American attention was on South-east Asia where Johnson had announced that there would be no limit to the number of troops sent.

This was the context of American actions during the crisis which resulted in the Six Day War of 1967 and changed the map of the Middle East. Warned, misleadingly it appeared, by the Soviets of an imminent Israeli strike against Damascus, Nasser responded with well-publicised movements of armoured units into Sinai and an ill-phrased demand that UNEF withdraw from its observation posts along the Egyptian border. The Egyptian leader saw this as a carefully-measured move which would signal his concern without triggering a conflict, for his demand did not include the UNEF forces in the only areas that really mattered, the Gaza Strip and Sharm al-Sheikh. On 19 May, however, Secretary-General U Thant concluded that he had no option but to close down the entire UNEF operation. Although the decision has been ably defended, the Americans believed that he made a fundamental error in not taking the issue to the Security Council or the General Assembly, thus allowing time for negotiation.[2] Whatever judgement is reached, the result of U Thant's action was to transform a heightening of tension into the prospect of a Middle East war. Two days later, with UNEF no longer in Sharm al-Sheikh, Nasser announced the blockade of Israeli shipping in the Gulf of Aqaba. U Thant's move had left him no choice, but his action was a clear breach of the secret undertaking he had given Israel in 1957 that the Strait of Tiran would remain an international waterway and in the knowledge that Israel had always said that any such blockade would constitute a *casus belli*. Trapped by a situation not entirely of his own making, his conduct became an unstable mixture of extreme public bellicosity, which raised the feeling of tension in Israel, combined with private assurances channelled through the Soviets that he was not planning to attack.[3]

This amounted to a difficult situation for the American administration, whose ability to take decisive action was in any case severely limited. Because of poor relations with Nasser and the Syrian leadership, it had little influence in Arab capitals except perhaps in Amman, but even there King Hussein ultimately preferred to follow the path of Arab solidarity. Relations with Israel were cordial but the fact that the country's major arms supplier was France, not the United States, meant that there was little effective pressure Washington could exert. Just as Nasser wobbled uncertainly between fire-eating speeches and peaceful overtures, the moderate government of Levi Eshkol and Abba Eban was under severe attack from the influential supporters of Ben-Gurion and Menahem Begin who voiced the public's demand for an effective riposte to the Arab forces massing on the orders. In assessing this volatile situation, several things were clear. With troop levels in Vietnam building up to half a million, neither resources nor public opinion would support active American involvement in the Middle East. As the Soviet Union supplied the Egyptian and Syrian armed forces, any conflict might carry the risk of a clash between Washington and Moscow. Finally, the intelligence assessments given to the administration showed that if there were to be a war, the Israelis would win it quickly and decisively.[4]

With the closure of the Strait on 23 May, the position had become acute and the administration increased its diplomatic efforts accordingly. Johnson issued a statement confirming that he 'considers the gulf to be an international waterway and feels that a blockade of Israeli shipping is illegal and potentially disastrous to the cause of peace'.[5] His purpose was to try to reach a peaceful solution to the problem of the Strait, which was the most obvious point at issue. The focus was possibly wrong, for the blockade began to take second place to the Arab military build-up and the consequent Israeli mobilisation. But despite the increasingly war-like sounds coming from the Middle East, the Americans believed that they could still defuse the situation, for the Israelis had told them that they had time to negotiate a peaceful opening of the Strait and they had the Soviet assurance that Nasser did not intend a war.[6] But to the Israelis, fearful for the safety of their coastal cities, American policy 'showed ominous signs of caution'. Faced with Johnson's appeal that Israel take no unilateral military action and his statement that 'You will not be alone unless you go alone', Eban persuaded his colleagues to allow him to undertake a diplomatic mission to Washington, which would also take in Paris and London.[7] The meeting with President de Gaulle was unsatisfactory, for the French leader kept insisting that Israel must not go to war. Since the end of the Algerian war, the French had been trying to mend their fences with the Arabs, while continuing to be Israel's main source of arms. De Gaulle's subsequent belief that the Israelis had disregarded his advice led to the ending of that relationship, with profound consequences for American involvement in the Middle East, but that lay in the future. Harold Wilson was more sympathetic, promising British co-operation in an international attempt to reopen the Strait. Nevertheless, it was clear that the United States held the key to any diplomatic action.[8]

Eban's negotiations with Johnson, Rusk and Defense Secretary Robert McNamara on 25 and 26 May were designed to test the force of the commitments Eisenhower and Dulles had made in 1957. The information he was receiving from home about the aggressive nature of the Egyptian military deployments did not tally with American information, but he was able to sense the administration's sympathy. While Johnson readily agreed that the Strait was an international waterway which had to be reopened, he could not accede to Eban's request that an attack upon Israel would amount to an attack upon the United States. In essence, the President wanted time to negotiate a compromise on the blockade or to give effect to the British suggestion of a multinational naval force for the Gulf of Aqaba. Repeatedly, he urged that Israel take no unilateral military action.[9] But the military pressures on the Israelis to act were growing, not least on account on the massive strain mobilisation was placing on the country's economy. As Egyptian, Syrian, and Iraqi military measures continued to build up, on 29 May Nasser told his National Assembly: 'Now we are ready for the confrontation. We are now ready to deal with the entire Palestine question'.[10] The following day, King Hussein signed a pact with Nasser and put his forces under an Egyptian general.

Even in this unpromising climate, the Americans tried to find a negotiated settlement, seemingly reassured that they still had time to do so. A possible way out of the crisis appeared on 3 June when American diplomats in Cairo arranged for Vice-President Zakariyya Muhieddin to come to Washington on the 7th; his mission, it seems, was to discuss the opening of the Strait. Combined with Johnson's insistence that Israel should not go on its own, this apparently offered hope for finding a way out of the crisis. But Israeli leaders could not see any benefit to them from Muhieddin's forthcoming visit and had been unimpressed by the lack of progress towards any international naval presence in the Gulf. The following day, by divided vote and without consulting or informing the Americans, their cabinet decided on war. In the early hours of 5 June, their air force delivered one of the most decisive strikes in history, winning in a few hours control over the skies of the Middle East.[11] Victory in the air ensured success on the ground. When the ceasefire came into place six days later, the Israel Defence Forces were in control of the Gaza Strip, the Sinai desert, east Jerusalem and the West Bank, and the Golan Heights. The dimensions of the Arab–Israeli conflict had been changed and it became the fate of American leaders and diplomats over the next two decades to preside over the consequences of what had happened.

Wars, especially short ones, generally relegate diplomacy to second place behind events on the battlefield. With the Israeli armed forces moving with such speed, the US administration's main consideration was to make sure that the Soviet Union did not come to the aid of Egypt and Syria in a way which would result in a confrontation. They had to take considerable trouble to convince the Soviets they had no fore-knowledge of the Israeli attack and no deception had been involved. But although the exchanges involved the first use of the 'hot line' between Washington and Moscow, it was clear that the Soviet Union had no interest in becoming involved in a war over the Middle East.[12] This helps to explain why Johnson gave such strong support to the Israelis, despite his earlier warnings to them not to start hostilities. Relieved that a major international confrontation was not likely to develop and that the swiftness of the Israeli victory meant that the United States would not be asked to intervene on her behalf, Johnson could afford to take a pragmatic view of the crisis. Moreover, American public opinion, like that in most Western countries, was strongly behind the Israeli action. This was most marked in the Jewish community which subscribed massively to help the war effort, but it was also felt by a majority of Americans who saw Israel's action not as aggression but as the justified reaction of a small country which had not hesitated to play a bold hand in the face of threats.

This broad base of support could only have been eroded by the most serious incident in the history of Israeli–American relations, the extraordinary attack on the electronic surveillance vessel USS *Liberty* cruising off the Gaza Strip on 8 June. As the Middle East crisis developed, the *Liberty* had been diverted from the African coast to the eastern Mediterranean where she entered the war zone without escort. On the morning of 8 June, she was spotted by Israeli reconnaissance aircraft and then attacked by flights of Mirage and Mystère aircraft which strafed her with rockets and napalm. This attack was subsequently pressed home with torpedoes and gunfire by three patrol boats. When news of the ship's plight reached the Sixth Fleet, a relief flight was sent off by the carrier *America* but was then recalled on orders from Washington. By the end of the incident, 34 American sailors were dead and 171 wounded. Mystery has continued to haunt the *Liberty*. The Israeli explanation that the attack was the result of over-eager commanders mistaking her for the Egyptian transport *El Quseir* is plausible, for such things happen in war. But senior members of the administration and naval officers found it unconvincing, as the ship was flying the American flag and the assault was so prolonged. Some believe that the ship was the victim of a deliberate attack to prevent the United States gathering intelligence of the forthcoming operations against the Golan Heights, though against that it must be said that the Americans had no obvious reason to feel solicitous towards the Syrians. Whatever the circumstances, the US administration made a conscious decision to play down the affair in public and not to follow it up with the Israelis. The *Liberty*'s survivors were left frustrated that their ordeal had been sacrificed to the needs of diplomacy and a scar had been cut on Israeli–American relations which never quite healed for the duration of the Johnson presidency.[13]

As the war ended, the main aim of Israel's supporters in the United States was to ensure that Johnson and Rusk did not assume the role of Eisenhower and Dulles, forcing an unwelcome withdrawal from occupied territory.[14] In fact, the perceptions in Washington and Jerusalem were not far apart. With the exception of east Jerusalem, which was formally annexed on 27 June, the Israeli position on the occupied territories had not yet hardened into rigidity. Eban's belief was that the need to regain the territories would at last induce the

Arabs into direct negotiations which would allow Israel to trade land for a peace settlement. The government agreed that it was prepared to relinquish the conquered territories in return for security adjustments and special arrangements for Sharm al-Sheikh. The future of the West Bank was not so clearly spelled out, but at all events, the new conquests would not become Israel's permanent frontier.[15] The hope in Washington was that the scale of the Israeli victory would force the Arab states to accept an over-all peace settlement for the area. This formed the basis of the 'five principles' for peace in the Middle East which Johnson broadcast on 19 June. This was partly intended to pre-empt a Soviet move in the Security Council to force a unilateral Israeli withdrawal. Johnson's principles involved an end to threats against the existence of any nation, 'justice for the refugees', an end to interference with maritime rights, restrictions on the arms race in the region, and finally peace based upon 'recognised boundaries.'[16] While the Israelis were relieved that Johnson's address showed that there was to be no repeat of 1957, no momentum for a peace settlement developed.

It became increasingly apparent that the conditions were not right. Israel's victory had been too overwhelming. Convinced that she was the region's superpower, 'the Sparta of the Middle East', she saw no need for hasty or dramatic compromises. The Arabs' defeat had been too humiliating. They had nothing to bargain with, except direct negotiations and recognition of Israel. Refusal to concede these too readily lay behind the resolutions of the Khartoum summit in September which resolved on 'no peace with Israel, no recognition of Israel, no negotiation with it, and insistence on the rights of the Palestinian people in their own country'.[17] The United States was in no position to encourage or cajole them, for Egypt and other Arab countries had severed relations during the war. Nevertheless, American initiative was important in the series of moves leading up to the passing of Security Council Resolution 242 on 22 November 1967. Although the resolution was sponsored by Britain's Lord Caradon, it was based upon earlier drafts introduced by the Latin Americans and by the Americans, and Washington's ambassador to the United Nations, Arthur Goldberg, has argued that through its diplomatic efforts the United States had the primary role in its adoption.[18] The resolution represented something of a triumph for East–West relations and was as much as could be achieved in terms of Arab and Israeli acquiescence. In some respects it was far-reaching. By accepting it, Egypt and Jordan were acknowledging 'the sovereignty, territorial integrity and political independence of every State in the area', in short Israel's right of existence. They also recognised the need to guarantee freedom of navigation in the area. For its part, Israel was accepting the need for 'a just settlement of the refugee problem', but that was suitably vague. The terminology, which pre-dated the post-war Palestinian revival, was deeply resented by them and was to cause problems for American diplomacy at a later stage. But the crucial elements were 'the inadmissibility of the acquisition of territory through war' and 'withdrawal of Israel armed forces from territories occupied in the recent conflict'. The absence, in the English version at least, of any qualification before 'territories' led to widely differing interpretations, with the Arabs insisting that it meant 'all' of the territories, while the Israelis maintained that it merely meant 'some'. Abba Eban has argued that his government would never have agreed to the resolution without assurances from Washington and London that they had deliberately excluded the words 'all the' from its terms. Lord Caradon, on the other hand, maintained that the terms 'inadmissibility of the acquisition of territory through war' meant that Israel was not entitled to keep her conquests, beyond rectification of such anomalies as the Latrun salient and the Mount Scopus enclave.[19] But for all its ambiguities and ultimate shortcomings, Resolution 242 was to be the starting-point for every attempt to resolve the Middle East conflict over the next two decades.

Resolution 242 was to be tied in to a major United Nations' initiative to resolve the dispute. Ambassador Gunnar Jarring, a tenacious Swede, was appointed Special Representative, but he was condemned to follow a lonely and ultimately barren road, for he carried no sanctions as a negotiator. If anything, his mission confirmed the impotence of the United Nations in this kind of negotiation. Even so, in February 1971 he presented a final plan to the Egyptian and Israeli governments which, though unsuccessful at the time, contained many of the key elements of the subsequent Camp David accords. But as no diplomatic agreements emerged, Israel, faced with the realities of being an occupying power, began to lose the moral high ground she had enjoyed in May and June 1967. This started with the destruction of the ancient Moghrabi quarter beside the Western Wall where bulldozers had gone into action even as the war ended. It continued with the annexation of east Jerusalem, which no country recognised, and the creation of a second Palestinian refugee exodus.[20] The erosion of international goodwill towards Israel meant that she became increasingly, and by 1973 almost totally, dependent on Washington for diplomatic support, with consequences of the first order for America's stance in the Middle East. Parallel with this went a radical transformation in the position of the Palestine Liberation Organisation. Previously little more than a creature of Nasser's foreign ministry, in 1968 it was re-organised with Fateh's Yasir Arafat as Chairman, adopting a revised national Charter which looked forward to the total liberation of Palestine. In the next few years, the growth of guerrilla activity was to thrust the aspirations and frustrations of the Palestinians before the world's consciousness. Although American diplomacy consistently kept the PLO at arm's length, its presence was always there, unacknowledged but pervasive.

The United States was becoming inexorably involved in the Byzantine ways of Middle East diplomacy. What confirmed this was the revolution in Israel's supply of arms, especially aircraft. The Israelis had been anxious to move away from their dependence on the French, whose Mirages and Mystères formed the basis of their air force. The first breakthrough came when President Kennedy authorised the sale of Hawk missiles and this was followed in 1966 by Skyhawk fighter-bombers. Although their delivery was embargoed during the June war, the aircraft were released in October. But, with de Gaulle hostile to Israel for defying his advice not to go to war, Israel's problems became acute. Losses had to be made good and the Soviet Union was engaged in re-equipping the Egyptian and Syrian air forces. The Israeli request was for the Phantom fighter, a highly sophisticated supersonic machine capable of using an impressive range and combination of weaponry. In early 1968, Eshkol visited Johnson and received an assurance that the Phantoms would be available but, when nothing seemed to come of this, a lobbying campaign was mounted in Congress. The opening move was an amendment by Representatives Lester Wolff (Democrat, New York) and Seymour Halpern (Republican, New York) to the appropriations bill demanding that Johnson sell 50 Phantoms to Israel. With suitable amendments in the Senate, this enabled Johnson to make the sale public when he signed the appropriations bill.[21] It was one of the most significant acts in the Israeli–American relationship. As the French arms connexion withered away, the United States became essential to Israel's security. As American and Israeli pilots exercised their Phantoms together over the Middle East and eastern Mediterranean, an important bond developed which did much to sustain the growing links between their countries. But alongside these growing links with Israel came new commitments elsewhere in the region. Since the end of World War 2, the USA had felt no need to involve herself in the Gulf, whose security seemed guaranteed by the British. This ended in 1968 when Harold Wilson announced that Britain would no longer sustain a military role 'east of Suez' after 1971. Faced with Vietnam, this was not a burden the Americans wanted to assume and they began a policy of building up the military strength of Iran and Saudi Arabia to replace the departing British . As the Saudis felt very keenly the Israeli presence among the Holy Places of east Jerusalem, this could not but complicate the picture.

This period of increased involvement in the Middle East came at a time when many American Jews were taking stock of their position. While they could take satisfaction from their material and cultural position at home and pride from Israel's success abroad, doubts and anxieties subsisted. The issues of urban transition, race and the Vietnam war all seemed to hold dangers. Jews were amongst the most urban of immigrant groups. Compared with the restrictions of the East European *shtetls*, American cities had offered economic opportunities, cultural satisfaction and education. But the 1960s was the decade of urban decay as upwardly mobile groups moved to the suburbs, their places taken by blacks and Puerto Ricans. As urban violence grew out of such disadvantaged communities, city life lost much of its allure and Jews were forced either to join the white migration to the suburbs or, as in parts of Brooklyn, organise their young men for self-defence. The choice was unappetising.[22]

Jews seemed to be particular casualties of the Black Revolution. This was a cruel paradox for they had been well to the fore in the Civil Rights campaigns of the early 1960s and leaders like Martin Luther King had commended the Jewish passion for education as the model for black progress. But tensions there were. Although Jews had abandoned many inner city neighbourhoods, Jewish landlords and shopkeepers remained, resented by many blacks who contrasted them with their own position. In the racial riots which spread across the nation in the mid-1960s, such property often fell victim to black discontent. After 1967, many blacks displayed an active sympathy with the Palestianins, whose position they felt was similar to their own. This was most noticeably, though not exclusively, marked amongst groups like the Nation of Islam who looked to Muslim solidarity. It was particularly unfortunate that when black activists confronted white authority it was often Jews they encountered: in 1970, the Black Panthers resented the fact that it was Jewish judges who were 'responsible' for the jailing of Huey Newton and Bobby Seale.

Nothing symbolised this tension more than the 1968 teachers' strike in New York. At issue was the possible suspension of a group of teachers in the Ocean City–Brownsville school district of Brooklyn. It had become a predominantly black area where Jews were strongly represented in the teaching profession. Before the dispute ended it had been characterised by black accusations of Jewish racism and Jewish counter-charges of anti-Semitism. In the tense debate between Jews and advocates of black advancement, education was to the fore. For the latter, blacks could only advance through a policy of affirmative action aimed at compensating for decades of discrimination. The philosophy behind Johnson's Executive Order 11246 in 1965 was to give disadvantaged groups preferential treatment where qualifications were equivalent or by accepting 'lower' qualifications from such applicants. Four years later, blacks and Puerto Ricans demanded that they be allocated 50 per cent of the places at the City College of New York. Affirmative action touched a raw nerve with the city's Jews, for the College had provided the route by which thousands of them had entered higher education without any compromise on educational standards. The whole issue of positive discrimination seemed to beckon a return to the bitterly resented quotas of the inter-war years. With barely 3 per cent of the population, but heavily represented in the student body and faculties of the major universities, Jews felt that they might become the principal victims of such a policy.

Finally, there was the Vietnam war, fast becoming the first serious defeat in the nation's history. Opposition to it had come most vigorously from the elite college campuses where Jews were strongly involved and many of the leading anti-war activists were Jewish. Many Jews were deeply apprehensive that non-Jewish Americans would contrast unfavourably this 'doveish' stance over Vietnam with vocal support for Israel's war effort in 1967 and 1973, provoking the accusation that they were 'more loyal to Israel than America'. Hence, as Vietnam collapsed in 1975, Professor Nathan Glazer speculated that Jews, traditional scapegoats, would be identified in the public mind with America's defeat.[23] Paradoxically, the war had spawned a New Left which was hostile to Israel as a prop of Western imperialism and this, too, gave rise to anxiety. Although neither of these fears developed any substance, a more realistic apprehension in Jewish circles was that in the post-Vietnam retreat the country was returning to an isolationism which would mean a reduction in the vital support for Israel.

If it was a period of anxiety for many American Jews, the community as a whole could take pride in Israel's achievements. Her success and survival was the guarantee that 'never again' would Jewry be placed in peril. Their commitment to Israel, enthusiastic and virtually universal, was expressed through philanthropy and lobbying, both established American institutions. Philanthropy is a vital part of the Jewish inheritance, symbolised by the *pushkah*, or collection box, of the East European *shtetls*, and the *halukkah*, which had provided the necessary support for the pious Jews of Jerusalem, Safed, Tiberias and Hebron. Such traditions, and the clubbable nature of American society, meant that the Jewish community's potential for fund-raising was considerable. Their generosity reached new peaks during the crises of 1967 and 1973. It confirmed the intensity of feeling towards Israel which had such an effect on America's Middle East policy.

The political dimension of this was channelled through the most powerful ethnic lobbying group in Washington, the American Israel Public Affairs Committee (AIPAC). Formally established in 1959 under the direction of I. L. Kenen, AIPAC was the successor to the great lobbying campaigns of 1944–48. Kenen cut a high political profile, ensuring that key figures were well briefed on Israel's position and could intervene at critical points to ensure continued support. Whatever reservations they held about the influence of lobbies, hard-pressed congressmen and their staffs found AIPAC's position papers a usefully packaged source of information. Kenen also edited *Near East Report*, which attempted a systematic rebuttal of Arab arguments against Israel. Kenen retired in 1974, being succeeded by Morris Amitay and then, in 1980, by Thomas A. Dine, a former aide to Senators Edward Kennedy and Edmund Muskie. Two years later, Dine was included in *Washingtonian* magazine's list of the hundred most influential people in the capital. In 1983, Dine stated AIPAC's purpose before the House Committee on Foreign Affairs' Europe and Middle East Subcommittee: 'The American Israel Public Affairs Committee is an organization of Americans who value and are deeply committed to strengthening the already strong moral and strategic bonds between our country and Israel. As you know, on AIPAC's Executive Committee sit the presidents of 38 major American Jewish organizations, representing a membership of 4.5 million throughout the United States.'[24] He was referring to what gave AIPAC its muscle: American Jewish devotion to Israel. In the immediate post-war years, the Jewish vote was the potential sanction but this became overshadowed by the importance to candidates of the community's high degree of political involvement, directed through local Political Action Committees sympathetic to Israel. These committees could deploy money in support of approved candidates like Hubert Humphrey or Henry Jackson. But political figures like Senators J. William Fulbright and Charles Percy and Congressmen Paul Findley and Paul McCloskey were made to feel the full weight of Jewish disfavour over their perceived disapproval of Israeli actions.[25] In 1976, Senator Charles Mathias (Republican, Maryland) summed up his view of the lobby's influence. Conceding that most congressmen strongly supported Israel, he concluded that 'congressional conviction has been measurably reinforced by the knowledge that political sanctions will be applied to any who fail to deliver'.[26] A lobby's success may only be measured by results and Thomas Dine reportedly observed that being strong and criticised was preferable to being weak and ignored.[27] This was the vehicle which was to act so decisively to safeguard Israel's interests in the new relationship developing after the 1967 war.

Richard Nixon's victory in 1968 brought new personalities and priorities into the direction of Middle East policy. He entered office at a time when the mounting casualties and unending nature of the Vietnam war were putting new strains on the country's relations with the rest of the world. The 1968 primaries had almost torn apart the Democratic Party, with its strong internationalist traditions. Most Americans now saw that they could not confront communism at every point in the globe, not least because there was no communist monolith to confront. Just as the Boer commandos had done to Queen Victoria's army, the Viet Cong were exposing the illusion of world power, and this at a time when the Soviet Union was at last achieving nuclear parity. Few were neutral about the man chosen to define the American response to these uncomfortable new realities. Despite the miseries endured by the Democrats, Nixon was elected by the smallest proportion of votes in any presidential contest since 1912, his plurality over Hubert Humphrey only 500 000 on a poor turn-out. As American Jews had overwhelmingly supported Hubert Humphrey, he felt that this gave him the possibility of flexibility in his Middle East policy. Distrusted by the Democrats and most of the liberal establishment as an impenitent conservative and anti-communist, he was to display both a skill in crisis management and the ability to reach out in search of new directions in foreign policy. His moves towards China and the Soviet Union were to confound his early critics. By his own admission an 'outsider' to the foreign policy establishment, Nixon had spent much of his long period out of office in travel abroad, meeting foreign leaders and seeing at first hand many of the issues he was later to confront. As President he was determined to keep the direction of foreign policy firmly under his own hand, constructing a dyarchy which he hoped would enable him to exercise maximum control. Such dual government of foreign policy, with its attendant tensions, seemed to typify this elusive, but gifted, man whose presidency was to end in such protracted ruin.

Nixon wanted a Secretary of State who would be a determined executor of his policies. He chose a veteran Republican, William P. Rogers, well known to him as Eisenhower's Attorney-General and New York corporation lawyer. Rogers was valued both for his administrative skills, which Nixon hoped would keep the State Department in line, and for his reputation as a tough negotiator. But it was left very clear that the initiation of policy was to rest with the President. Mistrustful of the State Department, Nixon set in hand an alternative structure which could offer him advice and respond to his ideas. This was a refinement of the National Security Council which Truman had established in 1947 and whose fortunes had varied under his successors. Eisenhower had created a special executive officer for the council, rather clumsily titled Assistant to the President for National Security Affairs, but commonly referred to as National Security Adviser. As the holder was not subject to Senate confirmation and held no administrative portfolio, he was, or was intended to be, 'the creature of the President', with no other power base. As such, he could act as a special channel of negotiation carrying the chief executive's authority, offering possibilities ideally suited to Nixon's personal style of diplomacy.[28]

His 'uncharacteristically impulsive' choice of Henry Kissinger introduced into public service the man who was to play such a pivotal part in Middle East policy. In retrospect it is clear why Kissinger had the potential to become one of the most outstanding, if at times controversial, diplomats of the post-war world. As a Harvard academic he had no political constituency to which he was beholden. His historical training and grasp of international relations gave him a perspective on events which career bureaucrats rarely have time to develop, refined as he presided over his prestigious seminar on national security at Harvard. After an unsatisfactory period with the

Kennedy administration, he developed close links with the perennial Republican presidential hopeful Nelson Rockefeller, becoming his adviser on foreign affairs. Kissinger knew better than most Americans what his country stood for. As a nine-year-old Bavarian Jew when Hitler came to power, he had seen human behaviour at its worst, his father dismissed from his teaching post, himself sent to a segregated school, years which he recalled as 'cruel and degrading'. [29] These experiences had not given him any special interest in Zionism or the Middle East, beyond some private visits to Israel. But the Middle East was to be profoundly affected by the policies he adopted.

The Middle East was not one of the administration's priorities. The Vietnam war was bound to head its agenda, with relations with the Soviet Union and the Western allies, neglected under Johnson, not far behind. Precisely because it was not a priority, the Middle East was left to Rogers and the State Department. By the spring of 1969, Jarring's lack of progress was clear. Israel's conditions were unchanged and, indeed, hardened under her new Prime Minister, Mrs Golda Meir, who succeeded Eshkol in March. The seventy-year-old veteran was determined to be no caretaker and proved a doughty defender of her country's interests. She had to be, for the Soviet re-supply of Egypt and Syria was starting to show results. By 1969, 400 new aircraft had been supplied to Egypt alone and thousands of advisers were in both countries. Heartened by this accession of strength, in April the Egyptians announced that as Israel had failed to implement Resolution 242, they would no longer observe the ceasefire arrangements, though these had long held little meaning. Fighting along the canal steadily built up, assuming serious proportions throughout the summer. The only glimmer of light was a speech by King Hussein at the National Press Club in Washington on 28 April, in which he confirmed his readiness to acknowledge Israel's existence within secure boundaries in return for a total withdrawal to the 1967 borders. Privately, he assured Nixon that while he and Nasser could not yet sign a peace treaty, they were prepared to reach a settlement with Israel. Egypt was willing to concede free passage through the canal and the Strait of Tiran and demilitarised zones in Sinai. He also suggested that in return for sovereignty over Gaza he would be prepared to make concessions over the West Bank. These assurances seemed to point to possible dialogue, but the signals coming from Cairo remained confused. When Nasser's foreign policy aide, Mahmoud Fawzi, came to Eisenhower's funeral, he failed to convince the Americans that Nasser had moved sufficiently far from his anti-Americanism and dependence on the Soviets for anything constructive to emerge, especially as he made it clear that the time had not come to resume diplomatic relations.[30]

But the new administration was not operating in a vacuum, as others felt that they, too, had a stake in Middle East affairs. De Gaulle, who shared Nixon's disdain for the United Nations, was anxious for Four Power talks, while the Soviet Union wished to pursue a dialogue with the Americans. The former did get under way in April but only really confirmed that Britain and France had ceased to be players of any consequence. The talks with the Russians, largely conducted by Rogers' energetic Assistant Secretary Joseph Sisco, were more significant, especially as the escalation in fighting over the summer made it vital that each side should know the other's position. Believing that America's conditions should be made clear from the start, Rogers presented a detailed plan to a meeting of the National Security Council on 25 April. This reflected the State Department view that, at least on the Israeli–Egyptian front, the border should revert to its pre-June 1967 position. Only in this way, he argued, could the United States identify what the main protagonists would settle for. Kissinger's objections to this were basic to his whole subsequent approach to the problem. Arguing that the two sides were already too far apart, these proposals would only confirm what Egypt and Israel were unable to accept, especially as the former's position still lacked definition. The United States would have given away its position on frontiers, to no purpose except pushing the two sides further apart. But Kissinger did not yet command sufficient authority and Sisco was subsequently allowed to negotiate with the Russians on this basis. On 28 October, he confirmed to Ambassador Anatoly Dobrynin that the USA wanted a return to the pre-1967 borders reinforced with security guarantees.[31]

The bait of the return of the Sinai failed to lure the Egyptians. Publicly, it provoked Nasser to rail at the USA yet again; privately, his Foreign Minister, Mahmoud Riad, was more circumspect, not rejecting the proposals but spelling out Cairo's belief that the Americans were aiming at a partial settlement which would split Egypt from the rest of the Arabs.[32] The State Department's response was that something dramatic would have to be done for the impasse to be broken, preferably before the Arab summit due to meet in Rabat on 20 December. Their strategy was twofold. They argued that the various elements in American thinking, so far secret, should now be brought into the open in a major policy statement which might attract moderate Arabs and force the Israelis to re-assess their position. Secondly, the charge that they were trying to divide the Arabs could be met by making it clear that they also favoured a return to the pre-1967 Israeli–Jordanian frontier, subject to minor modifications. In this way, no one could doubt American intentions.[33] Kissinger was unconvinced, portraying it in his memoirs as an attempt by Rogers and Sisco to challenge Nixon's use of the National Security Council as an instrument of policymaking. If so, it was a mistake, for the President was well aware that, as the proposal would be quite unacceptable to the Israelis, it stood no chance of being implemented. Nevertheless, he permitted Rogers to go ahead on the grounds that it offered the Arabs some hope over the occupied territories. This was an unpromising start to a major initiative, if perfectly consistent with the President's view of the State Department.[34]

The setting for Rogers's speech on 9 December 1969 was as unpromising as its prospects. A conference on adult education in a Washington hotel was treated to what must have seemed an arcane review of recent Middle East diplomacy – to the accompaniment of a band in the next room. But it was a serious statement of how policymakers saw the reconstruction of the Middle East and, as it was never repudiated, it is important to understand what it said and what it did not. From the assurance that American policy would be a 'balanced one', Rogers identified roadblocks – peace, security, withdrawal and territory – which were preventing a settlement. Peace would have to be guaranteed in specific terms, especially in regard to navigation rights in the canal and the Strait of Tiran, but it would also involve a change of attitude. Security could come from effective demilitarised zones. On the key issues of withdrawal and territory, he was emphatic that 'any change in the pre-existing lines should not reflect the weight of conquest. We do not support expansionism.' But the pre-1967 borders were armistice lines which could be adjusted, if only through 'insubstantial alterations required for mutual security'. This was clear acknowledgement of the American view that Israel could not continue to occupy her conquests.

Perhaps even more alarming to the Israelis was what he had to say about Jerusalem and the Palestinians, the latter apparently added to his speech at the last minute. Use of the term in itself marked a substantial change from previous statements, which had referred to 'refugees', and was a measure of how far the Palestinians had come into public awareness. 'There is a new consciousness', he said, 'among the young Palestinians who have grown up since 1948 which needs to be channeled away from bitterness and frustration toward hope and justice.' Beyond taking into account the 'desires and aspirations of the refugees', it was not clear how this was to be done, but at least the marker had been put down. Confirming that the Americans could not support the unilateral annexation of east Jerusalem, he conceded that it should remain a united city, but that 'there should be roles for both Israel and Jordan in the civic, economic and religious life of the city'. Finally, he made clear his hope that Jordan would be included in the diplomatic discussions.[35]

Some momentum developed. Nixon sanctioned release of the Jordanian section of the proposals which had been put to the Four Power talks and this provided an important gloss on what Rogers had said. It confirmed that Israel should withdraw completely from the Sinai, as that was clearly recognised to be Egyptian territory, but that adjustments could be possible to the Jordanian frontier. Officials were indicating that Rogers' 'insubstantial alterations' meant straightening out such old problems as the Latrun salient. This was bound to heighten Israel's sense of alarm, for it fell far short of what her security chiefs felt they needed.[36]

Reaction was much as Nixon and Kissinger had predicted. The press was inclined to be supportive, with the *New York Times* hailing it as a 'Call to Reason in the Middle East', an acceptable compromise which would win Rogers few friends in the region.[37] The Egyptians, who had known its details for some time, put the plan into a parking orbit to see what else was sent up to join it, as the *New York Times'* Raymond Anderson vividly put it. The Israeli response was drafted by Eban who viewed the plan as 'one of the major errors of international diplomacy in the postwar era', for the simple reason that it removed in advance his principal negotiating weapon by stating where Israel's borders should be.[38] His government was in no mood to yield to what they saw as an American attempt to reach a joint solution with the Soviet Union at their expense, and they responded appropriately. The day after the speech, Deputy Prime Minister Yigal Allon assured that the government would assist any Jew wishing to rent or buy property in east Jerusalem, including the Old City, confirming that 200 families had moved into the Ramat Eshkol project on land expropriated from the Arabs.[39] This heralded one of Israel's responses to Rogers, the construction of 'new realities' aimed at rendering his ideas on Jerusalem redundant. Restrictions on building were discontinued, with effects as aesthetically displeasing as they were unwelcome to the Arabs of east Jerusalem. The authorities were no longer required to carry out archaeological excavations before building and the city's skyline was damaged by adding floors to apartment buildings being constructed on French Hill to the west of Mount Scopus. The purpose of these moves was to build up the Jewish population as quickly as possible. Budgetary restrictions on building in the Jewish Quarter of the Old City were removed, 4000 acres of mainly Arab land were expropriated and sanction given for the construction of 25 000 apartments for Jews in east Jerusalem.[40] East Jerusalem was to be in undiluted Israeli control.

After an emergency cabinet meeting to review the plan, the Israeli government issued a clear warning to the Americans not to set pre-conditions, stating that 'The prospects for peace will be seriously marred if states outside the region continue to make territorial proposals and suggestions on subjects that cannot promote peace and security.'[41] Determined to resist, but knowing that they were vulnerable to pressure on aid requests already submitted to Washington, a political offensive was triggered. An early indication that they would get support came in a statement by Hubert Humphrey castigating the Secretary for requiring Israel to retire behind her old frontiers.[42] This theme was taken up by AIPAC. On 25 and 26 January 1970, 14000 prominent Jews conducted a mass lobby in Washington. Pro-Israeli resolutions attracted wide support in both Senate and House. A letter circulated over the names of the veteran Celler and Senators Joseph D. Tydings (Democrat, Maryland) and Clifford P. Case (Republican, New Jersey), urging direct negotiations between Israel and the Arabs, was signed by seventy Senators and 280 Representatives. Two other resolutions in the House also enjoyed wide support, one by eighty-four Republicans and four Democrats, the other by sixty-four Democrats.[43] Impressive though this mobilisation of political muscle against Rogers clearly was, it was actually superfluous, as Nixon had already privately assured the Israelis that the plan would not be pressed.[44]

The Egyptians were content to let the plan draw the Israelis' fire. With a shrewd appreciation of the subtleties of the American decision-making process, they knew that the extent of opposition in Congress meant that it only represented State Department thinking. Past experience showed that Israel's supporters had the political strength to kill it. Because it pointed the way to a comprehensive settlement, the Egyptians did not reject the plan but they did not believe it had enough credibility to accept it. Egypt was not being tempted to move closer to the United States and when the Rabat summit collapsed on the issue of aid to Egypt, Syria and Jordan, Nasser was left dependent on his old allies in Moscow. Confirming the diplomatic stalemate, on 23 December the Soviet Union rejected the plan, effectively stifling the Four Power and Two Power talks which had been limping along for most of the year. In short, a year of effort by the US administration had yielded nothing but the tightening of Israel's grip on east Jerusalem and confirmation of her political power on Capitol Hill. It was a clear defeat for Rogers and the State Department.

The USA was now too deeply enmeshed in the Middle East to walk away from its problems. Tension steadily rose in 1970, reaching a climax in September in a crisis so fraught with implications that Nixon compared his handling over it with that of Kennedy over Cuba. It centred on Jordan where King Hussein's regime had been trying to fight off the challenge to its authority posed by the organised Palestinian guerrillas, supported by Syria and Iraq. The immediate crisis was triggered on 6 and 9 September when a rash of aircraft hijackings carried out by the left-wing Popular Front for the Liberation of Palestine left American, Swiss and British airliners captive at Dawson Field in Jordan. Although the planes were blown up, all the hostages were subsequently released, but Hussein was now determined to be undisputed master in his own house. On 17 September, his army commenced operations against guerrilla bases and strong-points, winning important successes in bitter fighting. Three days later, Syrian armoured columns crossed his northern border offering a challenge which his forces would be hard-pressed to meet. It was an alarming situation for, behind Syria, stood the Soviet Union. Syria's move appeared to threaten either the overthrow of a pro-Western regime or Israel's intervention, with the threat of a new Middle East war. The American reaction was closely co-ordinated with the Israeli's. On the American side, airborne forces in Germany and at home were placed on a well-publicised alert, the aircraft carriers of the Sixth Fleet were increased from two to five, and key elements of the fleet were moved into the eastern Mediterranean. Israeli air and ground forces assembled to strike at the Syrian flank. The pressure worked. Heartened by the American moves, and aided by the fact that the Syrian air force was not supporting the army's move, Hussein was able to regain the initiative from his powerful adversary. By 23 September, it was clear that the Syrian tanks were withdrawing. In a sense, it was a reassuring experience, for it showed that Nixon and his team could act decisively to defuse a crisis, but it confirmed how volatile the Middle East had become and how intimately the USA, still deeply involved in South-east Asia, had become engaged in its affairs. But disengagement from Vietnam was no easy matter. The Paris agreements did not come until January 1973 and during this lengthy period the frustrations felt in Arab capitals over the continued occupation of their territory built up to a degree which made a further round of conflict virtually certain.

5 Crisis Management: Nixon, Kissinger and the 1973 War

At 2 p.m. on Saturday, 6 October 1973, some 700 Syrian tanks, well supported by infantry, attacked Israel's positions on the Golan Heights, as their airborne forces prepared to capture the vital Israeli observation posts on Mount Hermon. At the same time, over 1000 Egyptian guns bombarded the even more scantily held positions of the Bar-Lev Line on the Suez Canal and commando units spearheaded an immaculately conceived canal crossing which, by that night, had major elements of the Second and Third Armies consolidating inside their bridgeheads north and south of the Bitter Lakes. Such was the scale of the offensive, and the desperate courage with which it was met, that forty-eight hours later Israel had lost 500 dead. Most harrowing of all for government and public alike was the apparent failure of the air force, the key to success in Middle East warfare, to make any real impact on the battlefield. Well supplied with Soviet surface-to-air (SAM) missiles, in the first week of hostilities Syrian and Egyptian soldiers destroyed 80 aircraft, an attrition rate in planes and experienced pilots which could not be long sustained. Although the fortunes of war were to waver before finally turning, the success of the Egyptian and Syrian forces in preparing and carrying out this offensive destroyed one of the basic assumptions which had informed Israeli and, to a lesser degree, American diplomacy since 1967, namely, that Israel had such a measure of qualitative superiority over her antagonists that she had nothing to fear on the battlefield.

The Nixon administration had been no more successful in averting this latest Middle East war than its predecessor had been in 1967. Basically, its chances of doing so had never been high, for it was a war which the two countries had been determined to wage to restore Arab honour and secure the return of their territories. Nasser was succeeded in September 1970 by Anwar al-Sadat, who emerged as a leader of a different stamp. Dedicated to recovery of the Sinai, Sadat saw the USA as the only power which had the ability to put the necessary pressure on Israel. In an attempt to impress Washington, in

July 1972 he ordered the Soviet Union to withdraw its military advisers, some 15 000. It was the kind of dramatic gesture for which he would become famous, but the Nixon administration was not yet ready to respond, especially in the shadow of a presidential election in which the President had high hopes of weaning large numbers of Jews away from their traditional Democratic allegiance. Even so, it was a *démarche* which could not be ignored and unofficial channels of communication were opened up between the two countries which had not enjoyed formal diplomatic relations since 1967.[1] But the USA had other priorities in the early stages of Nixon's second administration and in the absence of diplomatic moves Sadat and Syria's President Hafiz al-Assad prepared their armed forces and generated the right amount of disinformation to lull both Israel and the international community into a sense of security. As a result, America's intelligence-gathering agencies failed to appraise accurately the moves Egypt and Syria were making. They may be excused, for Israeli intelligence, whose overriding task it ought to have been, only reached the right conclusions when it was too late to make any adequate diplomatic or military response.

The offensive came at a time when particular disarray in Jerusalem and Washington greatly increased its chances of initial success. As Sadat and Assad were completing their preparations, Golda Meir was in France to address the Council of Europe in Strasbourg. As she did so, Arab gunmen attacked a train carrying Jewish migrants from Russia to the Jewish Agency's transit camp at Schonau near Vienna, demanding that the Austrian government close the facility. Her visit to the Austrian Prime Minister Bruno Kreisky failed to prevent this. Israeli indignation at this latest act of terrorism, combined with the unhelpful attitude of the Austrians, served as a critical diversion from what was happening along the canal and the Golan. Meir was not able to meet with her defence chiefs until 3 October, though even then no one anticipated an immediate attack and further discussion was postponed. Other key figures were away from their posts. Foreign Minister Eban was at the United Nations in New York as part of a diplomatic offensive to improve Israel's standing with Third World countries. The ambassador to Washington, Simcha Dinitz, had left for Israel because of his father's death.

The American government, too, was caught unaware and preoccupied with other things. Kissinger had only recently become Secretary of State and, like Eban, was in New York when news came that war was imminent. The President was at Key Bicayne in Florida worried by problems more urgent to him than possible military moves in the Middle East. His 1972 campaign had thrown up the Watergate scandal which was reaching a particularly sensitive pitch, so ominous that, on 20 October, Special Prosecutor Archibald Cox was dismissed, followed by the resignation of Attorney-General Elliott Richardson, provoking resolutions in Congress for the President's impeachment and a storm of protest in the press. Nixon had gone to Florida to ponder the serious tax charges which were being pressed against Vice-President Spiro Agnew. On 10 October, as war raged in the Middle East, Agnew submitted his resignation and the following day pleaded guilty in court to failing to report income.[2] His successor was Gerald Ford, the much-respected Republican House minority leader. To complicate matters further, two days before the outbreak of war Senate–House conference committee approved the terms of what came to be known as the War Powers Resolution. Designed to prevent a repetition of the Vietnam involvement, it aimed to impose a sixty-day limit on the deployment of troops in the absence of a declaration of war. Bitterly opposed by Nixon as restrictive of executive power, it was passed by Congress over his veto on 7 November, an indication of the extent to which Watergate had impaired his authority. In short, throughout the entire Middle East crisis, the United States was led by an administration whose claims to credibility and respect were increasingly open to question. Its head, though distracted, could still take decisions and give leadership, but it was a situation destined to give Kissinger a unique chance to use his new office to full advantage in a major crisis.

With the Egyptian and Syrian forces moving into position, there was little the Israelis or Americans could do. The first clear danger signal came on Friday, 5 October, with the news that the families of Soviet advisers in Syria were being flown out; Golda Meir was alarmed by this but her defence chiefs were not. With the benefit of hindsight, she was to admit that she should have ordered mobilisation at that point but, reassured by professional opinion that war was not imminent, she held back from triggering a step which would have been seen as provocation or war-mongering.[3] It was a particularly dangerous time for Israel. The annual Yom Kippur fast was starting that evening with essential services reduced and many servicemen on leave with their families. With the Prime Minister worried but bowing to advice that the Egyptian and Syrian armies were engaging in defensive manoeuvres, it was perhaps inevitable that the one attempt to use the Americans to send warning signals proved to be a fumbling affair.

On the Friday morning (Eastern Time), a message arrived with the *chargé* in Washington, Mordechai Shalev, that he was to arrange a meeting with Kissinger, the reason for which was to follow in an explanatory message. The Secretary's whereabouts were unknown but if he were in New York, then Eban was to be included. Eban was informed of this but as neither man had any inkling of what the meeting was to be about, he saw no urgency about interrupting Kissinger's busy schedule. Shalev could not leave Washington until the message had arrived; by the time it came in the late afternoon it was too late to arrange a meeting. Jerusalem informed Eban that the information would be given to the Secretary in writing, not a move calculated to instil a sense of crisis. The material Shalev received was not clear-cut. Kissinger was to be asked to assure Egypt and Syria that Israel was not about to attack but that if they started hostilities then there would be an effective military response. But any sense of urgency was undermined by an accompanying intelligence appraisal that war was not imminent. Shalev passed the document to Kissinger's aide, General Brent Scowcroft, for transmission. Respecting the quality of Israeli intelligence, neither Kissinger nor Scowcroft got a sense of impending crisis, a view shared by their own analysts. As a result, Kissinger did not read the messages until the following morning. As the 5 October ended, no message had been sent which might have given Sadat and Assad cause to re-consider.[4]

Early the next morning, Meir was woken with the hard intelligence that an attack would come late that afternoon. An emergency cabinet meeting reviewed the options. Immediate mobilisation was obvious, though there were differences over the degree to which it should be done. The only hope of now averting attack lay in showing Sadat that he had lost the element of surprise needed for crossing as formidable an obstacle as the canal. The Chief of Staff and air force commanders pressed for a pre-emptive strike against Syrian missile sites. Tempting though this was, it was ruled out for compelling political reasons. Once war broke out, Israel would have to rely on the USA for diplomatic support and military supplies. Perhaps mindful of the accusation that in 1967 they had launched their air force at a time when Washington still had reason to expect a diplomatic solution, the government was determined that the source of aggression should be clear, even at the cost of Israeli lives in the early hours of the fighting.

The need to ensure Washington's goodwill also led to an order for less than total mobilisation; the Americans could use this to show Israel's peaceful intentions. These were hard choices, fully justified by the reality of the country's position.[5]

Israeli intelligence had mistaken the time of the attack by four hours, leaving diplomatic moves that morning no real chance of success. Summoning Kenneth Keating, the ambassador in Tel Aviv, Golda Meir informed him of Arab intentions, telling him that there would be no pre-emptive strike and asking the Americans to intervene in Cairo, Damascus and Moscow. Actually, no time remained. When Kissinger was roused in his New York hotel at 6.15 a.m. with news of what was about to break, less than two hours of peace were left. By 7.00 he had contacted Soviet ambassador Anatoly Dobrynin in Washington, Egypt's Foreign Minister, Mohammed el-Zayyat, also in New York for the UN session, and Shalev, but by 8.30 a.m. the latter had informed him that the war had been going on for the past half hour. With the Egyptian and Syrian forces at such a pitch of readiness, there had never been any real hope that American action could hold them back.[6]

The critical American and Israeli failure had been one of intelligence; not its collection, for the Israelis had been carefully monitoring the Egyptian and Syrian troop movements, but its evaluation. What both countries' analysts had failed adequately to take into account was the readiness of Sadat and Assad to fight a war for the limited aim of restoring Arab dignity with the possibility of a modest return of territory lost in 1967. In so doing, Sadat believed, they would be opening up the impasse which had crippled diplomacy since Israel's victory.[7] Even as the war was going on, on 16 October he signalled his purposes in an address to the People's Assembly. In return for Israel's withdrawal to her 1967 frontiers, he would attend an international peace conference and try to persuade representatives of the Palestinians that everyone should work for a peace 'based on the legitimate rights of all the peoples of the area'.[8] It was a remarkable statement, so bold that it helps explain why American and Israeli analysts had failed to read his purposes. Almost from the start of hostilities, the Egyptian leader was sending messages to Washington that this was not *guerre à outrance*. The heady rhetoric of 1967, so damaging to the West's perception of the Arabs, was notably absent. Instead, on the first evening of the war, Zayyat assured Kissinger that Egypt was fighting to convince the Israelis that their true security could only be based upon mutual respect. The following day, Sadat activated his unofficial channels of communication to the Americans, which he was to maintain throughout the hostilities, even when Washington's supplies were turning the war against him. His terms were familiar: an Israeli withdrawal from the territories taken in 1967 followed by a peace conference. Much more significant was his assurance that this was to be a limited war. Kissinger picked up the signals correctly. Egypt was fighting the war for clearly defined diplomatic aims and the United States, despite her close ties to Israel, was being asked to assume a key role in this process. It was information which enabled him to turn the conflict into the first step toward a peace settlement. Hitherto dismissive of Sadat as a light-weight, Kissinger increasingly saw him as a 'statesman of the first order'.[9] Although he did not know it, in sending these messages Sadat robbed the Israelis of much of the benefit of their decision not to mount a pre-emptive strike, for in the following days American spokesmen pointedly refrained from condemning Arab aggression.

For the first three days of the war American policy rested on the assumption, reinforced by Israeli assurances and their own intelligence, that the Israeli forces would quickly regain the initiative and repeat the successes of 1956 and 1967. But by 9 October it was painfully evident that this was not happening. While the Israelis had headed off disaster on the Golan Heights it had been at considerable cost and the Syrians showed no sign of weakening; on the Suez front, that day saw the collapse of the first major counterattack with the destruction of the 190th Armoured Brigade. In urgent conversation with Kissinger, Dinitz revealed the extent of the disaster his country was facing: forty-nine aircraft and 500 tanks had been lost, so far without result. It was an attrition rate which Israel, geared to the concept of a short, sharp war, could not long sustain without supplies from the USA. So critical was the situation that Golda Meir was prepared to fly secretly to Washington to plead with Nixon. Kissinger could not but respond. Failure to do so would be seen as desertion of a friend in time of need, a defeat for American arms by those of the Soviet Union and the consequent inability of America to influence the aftermath of the war. Yet the issue was not straightforward. To assist Israel too overtly might forfeit the openings which were being signalled from Cairo and trigger an oil embargo, which the administration was anxious to avoid. With Nixon and Kissinger agreed that a military stalemate offered the best way toward peace, any action would have to be finely judged. On 9 October, Nixon decided that an Israeli military defeat had to be avoided and her losses made good.

Aircraft, ammunition and other military hardware presented no insuperable logistic problem; as far as tanks were concerned, Israel was to be assured that her losses would be replaced after the war and hence she should not hold back her reserves. Organisation of the airlift was delegated to Kissinger and Defense Secretary James Schlesinger, each of whom was to attract controversy over his role.[10]

Israelis viewed what happened over the next few days with mixed emotions. Golda Meir has recorded how she wept at the news of the arrival of American C-5A Galaxy transports at Lod, but that was not until 14 October, and others were less effusive about the speed and quantity of what was being provided. Moshe Dayan complained that his forces received half the Phantom jets, a fifth of the tanks, a third of the field guns and a fifth of the anti-tank missiles his ministry requested.[11] But it was the pace of the operation which really alarmed the Israelis. By 12 October, faced with unprecedented aerial losses and ammunition stocks due to run out in days, supplies were still restricted to what could be carried in El Al's seven jets. Dinitz was informed by the Pentagon that the Americans would fly urgent material but only as far as the Azores; worse was the news that Israel would be sent one-and-a-half Phantoms a day up to a maximum of sixteen. Kissinger blamed the Pentagon for these delays but many Israelis were unconvinced, doubting that Schlesinger had the authority to obstruct a presidential order. In a widely-quoted *Commentary* article in September 1974, Edward Luttwak and Walter Laqueur argued that once Kissinger grasped the degree of military dependence on Washington he saw the opportunity to regulate the amount of assistance to ensure that Israel did not win a decisive victory.[12]

Although such an interpretation sits easily with what he hoped would happen, Kissinger later took pains to counter the charge that the apparent lack of urgency was the result of diplomatic guile. Rather, he argued that Nixon's assurances on total resupply led the Americans to assume that Israel would have the confidence to commit all her reserves, securing her position on both fronts. In the meantime, the Pentagon could charter aircraft capable of delivering supplies in a way which would avoid too close an identification with the USA. Such discretion was thought desirable to help maintain links with the Arabs, avoid an oil embargo and prevent a similar Soviet operation. By 13 October, when it was clear that charter aircraft were not forthcoming, Nixon gave orders for three Galaxies already loaded with supplies to fly direct to Israel. Knowing that once the airbridge had been established it then made no difference how many planes were sent, Nixon sanctioned an all out effort. By the time the transports arrived the following day, the Israelis had begun to turn the military situation to their advantage and it is easy to understand their resentment at the agonising delay while they fought the most desperate battles in their country's history. Such sentiments, however, fail to acknowledge the value to Israel of American satellite intelligence and it is interesting that for his part Sadat was to tax the Soviets with similar charges of overdue and inadequate supplies.[13] Once the airlift began, it was impressive. With twenty transports a day landing at Lod, no one in the Middle East could doubt America's capacity to sustain her allies.

On 14 October, Egyptian armour advanced in force out of the missile screen which had dealt such havoc to Israeli tanks and aircraft. In the largest tank battle since World War 2, the Israelis could at last fight the kind of engagement they wanted. The following evening, a small task force under General Ariel Sharon crossed the canal just north of the Great Bitter Lake, consolidating its position against bitter odds. Within days, in a startling reversal of fortunes, thousands of troops had entered Sharon's bridgehead and, advancing south toward Suez town, encircled virtually the entire Egyptian Third Army. Although neither opponent had yet broken, the prospect opened up that Israel, now the beneficiary of the massive American airlift, might once again humiliate the Egyptians. For different reasons, neither Washington nor Moscow wished to see this. The danger now arose of a major Soviet intervention on behalf of Cairo and Damascus. As a major American concern throughout the crisis had been to preserve the process of *détente* with the Soviets, a positive move to end the fighting was needed.

Pressure was also coming from a different source, for the airlift had, as the administration feared, led to an Arab oil embargo which the West had no concerted plan to counter. Meeting in Kuwait on 17 October, the ministerial council of the Organisation of Arab Petroleum Exporting Countries (OAPEC) condemned the USA as a prime factor behind Israeli intransigence. As a result, they had decided to reduce oil production by 5 per cent of the September total and by a further 5 per cent each month until Israel had withdrawn from her 1967 conquests and 'the legitimate rights of the Palestinians are restored'.[14] Two days later, Nixon requested a supplementary appropriation of $2.2 billion from Congress to pay for the supplies going to Israel. The Arab response was swift and angry, a total oil embargo on the USA and the Netherlands; because of the importance of the port of Rotterdam this was potentially a body blow to the economy of Western Europe. Although the economic needs of certain smaller Arab exporting states meant that the embargo was never as total as OAPEC said it was, nevertheless a sense of panic swept the world energy market.[15] As the Europeans and Japanese struggled to secure supplies and pointedly distanced themselves from Washington's policy on the war, it was clear that the OAPEC states had unveiled a weapon of formidable power. Although its full ramifications would not be seen for some months, the 'oil factor' was a critical new feature of Middle East affairs.

With these worrying new developments, the Americans began to work for a ceasefire. From the start, the Russians had been trying to encourage Sadat in this direction but an attempt by Kissinger on 12 and 13 October to arrange a ceasefire through British mediation foundered on continuing Egyptian military confidence. But Cairo's perceptions soon changed. With the tank battle of the 14th, Nixon and Kissinger sensibly judged that a struggle of such ferocity could not last much longer. The scale of the airlift provided Sadat with a plausible reason for ending the conflict, on the grounds that he could fight Israel but not the resources of the USA.[16] But wars are easier begun than ended, especially in a way which preserves the self-respect of all the parties, which Kissinger knew was necessary to turn a ceasefire into a full diplomatic settlement.

His problem now lay with Israel, for with the consolidation of Sharon's bridgehead, Golda Meir's government felt no urgency to stop fighting, or to agree to any preconditions it might later regret. Hence, on 18 October, Meir rejected Kissinger's soundings for a ceasefire based upon Resolution 242. Later that day, the Soviet leader Leonid Brezhnev suggested a draft resolution for the Security Council; namely, for a ceasefire 'in place', an imminent Israeli withdrawal from occupied territories under the terms of Resolution 242, and the start of consultations for a peace settlement. Knowing that the first was unacceptable to Israel but sensing possibilities in the last, Kissinger felt that the path to a ceasefire was opening up. The second element would be rejected in Jerusalem but Israel was now too beholden to the United States for any toleration of her total intransigence.[17]

The way forward was opened by the Soviets whose satellite intelligence was telling them what the Egyptian high command seemed slow to grasp, that Sharon's canal crossing beckoned military disaster. On 16 October, Soviet Prime Minister Alexei Kosygin felt it necessary to fly to Cairo with intelligence photographs showing the scale of Israel's success. Although Sadat later tried to pretend that the crossings presented no fundamental threat, on 19 October Kosygin flew home convinced that Egypt would accept a ceasefire as long as it provided for a Middle East peace conference which would include the Palestinians. At this point, Sadat told the Syrians that, faced with the reality of American power, he could not fight on and had informed the Russians that he would accept a ceasefire. [18]

That day, the Soviet leaders asked Nixon to send Kissinger to Moscow for urgent talks. On 20 October, he flew to Russia endowed with a plenipotentiary status which he had not wanted but which the President, preoccupied with the Cox–Richardson debacle, insisted he should have. The reason for his reluctance was that he wanted to have the ability to play for time to enable the Israelis to make good their positions. In any event, the Russians were so intent on saving the Arabs from military disaster that they wanted a quick ceasefire agreement that could go to the Security Council. Brezhnev quickly accepted that his existing three proposals were unrealistic. Kissinger then presented a draft resolution which he and Sisco had composed. It was readily agreed to by the Russians and, approved by the Security Council as Resolution 338 the following day, became a key document in all subsequent negotiations. The first part called on the combatants within twelve hours to observe a ceasefire 'in all the positions they now occupy', thus freezing Egyptian gains in Sinai and the Israeli bridgehead. It then called on them to proceed with the implementation of Resolution 242 'in all of its parts', something which could offer the Arabs the hope of return of their territories. Finally, in an attempt to open up the prospect of direct Arab–Israeli negotiations, these were to 'start between the parties concerned under appropriate auspices aimed at establishing a just and durable peace in the Middle East'. [19] It was a finely judged formula which hoped to exploit the new military and diplomatic situation in the Middle East, if the antagonists could be brought to overcome their distrust. Given the ferocity of what had happened, no one thought that was imminent.

While the Israeli government welcomed the prospect of direct negotiations, which they had been trying to secure for years, they naturally resented what they saw as the superpowers imposing a settlement so clearly designed to deny them the fruits of their recent military enterprise. Especially galling was the short time they were given to agree, resulting from an American communications failure in Moscow which they found implausible. This gave the resolution the air of an ultimatum, restricting the opportunities for their forces to expand their positions in anticipation of the ceasefire. As a result, Golda Meir asked Kissinger to stop over in Israel to explain the situation. Knowing it would be a strained meeting, Kissinger nevertheless acknowledged the need to reassure the Israelis that he was not manoeuvring behind their backs. By the time he landed at Lod, the ceasefire resolution had already passed through the Security Council and, at least in theory, the war had only hours to run. Accounts of his meetings vary. Mrs Meir dismissed it in one cryptic sentence of her memoirs, a poor tribute to the detour the Secretary had made to see her.[20] In a personal meeting, which Eban confessed he did not envy him, Kissinger explained to the Prime Minister his belief that he had opened up new possibilities for negotiations on the basis of Resolution 242, which carried with it implicit recognition of Israel. Further fighting on the western side of the canal, which would have to be returned to Egypt in any case, would be futile. Israeli journalist Matti Golan reported defence chiefs as optimistic that both Egyptian armies would be encircled and destroyed in a few days. Kissinger was unpersuaded. To him these were weary men conscious that this had been a different war to 1967. He was at least able to convince the government that the two powers had not made a secret pact to compel an Israeli return to the old frontiers. More positively, he urged his idea of a Geneva conference under the co-chairmanship of the United States and the Soviet Union to ensure that the Arabs became fully engaged in negotiations. In Golan's account he was already articulating his belief that a carefully measured step-by-step approach offered the only realistic way forward.[21]

Kissinger later admitted that he had made one error in Israel. Embarrassed by the communications lapse which had delayed sending details of the agreement to the Israelis, he had hinted that they might compensate by over-running the time of the ceasefire. His own account limits this to a few hours; Golan maintained that Israeli commanders believed they had two or three days.[22] Observance of ceasefire deadlines had never been one of the Israel Defence Force's more obvious virtues and little encouragement was needed to ensure that the Third Army was in a stranglehold. When Egyptian artillery opened fire, possibly in response to the steady build-up of Israeli troops, the Israel Defence Force responded in force. With the ceasefire in ruins, Israeli forces pressed south from their positions on the Bitter Lakes to the Gulf of Suez. The city of Suez and the Third Army had been trapped, their lines of communication now in Israeli hands. Ceasefires are always fragile things but it was clear that the scale of the advance went beyond anything demanded by possible Egyptian artillery violations, which the Americans were sceptical about in any case. Israeli commanders clearly wanted to avenge their early setbacks and end the war with the appearance of victory. The government's aim was probably to create dispositions which would allow them to argue for a mutual withdrawal across the canal, returning the situation to the *status quo ante bellum*, possibly reinforced by a demilitarised zone on either bank. This was an outcome which the Egyptians could not contemplate. Nor was it likely that the Third Army would simply allow itself to be starved into submission. If a diplomatic solution could not be found quickly, it would have to fight while it was still able to do so.

From the American standpoint, the diplomatic outlook was no better. Tactically, the Israeli advance had wrecked the credibility of the finely judged package which had been negotiated in Moscow, raising obvious questions about how the Soviet leaders would respond. Would they credit that Washington had no leverage with a country so clearly dependent on a massive airlift? If not, then it said little for the resolution they had worked out in apparent good faith. One thing was certain: the Soviet Union would forfeit all claim to credibility in the region if it failed to prevent the strangulation of the Third Army. Strategically, Israel's actions threatened to undermine the ultimate aim of the USA throughout the crisis: the creation of conditions from which peace negotiations could develop. If the Third Army fell, so would Sadat, with all the contacts that had been maturing. All that could follow would be a more radical regime, renewed confrontation and increased Soviet influence. Clearly, the aims of American and Israeli policy were far apart and Kissinger knew that his friends would have to be brought to heel, as Israel wanted what he could not grant: 'a veto over all our decisions regardless of the merits of the issue, and a free hand to destroy the Egyptian Third Army'.[23]

The Americans also had the uneasy feeling that the Russians could turn the situation to their advantage. On the morning of 24 October, a message came from Brezhnev to the effect that he expected the Americans to use their influence to compel observance of the ceasefire. Sadat was already requesting that a joint American–Soviet force be sent to do this, raising the unwelcome prospect of Soviet troops at the heart of the Arab–Israeli conflict, something which might well compensate for Moscow's recent setbacks. These moves coincided with pressure of another kind, for intelligence reports reaching Washington indicated that some eighty-five ships of the Red Fleet, with amphibious potential, were deploying in the eastern Mediterranean and that seven airborne divisions had been put on heightened alert. Moscow was signalling that it had the potential to rescue the Third Army, if need be. Confirming this was a message from Brezhnev threatening that if they could not agree on a joint force, he would have to consider a unilateral move. It was a clear challenge to the United States at a time when Nixon's fortunes were touching their nadir for, the previous day, resolutions for his impeachment had been introduced in Congress. The response, though not without risk, was carefully measured to show the Soviets that the administration still had the will and capacity to react. Nixon instructed Kissinger to convene a meeting to prepare their response, to include 'even the shock of a military response'.[24]

Kissinger saw the Soviet moves as the result of feeling betrayed over the ceasefire and the realisation of what they had lost by the Arab defeat. The possibility of a Soviet airlift from their European bases could only be countered by a display of firmness which could allow diplomacy time to work. In the course of the night, orders were sent to forces throughout the world to step up their state of alert from DefCon IV and V to DefCon III, the condition of maximum readiness without the assumption that war is imminent. As further reports arrived of Soviet transport movements in central Europe, the 82nd Airborne Division was put on alert and orders were sent for two additional carriers to join the USS *Independence* on station in the eastern Mediterranean, all designed to show the Soviets that the administration was still functioning and could marshal resources in the area. The means of defusing the crisis were provided in a reply to Brezhnev which conceded that Soviet and American personnel could be included under the auspices of the United Nations Truce Supervisory Organisation, but only on a temporary non-combatant basis. In agreeing to this face-saving device, Brezhnev allowed the crisis to be defused. Even this degree of direct superpower involvement on the ground proved unnecessary, as the Egyptians decided that they did not want it. The US administration's nerve had held and its decision-making processes had worked effectively, even though the fate of the Third Army remained undecided.[25]

This latter could only be resolved by forcing the Israelis to confront the fact that the USA would not permit the army's destruction. On 26 October, Kissinger spelled this out for Dinitz in no uncertain manner:

the destruction of the Third Army would not be permitted as the result of Israeli violations of a ceasefire agreement the Americans had negotiated. If Israel did not allow the non-military re-supply of the Egyptian lines and open the way to negotiations, then he would take the matter to the uncongenial atmosphere of the Security Council. Kissinger was reticent about any pressure being applied on Mrs Meir and Dinitz, but resentful Israelis felt otherwise. In a *New York Times* interview in January 1975, Moshe Dayan stated that Kissinger had threatened the suspension of military aid. At any event, with transports still landing at Lod, the implication of the US administration's messages could not have been lost. A deeply resentful Prime Minister responded that she was having to yield to *force majeure* and that if the United States wanted to preserve the appearance of an Egyptian victory it would have to tell Israel what to do. Her tone reflected how many informed Israelis felt about Kissinger's conduct, but, as he wryly reflected, his job was to serve the interests of American foreign policy not to act as psychiatrist to the Israeli government. The way through the apparent deadlock was shown by the Egyptian concession that in return for a convoy under UN and Red Cross supervision being allowed through and an end to ceasefire violations, they would accept direct talks between senior Egyptian and Israeli officers at Kilometre 101 on the Cairo–Suez road. Once the Israelis accepted this, five days and a superpower confrontation after the passing of Resolution 338, firing ceased along the canal on 27 October. The next day, the relief convoy passed through the Israeli lines; more significantly, early that morning Lieutenant-General Abdel Ghany el-Gamasy and Major-General Aharon Yariv met at Kilometre 101, exchanged salutes, and began the delicate business of negotiating the military details of the ceasefire.[26]

These events had clearly altered the nature of the Middle East conflict and America's relationship with it. Israeli leaders proclaimed another victory; not only were their forces in 'Africa', as Golda Meir liked to call it, but on the Syrian front they had re-taken Mount Hermon and thrust a salient toward Damascus. But the reality was different and claims of victory had much to do with a public opinion shaken by the loss of 800 tanks, 115 aircraft and, above all, 2412 lives. Although Arab losses were higher, they had succeeded in their primary aim of restoring their military reputation. With careful training, the Egyptian army had crossed the canal, taken the Bar-Lev line and defended its bridgeheads against an enemy which lacked nothing in courage or technical competence. Even when the Israelis had recovered their poise, the Egyptian and Syrian armies had fought tenaciously. In short, the legend of Israeli invulnerability, so potent a factor in international diplomacy since 1967, had been swept away. As if to emphasise the Arabs' new position, the oil embargo meant that Washington and other Western capitals now had to take notice of them. Moves already under way in the Organisation of Petroleum Exporting Countries to increase oil prices were given new impetus once the embargo had exposed the West's vulnerability. When the war began, Saudi Arabian light crude, which determined the pricing structure, was set at $3.011 a barrel; by the end of the year it stood at $11.651 with every indication of further rises. The consequences for the world economic system could not but be far-reaching and, until the industrial nations adjusted their energy needs, the Arabs had a diplomatic weapon of potential power.

The crisis could not have touched the American political system at a worse time with the administration facing ruin over the Watergate and Agnew allegations and executive and legislature pitted against each other over the War Powers Resolution. Yet despite intelligence failures and confused responses at the start of the war, the US administration had performed well. In the midst of personal turmoil, Nixon had not failed to give a lead, reaching key decisions in a measured manner. Kissinger's management of events had displayed a skill in tactical manoeuvring combined with an ability to cast his mind past the hectic and confused events of the day to the possibilities which might lie beyond. Catching the signals coming from Cairo, so long regarded as the agent of Soviet policy, he had been ready to distance himself from, and even offend, his Israeli friends when their needs of the hour clashed with his perception of the future. In the process, he had confirmed that the United States was essential to Israel's security. The Americans were now the key players in the Middle East power game. The issues were unresolved and nothing more than a fragile ceasefire was in place, but with Arab self-respect restored, Israel chastened and America's skill in crisis management confirmed, the way was seemingly open for important moves toward a settlement.

6 Step by Step

Because of their inability to read the signals in time, American leaders had contributed to the outbreak of war, but once it started Nixon and Kissinger engaged in crisis management of a high order. By the war's end, no one could doubt that America held the key to progress in Middle East diplomacy. Behind Israel's military success lay America's airlift of essential supplies, while her leaders had responded to Kissinger's wishes, albeit reluctantly. For her part, Egypt, though not yet Syria, had used the conflict to signal her willingness to re-open a dialogue with Washington. In short, Kissinger appeared to be uniquely placed to push ahead for the kind of negotiated settlement envisaged in Resolution 338. In fact, his search for an acceptable settlement was to ensnare him into one of the most protracted, and personally demanding, diplomatic missions of the post-war era, in the course of which he was to incur the disfavour of many Israelis and the distrust of many Arabs. But by September 1975, he had negotiated three disengagement agreements, two for Sinai and one for the Golan Heights, which, if they amounted to less than the breakthrough for which many hoped, were only achieved at the price of a seemingly endless series of 'teeth-grinding' sessions in the capitals of the Middle East.

Central to Kissinger's approach was his appreciation of the intractable nature of the Arab–Israeli conflict and the apparently unyielding barriers of mistrust spawned by four wars within a generation. His analytical mind had taught him to discount such over-reaching formulae as the Rogers Plan which had tried to reach out to 'goals more yearned for than attainable'. Rogers had only succeeded in pushing the Israeli government further into its corner; in contrast, Kissinger hoped that by a series of carefully measured diplomatic agreements, guaranteed by the prestige of the USA, he could foster a growing sense of confidence amongst the major protagonists. 'Each step', he wrote in his memoirs, 'had to show that we could achieve results. Thereby each advance would build confidence and make further steps easier.'[1] This perception, founded on a hard-headed appraisal of the distance separating the Arabs and Israelis, was the corner-stone of what came to be known as 'step by step' diplomacy, the purpose of which was to bring together Jerusalem, Cairo, Damascus and Amman in a diplomatic consensus held together by the USA. The anticipated benefit for the Middle East was peace; for the United States it would confirm that she, and not the Soviet Union, was the region's power broker.

What Kissinger achieved as the result of his 'step by step' approach must be measured against the difficulties which he faced at the start. As Richard Nixon's domestic problems grew, so did Kissinger's stature within the stricken administration but that was uncomfortably linked in the Secretary's mind with an awareness of how fragile his political base was becoming. On quite another front, as the final collapse of South Vietnam grew more apparent, so did the question mark against America's willingness to stand by her friends. Many in the Middle East were to agonise over this. If the war had restored the Arabs' sense of dignity, Israel's self-assurance had been sorely dented. The war had confirmed most Israelis in their sense of isolation. While Israelis had always known that they were alone in the Middle East, the spectacle of the European countries carefully drawing back their skirts from the American re-supply operation could not but re-awaken barely suppressed fears of anti-Semitism. The USA was their only proven friend but even she had used that relationship to push the Israelis in unwelcome directions.

The Israeli government and politicians were not well placed to respond with the necessary poise and imagination to these changing circumstances. If a sense of national solidarity remained strong enough to return Golda Meir's Labour Alignment to power in the Knesset elections of 31 December, this quickly eroded as the public became more aware of the true nature of October's events. On 2 April 1974, the official enquiry into the war, headed by Dr Shimon Agranat, released its interim findings which identified serious lapses by the intelligence services and military command. Its first victim was the Chief of Staff, General David Elazar, but by 11 April Golda Meir had announced her resignation, a sad end to a long career of service to Zionism which had started in Milwaukee in another age. She remained as head of a caretaker administration until, on 3 June, Yitzhak Rabin, lately ambassador to Washington and architect of the 1967 victory, had secured enough support in the Knesset to succeed her. As the various groups in Israel's complex political system bargained, it did not contribute to the clear-sighted and confident leadership which Kissinger would have wanted and the delicate state of the country's international position warranted.

As Israelis came to terms with the war's aftermath, the PLO's sophistication and credibility grew. Its leaders hoped to capitalise on the new stature the Arabs enjoyed and do something to counter the identification in the Western mind with the acts of violence which had reached a pitch with the massacre of Israeli athletes at the 1972 Munich Olympics. Certain groups within the PLO had been arguing for some time that the aim of a united secular Palestine set out in the 1968 National Charter was unrealistic. By the spring of 1974, this assessment was gaining wider, if by no means universal, acceptance. It came to be known as the 'mini state' solution which looked forward to a Palestinian entity on the West Bank and Gaza, once these territories had been freed from Israeli occupation. Because this offered little to those refugees in Jordan, Lebanon and Syria, not to mention the influential Palestinian diaspora elsewhere in the Middle East, whose homes had been in Galilee, Haifa, Jaffa and the coastal plain, this became a matter of acute controversy. It was unclear whether such a Palestinian state was seen as an interim stage or, as seemed likely, would acquire a permanence which would guarantee the exclusion of those living outside the 1948 borders. Even so, at the Twelfth Palestinian National Congress in Cairo, in the summer of 1974, a new programme was sanctioned which approved the 'people's national, independent and fighting sovereignty on every part of Palestinian land to be liberated'. This formula allowed PLO leaders to signal their willingness to acquiesce in a 'two state' solution. The PLO's credibility was given a further boost at the Rabat Arab summit in October which recognised it as the sole authentic voice of the Palestinian people, apparently ending King Hussein's role as spokesman for the inhabitants of the West Bank. This was quickly followed by Arafat's visit to New York to address the General Assembly, an occasion which aroused predictable indignation amongst Israelis and American Jews and disappointment for those who looked in vain for a public indication of the 'two state' solution. Nonetheless, it marked the PLO Chairman's new status in the international community.

These were not welcome developments in Washington. Kissinger's strategy in the 'step by step' approach was the gradual fostering of confidence between the Israelis and Egypt and Syria, with Hussein giving useful support. The barriers of distrust were sufficiently formidable without adding a 'Palestinian dimension'. If the PLO's 'two state' proposal were to become a serious item of discussion, it would only make the Israeli government even more defensive, for the country's political consensus saw any such Palestinian state as a threat to Israel's immediate security and long-term survival. Simply put, the PLO's emergence as a significant factor in Middle Eastern politics was seen by the Americans as an undesirable complication. The two sides explored their position in November 1973 at a meeting between Vernon Walters and one of Arafat's senior aides. But further contacts were not encouraged as, in Kissinger's estimation, 'At this stage, involving the PLO was incompatible with the interests of any of the parties to the Middle East conflict'.[2] The idea that the Palestinians could be excluded led to the later accusation that American diplomacy had evaded the central issue in the Middle East conflict.

Such, then, were the factors which had to be juggled and the interests taken into account as Kissinger and his team prepared to move into a new phase of diplomacy. Speed was essential, for the Third Army remained in place, its plight a source of discomfiture to Egyptians which would not be tolerated indefinitely. As Sadat re-equipped his army, the possibility grew of a major operation to break the encirclement, or so he was prepared to signal. No less pressing for the USA and her allies were the continuing economic effects of the oil embargo. Unless this were ended, the European countries might start their own moves against Israel which the Americans knew would be counter-productive. So pressing were these issues that two weeks after the ceasefire, on 6 November, Kissinger arrived in Cairo to start discussions with Sadat, having already consulted in Washington with Golda Meir and Egypt's Acting Foreign Minister, Ismail Fahmy. It was his first visit to a country with which the United States no longer had formal diplomatic relations and, by its end, the first signs of a new era in American–Egyptian relations could already be seen.

This was a *démarche* which Sadat had been working toward for some time prior to the war. He had long concluded that Egypt's established diplomatic positions, especially the links with the Soviet Union, were sterile. His problems had been that the idea of Egypt's changing course so dramatically had strained credulity in Washington and that he had felt unable to make major moves until his country's honour had been restored. The first meeting between the two leaders showed the extent to which these issues were being resolved. The signals Sadat had sent to Washington during the war had indicated new possibilities, making Kissinger receptive to the positive mood he found in Cairo. As Kissinger was careful to acknowledge, that new atmosphere was only possible because Egypt's military success had restored her sense of confidence. The immediate test of the incipient relationship would be the relief of the Third Army. Here Kissinger was well prepared, for he had explored the issue with Golda Meir during her Washington visit. Despite the frostiness on that occasion, it was clear that uppermost in her mind was the return of Israeli prisoners in return for which Israel would allow non-military supplies to the Third Army. This formula contained sufficient elements of compromise to encourage American mediation. It formed the basis of the 'Six Points' agreed between Sadat and Kissinger. These allowed for the scrupulous observance of the ceasefire; discussions under UN auspices for the separation of forces and a return to the positions held on 22 October; the daily provision of food, water and medical supplies to Suez; the free movement of non-military supplies to the east bank of the canal; the replacement of Israeli checkpoints on the Cairo–Suez road by the UN; the exchange of all prisoners once the UN checkpoints had been established. As Kissinger acknowledged, it was a considerable act of faith for Sadat to accept this, as it meant that for the time being the Third Army was still surrounded. This was clearly a price which the Egyptian leader was prepared to pay for the sake of his new relationship. He explained to Kissinger that the Third Army was not the main issue, that his aims were the restoration of the 1967 border and peace with Israel. Central to the achievement of these aims was friendship with the United States, the essential first step being the restoration of diplomatic relations between the two countries. True to his reputation for bold moves, Sadat had succeeded in making this first meeting into a major diplomatic event.[3]

The 'Six Point' formula was taken to Jerusalem by Kissinger's aides Joseph Sisco and Harold Saunders and, on 11 November, agreement was signed at Kilometre 101 on the Cairo–Suez road by the Egyptian General Gamasy and Israel's General Yariv. Over the following days the two men conducted direct negotiations over the working of the agreement, in itself no small achievement, and prisoners of war were exchanged. Kissinger himself flew to Riyadh, as the Saudi monarchy was seen as an influential factor in Arab diplomacy. In the course of his meetings it became clear that the Saudis approved of his diplomatic efforts and would soon take steps to end the oil embargo.[4] Kissinger had every reason to be pleased with the result of his first mission to Arab capitals. The immediate source of tension along the Suez Canal had been neutralised, but of even greater significance was the knowledge that American military support for Israel during the war had not forfeited Arab goodwill. On the contrary, there was every indication that the Egyptians and the Saudis were looking to the United States to direct the search for a settlement.

Armed with this knowledge, Kissinger could set in motion the process for convening the major conference at Geneva under joint American–Soviet auspices which had been anticipated in Security Council Resolution 338. It was a delicate issue. Given the nature of superpower relations, the conference could not now be avoided, at least, not without giving considerable offence to the Russians. But if it were to develop any real momentum, it would pose a clear threat to Kissinger's aim of keeping the major diplomatic moves firmly in American hands, something he knew that the Egyptians wished to encourage. The imminent Israeli elections were a further complication, for clearly no major initiatives could be expected until they had been held. Even after that, it was clear that no Israeli government would welcome a conference the obvious purpose of which would be to negotiate a withdrawal from occupied territory. Finally, there were the unexplored topics of Syria's attitude and possible Palestinian representation or involvement.

It was in an attempt to probe these issues that Kissinger returned to the Middle East on 13 December, in a rapid tour which took him to Algiers, Cairo, Riyadh, Damascus, Amman, Beirut and Jerusalem. Once again, Sadat was supportive, making it clear that he was looking to American leadership and moving toward severing his links with the Soviets once he could show positive results from his new course of action. In an attempt to encourage the Israelis to take part in the conference, he indicated that he would not make the question of the Palestinians a priority, nor insist on the letter of invitation referring to them. These assurances undoubtedly helped Kissinger in his difficult discussions with the Israelis. The formula which he took to Jerusalem was that the letter of invitation would include a sentence to the effect that 'the question of other participants from the Middle East area will be discussed during the first stage of the conference', obviously leaving open the possibility of Palestinian participation. Israeli sources insist that they only accepted this on the basis of a secret assurance in a Memorandum of Understanding that the USA would veto any PLO participation without Israel's consent. With that assurance, Israel would attend the conference, thus confirming, however unwillingly, that she would enter into a new diplomatic process whose only aim could be her withdrawal from territory. Her price for that was clearly to be the exclusion of the PLO and the continuation of large-scale arms supplies from the USA to continue to ensure her military security. Such guarantees were to be repeated in subsequent negotiations. Finally, this exploratory trip to the

Middle East was notable for the contact Kissinger made with President Assad. Syria had long been a particular blind spot with American negotiators who tended to regard her as incorrigibly nationalist and pro-Soviet. On the surface, Kissinger's visit to Damascus was a failure for he could not persuade Assad to come to Geneva. But the Syrian leader also made it clear that he would not actually impede the workings of the conference and the meeting between the two leaders was the beginning of a mutual respect which, for a time, eased relations between the two countries.[5]

When matched against the intensive diplomacy which had preceded it, the meeting of the Geneva conference on 21 December seemed an anti-climax. It lasted for one day and, publicly at least, yielded nothing more than familiar statements by the major parties. Had it all been worth while? Kissinger believed that it had, if only for bringing together Egypt and Jordan with Israel in a single conference chamber. This seemed to set the scene for progress once negotiations began in earnest in the new year. Abba Eban's speech went out of its way to indicate territorial concessions consistent with Israeli security, but repeated his government's view that the future of the Palestinians lay with Jordan. Andrei Gromyko seemed to indicate a softening of the Soviet position on Israel by talking of its existence within the 1967 boundaries, rather than previous Soviet references to the 1947 partition plan. But the real importance of the conference was the way it confirmed America's new dominance of Middle Eastern diplomacy. Soviet self-esteem had been satisfied but Gromyko had to confront the obvious fact that the meeting would not have taken place without Kissinger's efforts, which confirmed that only the USA had the lines of communication to the major protagonists. Kissinger took care in his speech to outline the next stages in the negotiating process, as he saw them. The way was now open for the bilateral diplomacy which he felt held the key to progress.[6]

On 11 January 1974, Kissinger flew to the Middle East to start another round of intensive diplomatic effort, the main purpose of which was to achieve a separation of forces on the Canal. That the Secretary's prestige should be committed in this way was a measure of the progress already made since the ceasefire. He had developed a taste for this kind of negotiation and had a realistic view of what might be achieved, based upon the relationships he had been able to cultivate. Hence, when Moshe Dayan suggested that Kissinger take personal charge of the attempt to achieve a disengagement agreement, he did not hesitate. Dayan came to Washington in early

January with interesting proposals for a disengagement. He had never been persuaded by the arguments for basing Israel's defence line along the Canal, believing that the Mitla and Gidi passes held the key to a successful campaign in the Sinai, but after 1967 his arguments had not prevailed against those of his colleagues who had been seduced by its apparent attractions. The ease with which the Egyptians had breached the Bar-Lev line on 6 October had confirmed the soundness of his judgement. The proposal which he discussed with Kissinger was partly official and partly 'private' but clearly reflected an Israeli acceptance of a total withdrawal from the line of the Canal. What Dayan suggested was that the army withdraw from its bridgehead on the west bank of the Canal and that Egypt be permitted to occupy the whole east bank to a depth of 6–10 kilometres. The Israeli line would be to the west of the passes. Each side would have two security zones where the level of forces would be reduced and between the two there would be a United Nations 'buffer zone'. To preserve Israeli security, Egyptian forces east of the Canal would not exceed two to three battalions with no tanks. In return for this Israeli withdrawal, Dayan expected Sadat to end the state of belligerency and to permit Israeli ships and cargoes through the Canal. He also expected Israeli security to be guaranteed by the continuation of large-scale arms supplies from the USA. This was the first serious Israeli offer to evacuate conquered territory since 1957 and Kissinger knew enough about Egyptian intentions to know that it offered the prospect of securing an agreement.[7]

Success, however, was not pre-ordained, for the Israeli cabinet could not share Kissinger's warmth towards Sadat, whom they saw as the leader who had recently unleashed war against them and whose artillery consistently bombarded their forces throughout the entire period of the negotiations. For his part, Sadat wished to avoid concessions which might isolate him from the rest of the Arab world and could not move too far out of step with the feelings of his army. He realised that the Israeli proposal which Kissinger brought involved him in withdrawing his entire field army of some 70 000 from Sinai and accepting restrictions on his level of forces west of the Canal which would leave his military position worse off than it had been before the war. He opened the negotiations by insisting that he be allowed to retain one and a half divisions east of the Canal and that Israel would have to withdraw east of the passes. In order to ease the negotiations, he indicated his willingness to allow Israeli cargoes through the Canal and avoided raising the issue of the Palestinians.

These were the proposals which Kissinger took to Jerusalem at the start of what was to become known as 'shuttle diplomacy', an apt title coined by Under-Secretary Joseph Sisco to describe the process of conveying proposals and counter-proposals between the two sides. Kissinger found that the Israeli negotiating position had hardened since Dayan's visit. The government was conscious of the nervousness of public opinion over the proposed withdrawal to the east bank, voiced particularly strongly by General Sharon who was asking what Israel was going to gain by surrendering the hard-won positions of her soldiers. Against this, as Kissinger knew, were the crippling costs of the continuing mobilisation necessary to keep the Third Army surrounded and the prospect of renewed war should the negotiations fail. The government now seemed less certain of a total withdrawal from the west bank and was insisting that Sadat declare an end to belligerency and permit Israeli shipping through the Canal once it had been cleared. There was no question of withdrawal to the east of the passes, which the government was adamant would only come as the result of a final settlement. The crucial issue, however, was that of the level of Egyptian forces Israel was prepared to contemplate on the east bank. Israeli soldiers quickly grasped the significance of Sadat's insistence on 'divisions', for these would involve not just infantry but all the supporting arms, engineers, tanks and artillery. The Israeli proposal was for 'battalions' of Egyptian infantry.

On his return to Egypt on 13 January, Kissinger found Sadat prepared to make the crucial concession that Israel's line could stay west of the passes. Sadat also suggested that the security zones be simplified by reducing them from five to three, one for each side plus that manned by the United Nations. But he could not accept that Israel could dictate to him that certain types of armaments could not be stationed on Egyptian territory and insisted on the right to station thirty tanks on his zone on the east bank. Once again, the gap was narrowing, though Foreign Minister Fahmy and General Gamasy felt that Sadat was conceding too much. In fact, it was precisely these concessions which convinced the Israelis that Sadat was genuinely interested in a settlement, for they had never seriously believed that he would reduce his tank level on the east bank from around 700 to thirty. It was the type of bold gesture which Kissinger admired in handling negotiations, and it did produce a breakthrough. On his next visit to Israel, Kissinger negotiated an Israeli agreement that Egypt could station eight battalions and thirty tanks on the east bank. The only major obstacle to the conclusion of an agreement now appeared to be the distance which surface-to-air missiles could be stationed from the front line. It was a matter of major importance to Israeli commanders, for these missiles had done such destruction to their air force during the war. Because of this, they insisted they be based thirty kilometres to the rear; General Gamasy, recognising that this would deprive his forward troops of anti-aircraft cover, demanded twenty-five kilometres. The necessary final concessions came quickly. Sadat agreed to the thirty kilometre limit, and indicated that he would not actually exercise his option to station his thirty tanks on the east bank, while the Israelis allowed Egypt to include eight batteries of howitzers in her forces there.[8]

On the evening of 17 January, Nixon, sorely in need of a diplomatic success to set against his domestic travails, announced that the Egyptian and Israeli Chiefs of Staff would sign the agreement at Kilometre 101 the following day. The disengagement of forces was completed by 5 March, exactly on schedule. What had Kissinger and his negotiators achieved? They were not the authors of the plan; that credit must go to Dayan, for it reflected his conception of where Israel's true security lay. But Kissinger had been the crucial intermediary, able to interpret for each side the true position of its antagonist. In this way he was able to bring Sadat to the point where he could make the key concessions and, by reassuring the skeptical Israelis, soften their bargaining positions. In consequence, Israel made a significant withdrawal from her 1967 conquests, not to mention Sharon's bridgehead. In return, Israel had embarked on the uncertain course that might lead to a new relationship with her most powerful enemy. Her negotiators had only done so by ensuring that essential military safeguards were in place; indeed, Gamasy seems to have felt that Sadat's concessions had been so sweeping as to preclude a future military option. Even so, Israel had not made these concessions without anchoring herself more firmly to the USA, now her only certain ally. In order to secure Israel's agreement, Kissinger made another secret Memorandum of Understanding. Apparently, this contained Sadat's assurance that he could clear the Canal and allow the transit of Israeli cargoes; a guarantee of American action in the Security Council should Egypt demand the withdrawal of the UN force; and acceptance by both countries of American aerial reconnaissance of the Canal area. Above all, it contained the vital assurance that the USA would be responsive on a long-term basis to Israel's security needs, thus cementing what was becoming a central element in the relationship between the two countries.[9]

With the situation on the Canal stabilised, the Syrian front had to be the next priority, even though it would provide a much sterner test of Kissinger's diplomatic skills. Central to the success of the Egyptian negotiations had been the determination of Sadat to put his country on a pro-Western course, but Assad, an unyielding nationalist, shared no such inclination. Important as the Canal and the passes were, the Sinai had acted as a buffer between Egypt and Israel. On the Syrian front, the Israeli salient stretched out to within twenty miles of Damascus, while the Israelis were conscious of the vulnerability of their Chula and Jezreel valleys should the Syrian army succeed in breaking through on the Golan front. Behind all this lay a particular barrier of dislike and mistrust between the Israelis and the Syrians. Their negotiating positions were no more promising. For Assad, all the occupied territory, both the 1973 salient and the Golan Heights, were Syrian territory which ought to be returned to him. Behind this maximalist demand, lay the realistic view that as Sadat had succeeded in restoring the entire east bank to Egypt, Syria could not accept less than an Israeli evacuation of the salient and withdrawal from part of the Golan. In particular, he wanted the return of the provincial capital of Quneitra and key positions on Mount Hermon whose slopes dominated the approaches to Damascus. Inevitably, the Israeli positions were very different. Memories of the mid-1960s meant that there was no question of a total withdrawal from the Golan; indeed, for the Israeli government and people even a partial withdrawal from the territories they currently occupied would be to reward Assad for aggression. While no Israelis lived in Quneitra, true to their tradition of 'creating realities', they had placed settlements only four kilometres away whose fields almost approached the city. The Israelis were every bit as aware as the Syrians of Mount Hermon's incalculable strategic position, as well as of hills beside Quneitra around which the tank battles had flowed in October. When Kissinger left to begin his new phase of 'shuttle diplomacy' on 28 April 1974, these were the positions he had to try to draw together. As if to confirm the immensity of his task, artillery bombardments continued throughout his negotiations and radical Palestinians did their best to thwart what was being attempted. On 11 April, the border town of Kiryat Shmonah was attacked with the loss of eighteen civilians; the inevitable Israeli air strike on southern Lebanon followed. Then on 15 May, at a critical point in the negotiations, came the Maalot massacre with the death of sixteen schoolchildren. Adding to Kissinger's difficulties was the release of the so-called White House Tapes which ushered in the final phase of Watergate. All of this added up to one of the most unpromising diplomatic briefs of recent times and yet one which the Secretary of State had little option but to follow through. The one positive sign was that, on 18 March, the oil embargo, which at one time seemed to turn on an agreement with Syria, was lifted, though not without hints that it might be re-imposed were the mission to fail.

Kissinger set aside a week to reach an agreement; instead, the American party became involved in thirty-two days of extraordinarily taxing negotiations, the tone of which was set immediately on his arrival in Israel. Israelis, both government and public, knew that the sole purpose of his mission was to force an unwelcome withdrawal from hard-won positions on the Golan and they did not propose to make this easy for him. Their resentment was not helped by America's recent vote in the United Nations to condemn Israel for her retaliation in southern Lebanon. Kissinger's party was met with hostile demonstrations and testy meetings with Golda Meir's team. His negotiating technique with the prickly Israelis was to remind them of their isolated position in the world, and that it was in their interests to reach an accommodation with the Syrians for only in that way could the United States, Israel's only friend, continue to control the diplomatic process. It was the truth but the truth is not always palatable and, on 4 May, Kissinger had to hammer home his message in a 'threatening' letter from President Nixon to the Israeli premier. In these first discussions, once again it was Dayan who signalled the possible breakthrough by suggesting that Quneitra be partitioned between the countries, on the face of it a ludicrous proposal but one which showed the Secretary 'that Israel had crossed the psychological Rubicon'. Assad's response was predictably acid, insisting on the return of the salient and of half the Golan Heights. As the start to a successful negotiation it was unpromising but not disastrous.

On 13 May, after some very hard talking from Kissinger, the Israelis at last dropped their insistence on partitioning Quneitra but emphasised instead the importance of holding forward positions on the surrounding hills. On the 15th, as the Israeli cabinet tried to grapple with the situation in Maalot, Kissinger's old friend Simcha Dinitz explained that Quneitra had never been the major issue for the Israelis but that the hills were seen as vital to their defensive structure. Armed with this perception, Kissinger put forward a formula to both sides for a line just to the west of Quneitra, a demilitarised zone supervised by the United Nations, and arms restrictions on the Israeli troops on the hills to prevent them firing on the town. To his surprise, on 18 May, Assad accepted this formula. It proved to be the critical breakthrough, though not by any means the end of the negotiations, for the related problems of the extent of the United Nations zone, the positions on Mount Hermon, the limitation of forces, and support for the Palestinian guerrillas still held infinite promise of disagreement. Particularly difficult for the Syrians was the vulnerability of Damascus if they should agree to any limitation of forces beyond a ten kilometre zone. It was not until 26 May that Assad indicated that while he could not accept any formal limitation of forces beyond ten kilometres he would confine his army in front of Damascus to nine brigades, together with restrictions on the calibre of artillery to be deployed and the important concession of no surface-to-air missiles closer than twenty-five kilometres from the front line. The question of Palestinian raids, which in any case Assad had prevented along the Golan, was apparently solved by an American declaration that the ceasefire covered any such action. In fact, in the bitter aftermath of Maalot it was this which was to prove the final obstacle to an agreement. Before the Israeli Cabinet would conclude the negotiations, it was necessary for Kissinger to make a final trip to Damascus in an attempt to extract further assurances that the Golan front would not be used by the Palestinians. Assad explained that his depth of feeling on the Palestinians was such that he could make no public statement which would appear to abandon them, but repeated that he would not allow the frontier to be violated. For Israel, this had to suffice.[10]

The agreement, signed in Geneva on 31 May 1974, was Golda Meir's last act as Prime Minister and many would argue that it marked the zenith of Henry Kissinger's remarkable career as Secretary of State. It ended the dangerous Israeli salient which had thrust towards Damascus and allowed Assad to match Sadat's regaining of the Canal with the return of Quneitra, or such of it as Israel had left standing. Perched uneasily close to the Israeli line, the town was to present a ghostly reminder of the bitter quarrel between the two countries. The Druse villagers and farmers, whose communities remained behind the Israeli line for security reasons, were to remember Kissinger with deep bitterness as the fences erected under his disengagement agreement separated them from relations and the country they continued to regard as their homeland. But despite all the obstacles, Kissinger's stamina and determination had succeeded in stabilising one of the most contentious frontiers in the world until the Israeli annexation of the Golan Heights in November 1981. As with the Sinai agreement, Israel ensured that part of her price was the assurance of continuing American aid. Yet Kissinger's achievement left two unanswered questions. Would he try to build on the agreement to work for a broader Middle East settlement, or rest content with having defused the immediate crises? Just as intriguing was the relationship he had cultivated with President Assad. No major American figure before him had made such an effort to give due weight to Syria's perceptions and concerns. The obvious mutual respect of the two men seemed to hold out hope for a fresh dimension to American policy.[11]

As Kissinger explained before the Senate Foreign Relations Committee on the day that the Golan agreement was signed, the next step seemed logical: having dealt with disengagement on the Egyptian and Syrian fronts, Jordan should be next. Superficially this ought to have been the easiest of the three agreements to negotiate for both Israel and Jordan were bound to the United States by a multitude of obligations. Moreover, Israelis might have been persuaded that it was in their interests to reach an accommodation over the West Bank with King Hussein rather than with the PLO which was in the process of broadening its diplomatic appeal. The reality, of course, could not have been more different. The West Bank was not like the Sinai, or even the Golan. For most Israelis it was an essential security buffer, while for the National Religious Party, whose intentions were important for the future of Rabin's precarious government, it was Judea and Samaria, part of God's covenant with the Jewish people. The National Religious Party had not yet joined Rabin's Knesset coalition but he had hopes that it would do so and with his one-vote majority he had to be sensitive to their wishes. With these considerations in mind, he repeated a pledge given by his predecessor that there would be a general election before the conclusion of any agreement affecting the West Bank. Despite this clear signal that the government was in no mood to contemplate concessions on the West Bank, familiar signs of pressure from Washington began to appear. In testimony before the House Committee on Foreign Affairs, Joseph Sisco pointed to the new mood of accommodation in the PLO and hinted that this might open the way to its participation in the Geneva negotiations. When this was followed by delays in the delivery of American arms supplies, Washington's intentions seemed obvious, but Rabin's government still refused to respond.[12]

What sustained the Israelis in their resistance was the knowledge that they were dealing with a preoccupied and terminal administration, for the Watergate affair had at last moved into its final phase. Before it did so, however, there was a curious interlude in which Richard Nixon visited the Middle East despite, or perhaps because of, the humiliation which awaited him. The tour, which took him to Egypt, Saudi Arabia, Syria, Israel and Jordan, ought to have been a triumph for it was the first visit to the Middle East by a President since Roosevelt's occasional forays during World War 2. The cheering crowds assembled in Egypt confirmed the diplomatic revolution which had taken place since the October war; no less remarkable was the fact that an American leader could be welcomed in Damascus, an event which quickly resulted in the restoration of diplomatic links. Arab leaders, it seems, were impressed by his readiness to talk about a comprehensive settlement of the territorial legacies of the 1967 war. The only other major result of the trip was Nixon's offer to build a nuclear reactor in Egypt. Confronted by the enraged Israeli reaction to this, Kissinger suggested that the only way to ensure that it was not converted to military purposes would be American supervision of nuclear reactors in both Egypt and Israel.[13] The last thing that an Israeli government was likely to welcome was an American eye near their facility at Dimona in the Negev, and their rage was diverted to a campaign in Congress which succeeded in delaying the implementation of Nixon's promise by seven years. But with the President so obviously distracted by events at home, his tour was remembered as a rather forlorn episode in Middle East affairs rather than the triumph, which, had domestic events been different, it undoubtedly would have been. His departure from office on 9 August deprived Middle Eastern diplomacy of a man who had tried to open up new perspectives in American foreign policy, not least in that region.

Kissinger tried to breathe some life into his 'Jordanian option' in the autumn of 1974. He aroused a brief flicker of interest in the idea of restoring Jordanian administration to the city of Jericho, or even putting it under the United Nations, but even this failed to develop any momentum. When the Rabat summit recognised the PLO as the legitimate representative of the Palestinians, freezing out King Hussein, he finally recognised that the obstacles had become too great and that the time had come to return to the Egyptian front.[14] The inability to achieve any movement over the West Bank has been the basis of the charge that Kissinger was more concerned with the periphery of the Arab–Israeli conflict than with its substance, but that takes little account of the realities he had to face in American, Arab and Israeli politics.

With the new administration of Gerald Ford and Nelson Rockefeller settling down, Kissinger was not able to resume his attempt to build upon the Sinai disengagement agreement until the beginning of 1975, with mixed prospects for success. On the positive side, he could draw upon his unrivalled prestige and experience. His handling of foreign policy had made him into an international superstar with a reputation for winning agreements in the most unpromising circumstances. Fifteen months' sustained contact with the Middle East had acquainted him with the main obstacles to progress, enabling him to distinguish what leaders adopted as negotiating positions from what they really wanted. He was assisted by a talented and experienced staff, Joseph Sisco, Alfred Atherton and Harold Saunders, who had a highly-developed sense for assessing the nuances of Middle Eastern politics. Kissinger had good reason to hope that his reputation, knowledge of the issues and well-developed contacts could be mobilised in the search for a substantial move forward.

But in other respects the climate was far from encouraging. The winter of 1974–75 saw America's fortunes touch their lowest point since the great depression. No President in recent times had as unenviable an inheritance as Gerald Ford. Widely respected for his integrity and decency, it fell to him to help the nation regain its respect for the political process. His presidential pardon of Richard Nixon, a matter of common sense if the country were to put the enervating experience of Watergate behind it, cost him much of the public goodwill which, as the country's first unelected President, he needed so much if he hoped to carry any weight in international affairs. In South-east Asia, America's credibility was being seriously undermined as the hard-won Paris peace accords were systematically destroyed by the ruthless leaders in Hanoi. Disengagement from Vietnam had been negotiated on the assumption that Congress would sanction military and economic assistance which would enable South Vietnam to survive. But congressional opinion, hostile to further commitments in South-east Asia, was determined to assert a new place in the making of foreign policy. As a result, the administration's request for aid in fiscal years 1974 and 1975 was substantially cut, undermining the capacity and morale of South Vietnam's armed forces.[15] On 13 December 1974, the final North Vietnamese offensive began; Kissinger's sensitive Middle Eastern negotiations the following March were punctuated by a depressing litany of the fall of one South Vietnamese strong point after another. The lesson of these events for Egypt and Israel was clear: how trustworthy was the United States? If Israel was being asked to pull back from strategic positions in the Sinai under American guarantees, would these be honoured? Sadat had the problem of aligning Egypt with a country capable of abandoning its allies. Furthermore, as South Vietnam collapsed, Israel's leaders suspected that Ford and Kissinger badly needed a foreign policy success and were determined that this should not be at their expense.[16]

Nor did the situation in the Middle East inspire optimism. Lebanon was fast lapsing into the chaos which only formally began with the start of the civil war in April 1975. Arafat's visit to the General Assembly, which the Americans had resisted, resulted in the strongly pro-Palestinian Resolution 3236 (XXIX) which, amongst other things, requested the 'Secretary-General to establish contacts with the Palestine Liberation Organization on all matters relating to the question of Palestine'.[17] The success of the PLO's diplomatic strategy was not what the Americans wanted, for its immediate result would be a hardening of attitudes in Jerusalem and the undermining of King Hussein. On the night of 5 March, as Kissinger was flying to the Middle East, eight Fateh guerrillas landed on the Tel Aviv waterfront and attacked the Savoy Hotel leaving eighteen dead. No one doubted that the raid's purpose was to convince him that no settlement was possible without the PLO; the Palestinian news agency reportedly announced as much.[18] It did not make the Israeli government more conciliatory.

Rabin's government was the other problem Kissinger had to confront. The Labour Alignment showed all the signs of having been in power too long and, despite the change of leader, had never recovered from the setbacks of the October war. Rabin found it difficult to assert his authority over his principal subordinates. Foreign Affairs were taken from the highly-experienced Eban and given to Yigal Allon, by Israeli standards a 'dove' who was not averse to a substantial evacuation from the West Bank on suitable terms.[19] But Rabin's main problem was with Shimon Peres, his rival for the premiership, whom the compromises endemic in Israeli politics had forced him to nominate to the defence portfolio.[20] The resulting team was poorly co-ordinated, ill-suited for the hard decisions with which Kissinger would confront them. Though this was difficult enough, it was an open question whether Rabin's government judged it to be in Israel's interest to reach an agreement, believing it to be advisable to delay until the United States could solve its energy problems and, hence, would be less susceptible to Arab pressure. Rabin said as much in a press interview at the end of 1974 when he admitted that he would try to delay negotiations until after the next presidential election.[21]

In this unpromising climate, Kissinger arrived in Egypt on 8 March 1975, having made a brief exploratory visit to the region the previous month which had convinced him that there was a real chance of each side offering concessions. The publicly expressed position of the two parties was well known. Egypt's aim was the return of the Mitla and Gidi passes. Although not everyone was convinced that the passes held quite the military significance so often claimed for them, the Israelis had constructed early warning systems capable of alerting them to any Egyptian military build-up in the area of the Canal. The Egyptians were also determined to regain the Abu Rudeis oil field with unrestricted access. The Israeli aim was an agreement which would keep their forces to the west of the passes, thus retaining their electronic warning system. In return for such a withdrawal, they were demanding a public declaration of non-belligerency from Sadat, which would drive a wedge between him and Assad to Israel's strategic advantage. It was known that Sadat was not ready for such a public statement but preferred to give Israel indirect assurances as he had done the previous year.[22]

This is what Kissinger took to Jerusalem, together with an Egyptian proposal for a line putting the Israelis well to the east of the passes. He believed that Sadat had offered the substance of what the Israelis wanted, for in a recent interview with former New York mayor John Lindsay, Rabin had confirmed that if Egypt genuinely wanted peace she could have the oil field and the passes. He had previously conceded that it was unrealistic to expect a public declaration of non-belligerency. It was a belief shared by Kissinger, who argued that Israel would be better off with the reality of Egyptian goodwill rather than fighting for a public declaration of the kind that had failed to prevent war between India and Pakistan.[23] But his talks in Jerusalem soon showed that he was not going to carry these points easily. The Israelis returned to their familiar theme that in return for substantial withdrawal, Egypt was merely offering intangible assurances, a fear partly conditioned by the ease with which Nasser had swept aside the secret promises made in 1957.

By 19 March, the two sides were reportedly at the 'hard bargaining' stage. In fact, despite several shuttles, Kissinger was making no progress. Israel was prepared to make concessions on withdrawal but not if this involved surrendering control of her early warning system. Sadat was holding to the view that he could not adopt a declaration of non-belligerency while Israel was still occupying Egyptian territory; such a move would have to await a final settlement with Israel. But for the time being he was offering the Israelis the reality of an absence of war which could only be to their strategic advantage.[24] Kissinger, who took this point, became increasingly frustrated over his inability to convince Rabin's negotiating team that they were squandering the chance to secure their Egyptian front for the sake of a few kilometres.

The final confrontation came on 22 March in one of the bleakest exchanges in Israeli–American relations. It took place in the knowledge that a breakdown might throw the whole balance of that relationship into question. The previous day, a letter arrived from Ford threatening that if last-minute concessions were not made, then he would order a 'reassessment' of his Middle Eastern policy, including relations with Israel. Timed at a critical moment in the consideration of aid to Israel, the nature of his threat was clear. But Rabin's government had no desire to repeat the experience of 1957. Far from intimidating them, it hardened their determination to resist American pressure.[25] At the meeting, Kissinger could do little more than return to his earlier theme of taxing the Israelis with robbing him of control of the diplomatic process, the only result of which could be the replacement of his step-by-step approach by a more general settlement to force a return to the pre-1967 borders. This, he claimed, he had been trying to avoid. At a midnight press conference in the King David Hotel he announced his return to Washington to begin his 'period of reassessment'.[26]

His failure could not have come at a worse time, for he had barely reached Washington when the Buddhist holy city of Hue fell to the North Vietnamese. On 30 March, Da Nang, with all its memories as the key to control of the north of the country, was also taken, signalling South Vietnam's impending collapse. A month later, on 30 April, the victorious North Vietnamese army entered Saigon; nothing seemed to symbolise the impotence of American power more dramatically than in the frantic scenes at the embassy as Hanoi's tanks approached. On the day that Hue fell, King Faisal of Saudi Arabia was assassinated, creating yet more potential problems. Not only was his country easily the wealthiest in the Arab world, with economic leverage she had recently displayed, but Faisal had made her into a player of major significance in Middle Eastern politics. The new rulers, King Khaled and Prince Fahd, could not be assumed to have the diplomatic poise of their predecessor whose experience went back to the days of Neville Chamberlain and Franklin Roosevelt. Especially worrying was that Faisal, a powerful financial backer of Egypt, had been fully behind Sadat's strategy of seeking a solution with Israel through American mediation. Clearly, it was not the best of times to have returned empty-handed from a major diplomatic mission and, while his public statements carefully avoided laying blame, it was an open secret that Israel was the intended target of Kissinger's reassessment.

Any doubt that this might be the case was dispelled at the presidential news conference on 27 March when Ford identified Israeli inflexibility as the reason for the collapse of the negotiations.[27] Each side was well aware that any substantial reassessment could test the nature of the American–Israeli relationship. With Israeli's increasing isolation, her government could not contemplate any weakening in Washington's support. Kissinger's threat that his mediation would be replaced by a return to the Geneva conference also held dangerous implications, for there Israel would be faced with a number of Arab states backed by the Soviet Union and the probable demand for Palestinian representation. But the most potent source of leverage was known to be aid. The administration was about to lay Israel's request for $2.5 billion in military and economic assistance before Congress. While officials emphasised that nothing would be done to endanger Israel's security, the fate of that aid package was clearly going to reflect the nature of the reassessment. As part of the policy review, government departments and agencies were asked to report on how they felt about Middle East policy as a result of the collapse of the Kissinger mission. On 1 April, in a leak clearly designed to keep up the pressure on Jerusalem, Defense Secretary Schlesinger indicated his reluctance to enter into any new arms agreements with Israel while the reassessment was in progress. An Israeli team about to come to the United States to discuss the possible purchase of F–16 jets was asked to hold off.[28] In any case, the Pentagon and intelligence analysts were known to feel that Israel already possessed the capacity to win a prolonged war against Egypt and Syria, if necessary.[29] None of these signals was calculated to reassure Rabin's government.

On the broader issue of re-opening negotiations, Kissinger, Sisco and their team consulted widely with a number of respected figures from the defence and foreign policy establishments: Dean Rusk,

Robert McNamara, George Ball, Cyrus Vance, Averell Harriman, George Shultz among others; not a combination the Israelis found especially reassuring.[30] Three possible options were emerging. The first involved reviving the stalled Kissinger mission in an attempt to persuade Israel east of the passes in return for an acceptable Egyptian declaration, but it was not clear what fresh concessions each side could be expected to make. A second, rather vague, possibility was to attempt a more wide-ranging settlement between the two countries which might involve surrendering most of the Sinai in return for full Egyptian commitment on non-belligerency. The final option remained a resumption of the Geneva conference where negotiations over Sinai could be linked to the broader question of an Arab–Israeli settlement, possibly including, it was hinted, the Palestinians. In a CBS interview with Walter Cronkite on 21 April, Ford, his tone noticeably cool towards Israel, indicated that this was what he favoured. The broad outlines of the administration's thinking were emerging: an active diplomatic effort aimed at improving relations with the Arab states, along with a continued commitment to Israel's security. Any aid to the Middle East, including the package for Israel, would have to await completion of the review.[31]

In the meantime, the Arabs maintained the diplomatic momentum which they sensed was beginning to turn to their advantage. In early May, King Hussein went to the USA, spelling out publicly his and, he claimed, Egyptian and Syrian basic positions. In return for an Israeli withdrawal to her 1967 borders and recognition of Palestinian rights, he argued that the Arabs were ready to support a final peace based upon recognition of Israel's right to exist within recognised borders guaranteed with a declaration of non-belligerency. As if to confirm the administration's sympathy with this stance, the State Department announced approval of the sale to Jordan of a Hawk surface-to-air missile defence system worth $100 million. Israelis could not help but contrast this with the administration's refusal to enter into any new arms contracts with them.[32] Sadat, too, made one of his diplomatic moves, nicely timed to catch the Americans' imagination. Conscious that many allies were publicly expressing disquiet over Washington's sense of commitment in the wake of the collapse of Saigon, he announced that he would meet Ford in Salzburg in early June, affirming his belief that the Americans were the key element in Middle Eastern diplomacy. Again, Israelis took note of the fact that while details of this meeting had been worked out, a similar conference with Rabin was only being 'considered'.[33]

Such not-so-coded signals were pointing to what Jerusalem feared, the unwelcome prospect of being cajoled into a return to Geneva unsupported except by a 'cool' United States, with aid providing the carrot and the stick. Israel's aid request was being put on the same level as those of other Middle Eastern countries, to be delayed or cut according to Washington's degree of displeasure. No matter that Kissinger insisted that there was no question of a 'tilt' against Israel, that was not how the exercise was being perceived. The scene was set for a trial of strength that had been anticipated for some time, at least since Kissinger's successful application of pressure in October 1973 had forced Golda Meir's government to forfeit what they regarded as the ultimate fruits of their success. Many Israelis had become seriously alarmed over what they felt was a dangerous over-dependence on Washington for diplomatic and, more importantly, military support. If the latter could be regulated in the interests of American foreign policy, then Israel had been reduced to little more than a client state, a fate which Israelis, with their keen sense of independence, could not easily contemplate. Rabin's government believed that the implications of the reassessment must, and could, be fought.

Soundings taken amongst leading public figures and private opinion polls had convinced the Israeli government that if it acted decisively in Washington political circles, it had little to fear. While their refusal to co-operate with Kissinger had riled the administration, this was not widely shared in Congress or among the population at large.[34] In a sense, the period of 'reassessment' became more than a test of Washington's ability to put pressure on the Israelis; it showed how far the latter could still operate in American politics. Here, too, there had been some doubt. Since the aftermath of the 1973 war, many American Jews had been concerned that their leverage in Washington, based upon their political profile, might have been impaired by the country's need to accommodate itself to Arab oil interests, and that they would be blamed in the community at large for the energy shortages and economic hardships that were being faced. In its most extreme form, it was a fear that the new economic realities would lead to an abandonment of Israel and a backlash against the American Jewish community. Understandable enough in terms of the Jewish experience, they were wrong, for tests of public opinion showed that non-Jewish Americans were far less anti-Israeli or anti-Semitic than their Jewish fellow-countrymen thought they were. Three-quarters of Americans laid the blame for their economic problems on the Arab oil-producing countries, and two-thirds resisted the proposition that the country should secure her oil supplies by abandoning Israel. Moreover, most Americans instinctively disliked the radical figure Arafat had cut before the United Nations. Yet when as prominent a figure as the Chairman of the Joint Chiefs of Staff, General George Brown, could allude publicly to the power of the Jewish lobby being broken if the public suffered enough in the energy crisis, then Jews could not but feel uneasy. The proposed reassessment was the chance to test the political waters in Washington to see whether or not these fears were justified and to confirm Rabin's appreciation of the country's mood.[35]

With such issues at stake, the effort could not be half-hearted. On Kissinger's return, meetings took place between Israeli diplomats and their friends on Capitol Hill, out of which came a well organised and highly articulate campaign against what the reassessment seemed to threaten. This was to be done by three groups, the leadership of the Jewish community, influential visiting Israelis, and sympathetic Congressmen. The task was eased by the fact that it coincided with the annual fund-raising effort of the United Jewish Appeal, when Jewish families throughout the country were contacted. The campaign against the reassessment was initiated at a meeting in New York convened by the Conference of Presidents of Major Jewish Organisations attended by five of the city's Congressmen. Kissinger's dominance in foreign policy was bitterly, if predictably, denounced and Representative Benjamin Rosenthal made the increasingly familiar demand that Congress should assume a more positive role in policymaking.[36] Major political and public figures who criticised any weakening of the country's ties to Israel included Senator Edward Kennedy, New York Governor Hugh Carey, Daniel P. Moynihan, and the Chairman of the Senate Foreign Relations Committee, John P. Sparkman (Democrat, Alabama), who assured a B'nai B'rith meeting that any review of America's diplomatic options should be without prejudice to Israel's military or economic security.[37] Their efforts were reinforced by a record number of well-respected visiting Israelis, including Foreign Minister Allon, Abba Eban, Moshe Dayan, and two former intelligence chiefs, Aharon Yariv and Chaim Herzog. Dayan alone addressed meetings in twenty-one colleges; all emphasised the message that Israel had not been to blame for the collapse of Kissinger's negotiations and should not be the victim of any consequent reassessment.[38]

Important as all this was in demonstrating the depth of Israeli and

Jewish concern, the real battle was on Capitol Hill, where AIPAC's priority was to mobilise Israel's supporters in the Senate. The logic was clear: if enough Senators could be publicly enlisted, then the administration could not use the aid package to coerce Israel. The tactic that this should be done through a letter to Ford was worked out by AIPAC's Morris Amitay and a small group of aides to Senators Jacob Javits, Birch Bayh, Henry Jackson, Hubert Humphrey and Clifford P. Case. As the result of their discussions, Javits and Bayh met a group of Senators on 6 May where it was decided that a letter would be circulated under their sponsorship. When it was submitted to the President on 21 May, it bore seventy-six signatures, fifty-one Democrats and twenty-five Republicans, including twelve of the seventeen members of the Foreign Relations Committee. Prominent Democrats included Henry Jackson, Walter Mondale, Abraham Ribicoff, George McGovern, John Glenn, Thomas Eagleton, Stuart Symington, Daniel Inouye, Edmund Muskie, Alan Cranston, Herman Talmadge and Edward Kennedy, while Republicans included John Tower, Paul Laxalt, Robert Dole, Charles Mathias, Barry Goldwater and Edward Brooke. Most had signed without demur, though it was conceded that between ten and fifteen had to be lobbied by other Senators or Jewish constituents and Mathias has recorded the degree of pressure Senators were made aware of. The letter emphasised Israel's reliability as an ally in an area where the Soviet Union was arming the Arab states, and supported her position on defensible borders and the need for a peace treaty. Above all, it urged Ford that the aid package which he was to present to Congress would be 'responsive to Israel's urgent military and economic needs' and that the reassessment should be based upon the premise that the two countries stood firmly together. Of those who did not sign, Charles Percy sent an independent letter to Ford arguing that policy should not be based exclusively on the interests of one party.[39] But Rabin, AIPAC and their senatorial allies had seemingly won a signal victory, for the administration was being told that whatever aid package was presented to the Senate would be adjusted to meet Israel's needs. With three-quarters of the Senate behind her, Israel need not fear this kind of pressure. More generally, the letter confirmed what the Israeli government had believed to be the case, that the disapproval felt by Ford and Kissinger was not shared in political circles, nor by the country as a whole. The reassessment of policy had now been seemingly rendered academic and, as Ford prepared to meet Sadat and Rabin, little remained but a return to step-by-step diplomacy.

Two things had apparently been confirmed: Arab oil power had not deprived the Israeli lobby of its power in Washington and, as a result, Israel could feel rather more certain that she was not at the latter's beck and call. Many would come to see it as the most notable victory by an ethnic lobby in recent political history.

Yet that victory was more apparent than real; it reflected the world of Capitol Hill rather than the realities of power in the Middle East. In the weeks that followed Kissinger did not relax his pressure on Israel, though he did so in a less public manner, and he succeeded for the simple reason that Israel did depend on the USA for diplomatic support and aid. AIPAC's victory was a conjuring trick. As Kissinger's insistence on concessions grew, the Israeli Treasury Minister warned colleagues of the dire economic problems they would face if immediate American aid could not be secured. 'All of these pressures', wrote Matti Golan, 'forced Rabin and the others to face their moment of truth.'[40] Realising that they had no alternative but to give further ground in Sinai, the Israeli government decided to secure the best possible guarantees from the Americans on political, military and economic support. Unlike the previous disengagement agreement, where Kissinger had assumed the role of mediator, he now moved in to what, in effect, was a bilateral negotiation with Rabin's government, with Sadat largely acquiescing in what was being done.

On 21 August 1975, Kissinger arrived in Jerusalem to begin his latest shuttle. But almost all the important points had been agreed beforehand and enough had been leaked for him to be greeted by large hostile right-wing demonstrations, which castigated him for selling out Israel's interests. It cannot have been a pleasant experience for the Secretary, who had experienced Nazism at close quarters, to be confronted with placards denouncing him as a 'Kapo', but it did not deflect him from his view that Israel's best interests were served by an accommodation with her Arab neighbours. What angered the crowds was the knowledge that their government had already conceded what most people believed should not be surrendered short of a final peace agreement. A negotiating team led by Dinitz had already agreed with the Americans that they would pull back to the east of the Mitla and Gidi passes, whose strategic value and electronic surveillance facilities had caused the breakdown of Kissinger's previous mission. They had also yielded on the issue of the Abu Rudeis oil field which was to be returned to Egypt together with a road link. To return Israel's only guaranteed source of oil, which supplied some 55 per cent of her needs, in a world which had not long emerged from an embargo, was no small matter.[41] In return, Sadat was apparently giving very little. He was still set against a declaration of non-belligerency as long as Israel occupied part of his territory. The most he was prepared to give was a public assurance that Israeli cargoes would be allowed through the Canal. As the Israelis were well aware, he had already given this assurance secretly the previous year but had done nothing about it. All the Israelis were really gaining from Sadat was a further instalment of goodwill; at a meeting of the Organisation of African Unity in Uganda the Egyptians lobbied hard to forestall a resolution demanding Israel's expulsion from the United Nations.[42] But this seemed remarkably little in return for Israeli concessions no different to those for which the government had been prepared to jeopardise relations with Washington only a few months previously.

The real concessions, of course, came from Washington. The most immediately controversial was the commitment of American personnel to the Sinai. From the start, the Israelis had been worried about their electronic surveillance system in the passes and the price of their withdrawal was American involvement. Egypt and Israel were each to be allowed a surveillance station with Americans assigned to them; in addition, there was to be an American-manned surveillance station. To introduce American personnel into the Sinai so soon after Vietnam was a matter of the utmost delicacy, for the 'doves' in Congress would inevitably point to the sending of 800 advisers to South Vietnam as the start of that involvement. To head off such criticism, the Americans were to be described as 'civilians' furnished only with side arms, and it was emphasised how their presence was acceptable to both sides. This much was to be made public, but of even greater significance were the secret guarantees given to Israel. In order to compensate for the return of Abu Rudeis to Egypt, Israel was given comprehensive assurances about her energy needs. For a five-year period, if Israel were unable to secure sufficient oil, the USA undertook to make available for purchase the amount necessary for her needs. In addition, the Americans undertook to provide funds to enable Israel to build the facilities needed to store a greater amount of oil reserves, and they agreed to take Israel's financial losses in losing access to Abu Rudeis into account when deciding the level of aid. Israel's international position was also to be safeguarded, with the Americans agreeing to veto any Security Council resolution which ran counter to the agreement and to consult with the Israeli government in the event of any threat by a 'world power' with a view to providing support 'diplomatic or otherwise'. Far-reaching assurances were also provided on aid; namely, that the United States would be 'fully responsive, within the limits of its resources and Congressional authorization, on an on-going and long-term basis, to Israel's military equipment and other defence requirements, to its energy requirements and to its economic needs'. More specifically, Israel was assured that 'the United States is resolved to continue to maintain Israel's defensive strength through the supply of advanced types of equipment, such as the F–16 aircraft'. The next move with Egypt was agreed to be a final peace settlement and any negotiation with Jordan would be 'directed toward an over-all peace settlement', thus ruling out any piecemeal arrangements for the West Bank. A separate memorandum dealt with the conduct of the USA over the Geneva Conference where the two countries agreed to concert their policies. The crucial gain for Israel was Kissinger's assurance that 'The United States will continue to adhere to its present policy with respect to the Palestine Liberation Organization, whereby it will not recognize or negotiate with the Palestine Liberation Organization so long as the Palestine Liberation Organization does not recognize Israel's right to exist and does not accept Security Council Resolutions 242 and 338.' To reinforce this, the United States undertook to veto any attempt in the Security Council to change these resolutions in a way which was judged incompatible with their original purpose.[43]

The initialling of the second Sinai disengagement agreement by Egypt and Israel on 1 September 1975 marked the end of nearly two years' intensive Middle Eastern diplomacy. It is clear that its author did not intend this to be the case, but so it proved, for other foreign policy issues engaged Kissinger's attention and the election year of 1976 was not the time to press for Middle Eastern initiatives. After Vietnam and Watergate a majority of American voters saw in Jimmy Carter the freshness they were looking for and his victory brought the 'Kissinger era' in Middle Eastern diplomacy to an end. Others in the Middle East and the United States had played their part, Sadat, Meir, Dayan, Rabin, Allon, Dinitz, Assad, and his own team of tireless advisers, but as Kissinger had argued, threatened, cajoled and mediated he had made himself the ultimate architect of all that had been accomplished. On the nature of that accomplishment there was no unanimity. If many Israelis felt that he had reduced them from a client ally to a client dependency, there were those in the USA who were uneasy at the wide-ranging nature of the guarantees he had given. Israeli resentment over the degree of pressure he had exerted on them was matched by different complaints on the Arab side. 'For all the fanfare, Kissinger in the Middle East was basically Israel's envoy', Ismail Fahmy later complained.[44] More fundamental was the objection that his vision had been limited to adjustments on the periphery of the Arab–Israeli conflict rather than to its central issue. Such critics point to the failure of his Jordanian initiative to achieve any kind of momentum and his determination to exclude the PLO from the discussions. The West Bank and Gaza were left untouched for his successors. As Israeli settlements there expanded in the late 1970s, the problems they posed were to grow ever more intractable. The issue of east Jerusalem was avoided. These gaps essentially derived from Kissinger's 'step by step' philosophy, grounded as it was on a pessimistic view of the nature of the Arab–Israeli conflict. If Kissinger's negotiations demonstrated anything, they proved the depth of mistrust between the parties to the Middle East conflict and nothing short of a virtuoso performance had been needed to bring a measure of disengagement in Sinai and on the Golan. When Watergate and America's other international problems are also taken into account, the wonder, as Dr Johnson might have conceded, was that it was done at all.

7 Carter: The Search for Peace

Jimmy Carter promised a new start to a public grown weary by Vietnam and Watergate. Many American Jews were uneasy over his election, feeling that his origins and experience as a Southerner had isolated him from their community and its concerns; some also felt that he could not match their knowledge of Middle East issues. Nevertheless, the new President, on his own admission an 'outsider' in Washington, was probably much better equipped than most of his countrymen, and many of his predecessors, to approach the region's problems. A committed Christian, long fascinated by the land of the Bible, in May 1973 he had visited Israel, seeing for himself something of her achievements and security concerns and meeting a number of influential Israelis, including Golda Meir. In the course of the 1976 campaign, he made the customary, if by now ritual, declarations of 'unequivocal' support for Israel demanded of any candidate seeking Jewish votes and support. He also expressed strong disapproval of the Ford–Kissinger technique of appearing to threaten Israel if she did not do as they wished.[1] It soon became clear, however, that his Middle East policies were not to be bound by the conventions of campaign rhetoric. Not only was he determined to bring a fresh approach to the business of government, the Democratic Party had also been actively engaged in thinking about the Arab–Israeli conflict. Especially forthright was former Under-Secretary of State George W. Ball, who argued that Kissinger's shuttle diplomacy had been the triumph of tactics over strategy. In a graphic phrase, Ball concluded that 'Secretary Kissinger has pursued a practice that most medical doctors would deplore; he has sewn up part of the wound, leaving a raging infection inside'.[2] Although Ball did not become Secretary of State, possibly because of his views on the Middle East, the perceived need to move on from Kissinger's 'step by step' approach to a comprehensive settlement of the Arab–Israeli dispute was to distinguish the Carter administration.

The possible dimensions of this were set out in the report of a study group published by the Brookings Institution in 1975, which argued that a comprehensive settlement was urgently needed because the Sinai agreement had not addressed the fundamental issues. The key elements in the report were to linger in American thinking for many years. Like the Rogers Plan, it envisaged an Israeli return to the pre-1967 borders, with mutually agreed modifications. Israel's security would be guaranteed by demilitarised zones beyond her borders under United Nations' supervision. Most controversially, it explicitly acknowledged the need for a Palestinian state, either as an independent entity or in federation with Jordan, subject to Palestinian acceptance of Israel. The provisions on frontiers and a Palestinian state were alarming to the Israelis who were not reassured when two of the report's authors became leading policymakers in the new administration. Zbigniew Brzezinski became Carter's National Security Adviser, bringing with him William B. Quandt, who had recently written a fine study of America's Middle East policy under Johnson, Nixon and Ford. Quandt had also worked in the National Security Council with Harold Saunders from 1972 to 1974. Saunders had a sophisticated feel for the nuances of the Arab–Israeli conflict and, together with Alfred Atherton, represented continuity from the hectic days of Kissinger's diplomacy. Leading Carter's foreign policy team was Cyrus R. Vance, an experienced New York lawyer who proved to be an outstanding negotiator. If Brzezinski was suspect to the Israelis because of his association with the Brookings report, Carter's Vice-President, Walter Mondale, had strong links with the Jewish community. It was a team of many talents, combining fresh ideas with practical and academic insights.[3]

Carter was determined to make an early start on the Arab–Israeli problem. In the course of his campaign, he had discussed the Brookings report with Brzezinski and approved its findings. Its emphasis on the Palestinians fitted well with one of the main themes of Carter's approach to foreign policy, the pursuit of human rights, which he saw as bringing back a much-needed emphasis on morality in public affairs. 'Since I had made our nation's commitment to human rights a central tenet of our foreign policy', he recorded, 'it was impossible for me to ignore the very serious problems of the West Bank.'[4] His advisers were well aware that as any such approach must embroil him with the Israelis, and hence their lobby in Washington, it should be made as early as possible, far in advance of the next round of congressional elections. With that in mind, the early weeks of the new administration were full of diplomatic activity aimed at bringing together the various parties in a revived Geneva conference. The strategy was twofold. In mid-February, Vance undertook a trip to the Middle East in an attempt to identify the major negotiating positions and how they might be nudged closer together. Carter's role was to meet the Israeli Prime Minister and key Arab leaders in Washington to show how committed the administration was to the search for a settlement.[5]

Vance's exploratory mission confirmed the size of the obstacles in the way of an understanding. Rabin, an experienced soldier, was not attracted by the idea of an internationally guaranteed security zone around Israel's frontiers and was predictably hostile to any kind of Palestinian state, while Sadat was interested in the possibility of linking the West Bank and Gaza with Jordan. Making it clear that the Palestinian issue was the prime one, the Egyptian leader was prepared to put forward the idea of a joint Jordanian–PLO delegation for the Geneva talks. Before leaving Washington, Vance had hinted that he was interested in exploring the possibility that the PLO's attitude toward Israel might have moderated but he soon came up against the assurances Kissinger had given the Israelis on not negotiating with the organisation.[6] If Vance's trip merely confirmed the immensity of the task confronting the United States, at least he had made contact with the key leaders, assuring them of the new administration's determination to push ahead.

Carter's meetings with Rabin on 7–8 March were mutually unsatisfactory. With his government beset with troubles and facing an election in May, the Israeli premier was in no mood, or position, to offer concessions. It was immediately clear to him that Carter's position was that of the unpalatable Brookings report but what he was less prepared for was the shock of the President's insistence that a means should be found of involving the PLO in negotiations. At his press conference the following day, Carter, for the first time since the Rogers Plan, publicly indicated the nature of the settlement the Americans wanted. Like Rogers, he envisaged Israel's return to the June 1967 border, but with the refinement of a security zone which he was careful not to define too closely.[7] If Carter's strategy was to sting the Israelis into new ways of thinking, then he certainly kept up the momentum, for on 17 March he caused a stir by shaking the hand of the PLO representative at a reception at the United Nations in New York. The previous night, in response to a question at a meeting in Clinton, Massachusetts, he had declared that there would have to be a homeland for the Palestinians. In this, he was running ahead of his advisers, but Carter seems to have been set on shock treatment, for Brzezinski received direct orders to issue no elaboration of the Clinton statements.[8] The impression that the new administration was 'tilting' away from Israel was confirmed by their refusal to allow her to export twenty-four Kfir aircraft, equipped with American engines, to Ecuador, or to deliver CBU–72 concussion anti-personnel bombs which had been authorised by Ford. In sharp contrast to the growing chill with Jerusalem was the atmosphere created by Sadat's meeting with Carter on 4 April, which the latter was to describe as a 'shining light' bursting on the Middle East. Although no detailed concessions were forthcoming, beyond clear confirmation of Sadat's readiness to come to terms with Israel, the warm relationship the two men struck up was to be of fundamental importance in the next two years.[9]

Nothing could be done to prepare for a revived Geneva conference until after the Israeli elections in May. These resulted in the defeat of the Labour Alignment which had dominated Zionist and Israeli politics since the early days of the Jewish Agency but which recently had shown all the signs of a political movement too long in power. The Americans had found Rabin stiff in negotiations but he was more flexible than his manner suggested. His successor, Menahem Begin, was a man of a different stamp, the leader of a Zionist tradition which had hitherto existed only on the margin of American awareness. Begin's intellectual and political inspiration was Ze'ev Jabotinsky, founder in 1935 of Revisionist Zionism–opposed to the ideology and techniques of Weizmann and Ben-Gurion. As leader of the Irgun Zvai Leumi or Etzel, Begin had waged a relentless war first against the British and then the Palestinian Arabs, earning him both a unique place in Israel's history and the antipathy of Ben-Gurion and the Labour establishment which condemned him to the fringe of political life for thirty years. Never a man of compromise, Begin had a profound sense of his responsibility to safeguard the Jewish nation; partly this resulted from his religious faith and partly from the memory of losing most of his family in the Holocaust. The central part of his political platform threatened to confound American policy: his conviction that the West Bank, or Judea and Samaria, was an inalienable part of the Jewish inheritance. Although Labour leaders had shown few signs of wishing to relinquish the West Bank, their approach to it had been pragmatic, conscious as they were of its growing Arab population. Even so, almost from the start of the occupation Jewish settlements had been established along the Jordan valley with the aim of creating a security belt and also, under pressure from religious groups, at places like Kiryat Arba near Hebron. By the mid-1970s such religious pressure had found its focus in the *Gush Emunim* movement, whose settlements, if often poorly occupied, were the gauge of intense feelings held by many Israelis. It was a sentiment shared by the new Prime Minister, for whom the West Bank, if not Gaza, was not negotiable.[10] How this was to be reconciled with the Carter administration's aspiration to achieve something for the Palestinians of the occupied territories was far from clear.

The principal American hope was that, as a strong leader with a popular mandate behind him, Begin would be more able than his predecessor to deliver an agreement. It was, therefore, with rather mixed expectations that Carter met him in Washington on 19 and 20 July. Knowing that much would depend on the new premier, Carter made a special effort to cultivate him. The two men were able to agree on the need for a comprehensive peace based upon Resolution 242 and the normalisation of relations between Israel and her neighbours. Vance thought that Begin agreed to the principle of withdrawal 'on all fronts', which would have been a significant concession. On the West Bank and Gaza, however, Begin made clear his total opposition to any kind of Palestinian homeland and managed to secure a promise that Carter would stop using the term. His visit left Carter and his team reassured that there was the prospect of diplomatic progress, but his action on returning home of legalising three settlements on the West Bank did give them cause to think; it was not a breach of any undertaking but neither was it a gesture of goodwill. William Quandt has argued that it took the administration a long time to appreciate the depth of the Israeli leader's ideological commitment to the West Bank.[11]

Disillusion was, however, setting in as Vance prepared to return to the Middle East on 1 August in pursuit of the Geneva conference. Already annoyed over the settlements, the Secretary was 'furious' when the Israeli ambassador informed him that while Begin had agreed on the principle of Resolution 242 that did not imply withdrawal 'on all fronts', as he had supposed. Vance was concerned to find a mechanism which would allow the Palestinians to be represented at Geneva and give an opportunity to lobby for a new line of thought toward the West Bank and Gaza which his advisers had been developing. The former foundered on the deep divisions within the PLO and Begin's angry reaction to the prospect of having to negotiate with them. Atherton, Saunders and Quandt had been working on the idea of a transitional arrangement for the West Bank and Gaza, probably under United Nations' trusteeship, which would allow Israel and a Palestinian entity to come to terms with each other.

For the time being this idea failed to gain momentum, for Begin predictably bristled at the notion of giving up the territories and the Arabs were unwilling to concede that no better idea was currently on offer.[12] Progress toward Geneva was proving slow and was soon to be completely overtaken by events in the Middle East over which the USA had little control but which came to dominate Carter's search for a settlement.

In conditions of intense secrecy, contacts were taking place between Arabs and Israelis. At the end of August, King Hussein met Moshe Dayan, now Begin's Foreign Minister, in London. On 4 September, Dayan flew to Morocco for the first of a series of meetings with King Hassan and the Egyptian Deputy Prime Minister, Dr Hassan Tuhami, who hoped to convince him of Sadat's genuine desire for peace and belief that the Begin government was strong enough to negotiate it. Tuhami's positive reports helped Sadat come to his decision that direct contact with the Israelis offered a better way forward than Geneva. Sadat had become irritated over the slow progress being made toward Geneva and was, in any case, unhappy about the Soviet Union becoming directly involved once again as the conference's co-chairman. On 21 October, Carter sent him a personal letter appealing for his help in moving forward. Although it was couched in terms of Geneva, the letter helped stimulate his thinking toward a less orthodox approach. What seems to have confirmed his new line of thought were discussions with the Rumanian President, Nicolae Ceausescu, who reassured him that Begin was a courageous leader who could deliver an agreement. Sadat concluded that if he could reassure the Israelis by going to Jerusalem and conducting the face to face negotiations they had been demanding for thirty years, he could create the conditions for a successful peace negotiation.[13] So closely did he keep his own counsel that when he announced before the People's Assembly on 9 November that he was ready to go to the Knesset to talk peace, the American government, and many of his advisers, were 'stunned', as both Vance and Brzezinski conceded in their memoirs. The Americans were uncomfortably aware that Sadat's mission to Jerusalem had abruptly taken the game away from them. How Sadat and Begin, two 'unguided missiles' as one State Department official described them, would interact without American mediation seemed problematic at best. The Egyptian leader's unexpected move seemed to hold out awful prospects were it to fail; the resignation of his Foreign Minister, Ismail Fahmy, and the outraged response in other Arab capitals seemed to show how isolated he was. The risks were clearly immense and, as Sadat's visit to Jerusalem went ahead on 19–21 November, the Americans were largely reduced to hoping, and praying, for success.[14]

By any reckoning, Sadat's address to the Knesset was an event of rare drama watched by television audiences throughout the world. It was a wide-ranging appeal for a peace settlement which would include the Palestinians, ensuring Israel a recognised place in the Middle East. Begin's reply that everything would be open to negotiation seemed to many Americans to fail to rise to the occasion, but he was clearly determined not to be swept into concessions he might later regret. Within days of his return, Sadat sought to maintain the momentum by inviting the major parties to talks in Cairo. The US administration's reaction to all of this was cool, so cool as to cause the *New York Times* to observe that it 'could freeze the Nile', but there seemed little alternative except to follow where Sadat was leading.[15] In agreeing to send a delegation to Cairo, Carter knew that he was breaking with the Soviet Union and the other Arab states which had been working toward Geneva.

As the Americans had feared, only the Israelis and themselves accepted Sadat's invitation and little came of the meeting. But the Americans were steadily being drawn into what was now being termed the 'Sadat initiative', a clear indication of this being Vance's return to the Middle East from 10 to 14 December. Sadat assured him that his visit had created the conditions for an Israeli return to the 1967 borders and the resolution of Palestinian issues, but in Jerusalem Vance formed the view that the Israeli aim was a bilateral peace treaty with Egypt. Begin did insist, however, that he had proposals for a withdrawal from Sinai and arrangements for the West Bank and Gaza which he wanted to put to Carter. These were explained to the Americans on 16 and 17 December and, in a sense, they seemed to show new thinking on Begin's part. What he was proposing on Sinai was a phased withdrawal to the 1967 border, which was more than Kissinger had been able to secure in eighteen months of negotiations. For the West Bank and Gaza, he envisaged a form of 'autonomy' which would allow the inhabitants to govern their daily lives while retaining Israeli military rule. In addition, he would not press Israel's claim to sovereignty for five years to give this arrangement time to work. Carter and his advisers reacted with mixed emotions to this. It had elements in common with the transitional plan for the territories which they had been preparing and it seemed to be an acknowledgment on Begin's part that the

Palestinians had to be taken into account, no small departure from his previous positions. But there were problems. The Americans had envisaged a transitional arrangement supervised by the United Nations; this was to be under the Israeli military. More fundamentally, was Begin's proposal the first step toward a negotiated settlement for the territories or was it a cosmetic exercise which would perpetuate Israel's hold? Could it be reconciled with the American proposal or, as Brzezinski perceptively observed, would it simply result in the West Bank and Gaza becoming 'a Basutoland under Israeli control?'[16] The future shape of the Arab–Israeli conflict would be largely determined by the answers. For the moment the two sides thought they had the basis for an agreement; the process of disillusion was to be hard.

These discussions were the prelude to the unproductive and potentially disastrous encounter between Sadat and Begin at Ismailia on Christmay Day. Once again, the Americans' fears were fulfilled. Sadat's dramatic move had failed to produce a diplomatic break-through, leaving him increasingly exposed at home and abroad. The major issues were clouded by the presence of a cluster of Israeli settlements near Rafah in the Sinai. Always liable to be controversial, the government proceeded with their expansion, to the fury of Carter and Sadat. The measure of their concern was Carter's diversion from a brief foreign tour to land briefly at Aswan on 4 January 1978 in an attempt to demonstrate his solidarity with the Egyptian leader. While there, he re-stated publicly his conviction that a peace settlement would have to address 'the legitimate rights of the Palestinian people and enable the Palestinians to participate in the determination of their own future', a carefully coded message intended to reassure the Arabs while pleasing the Israelis by avoiding the use of the term Palestinian 'state'. The President's action and his statement were designed to help remove the dangerous impasse so apparent after the Ismailia summit and seemed to confirm a growing view that nothing could be accomplished without American mediation.[17]

Sadat increasingly shared this view. The collapse of talks in Jerusalem, when Sadat recalled his delegation, led to a message from Cairo that he was becoming 'disillusioned' with Carter's apparent inaction, in effect an appeal for help. The result was an important policy meeting on 23 January at which the idea of inviting both leaders to Camp David was aired for the first time but held over for the future. Instead, Sadat was invited to Washington. It was a

measure of the US administration's frustration with Begin's government that they were prepared to contemplate a joint strategy with
Sadat aimed at putting the Israelis under strong pressure to produce
concessions. The essence of this approach was that Sadat would come
forward with a proposal containing certain elements which the
Americans would ask him to concede, and then 'use the subsequent
Egyptian "concession" as the point of departure for joint public
pressure on the Israelis'. Essentially, what was agreed with Sadat was
that he would propose his peace plan after a meeting between Carter
and Begin. After Begin had rejected it, the Americans would be able
to put forward their own formula. As Quandt, one of its authors,
later conceded, it was all 'a bit too Machiavellian' and little was to
come of it.[18] Such was the state of American–Egyptian–Israeli
relations ten weeks after Sadat's visit to Jerusalem.

On the eve of Begin's visit to Washington, once again the world
was forced to contemplate the intensity of the Arab–Israeli conflict,
for on 11 March a group of Palestinians landed on the coast between
Tel Aviv and Haifa. Their first victim was an American photographer
Gail Rubin, niece of Senator Abraham Ribicoff. After seizing two
buses, their action ended with the death of thirty-five people. Three
days later an estimated 20 000 Israeli forces began an invasion into
southern Lebanon which was clearly more than a retaliatory raid.
'Operation Litani' soon had Israeli forces occupying the area to the
south of the Litani river. As casualties rose into the hundreds, with
thousands more made homeless, Carter and his aides were only too
aware of the potentially terminal damage to a peace process which
was only just alive. If Sadat stood silent, then it would appear that he
had collaborated in an attack on an Arab country which his Foreign
Minister castigated as 'organised genocide'. Although he had been
appalled by the PLO attack, Carter saw the Israeli attack as a
'terrible overreaction' which he was determined to end, especially
since he suspected it might be part of a plan to establish a permanent
presence. On 16 March, the State Department issued a terse
statement that 'we expect Israel to withdraw, and we have made our
views in this respect known to the Israeli government'. It appears that
Carter warned the Israelis that American-supplied weapons were
being used in Lebanon contrary to the terms under which they had
been supplied. If Israel did not agree to withdraw, Congress would be
formally notified of this, resulting in the ending of military aid. Like
Eisenhower in 1957, the pressure proved sufficient.[19] In an attempt
to stabilise Israel's northern border, the Americans sponsored the

formation of the United Nations Interim Force in Lebanon (UNIFIL), charged with confirming Israel's withdrawal, restoring security and assisting the Lebanese government with the restoration of its authority. Approved by the Security Council on 19 March, it began to assume its duties as the Israelis withdrew, the evacuation being complete by 13 June. As a quick piece of crisis management, the deployment of UNIFIL was a success but its subsequent mission was bedevilled by the efforts of the PLO, the Israeli-backed militia of Major Saad Haddad and the Israeli army, to ignore or thwart it. In June 1982, the Israeli armed forces simply rolled over it in their next invasion of Lebanon.

With Israeli–American relations reportedly at their lowest point since 1957, Begin's visit to Washington from 21–23 March was productive of little but mutual recriminations; indeed, Begin confessed that they were the three most difficult days of his life. Carter directly charged the Israeli leader with the 'six noes': that he would not withdraw from the West Bank; that he would not draw a halt to the construction of settlements; that he would not withdraw Israeli settlements from the Sinai; that he would not agree to put these settlements under the protection of the United Nations; that he would not concede that Resolution 242 applied to the West Bank and Gaza; that he would not allow the Palestinians to determine their own future. Faced with such a direct challenge, the Israelis, in Brzezinski's view, looked 'shaken', but Begin did not deny the validity of Carter's charges nor did he offer any hope of compromise.[20] Despairing of an effective Israeli response, the Americans prepared to ask Sadat to reveal his proposals in terms of what had been agreed in February. However, the idea had indeed been too Machiavellian for, when Sadat did make public his plan in May, the Americans found that they could not turn it to their advantage. Vance, it seems, had never really liked the idea and Carter had reached a stage in his presidency where to indulge in public criticism of the Israelis was politically undesirable; significantly, neither alludes to the February plan in their memoirs. Carter had in any case run up against the Israeli lobby and their supporters in Congress with his proposal to sell F–15 aircraft to Saudi Arabia. As far back as the previous October, leading Jewish Democrats had been warning about the serious effect his policies were having on their fund-raising and their prospects in the 1978 congressional elections. A major fund-raising dinner in Los Angeles, addressed by Carter, ran up against the unwillingness of Jews to attend. Only lobbying by Mondale helped save the situation but, even so, the function raised $650 000 rather than the $1 million expected. Far from improving, in May, fund-raising dinners in New York and Los Angeles had to be postponed because of cancellations.[21] Domestic difficulties and the continuing diplomatic stalemate, confirmed at a meeting which Vance had with Dayan and the Egyptian Foreign Minister Mohamed Ibrahim Kamel at Leeds Castle in England, were urgently dictating a fresh move.

On Vance's return, Carter began to think seriously about bringing Begin and Sadat together in a summit meeting and, on 31 July, finally decided that the two leaders would be invited to Camp David where the Americans could, to a degree at least, set the agenda. The Camp David summit, which lasted from 5–17 September, proved to be the most concentrated attempt to build the foundations for an accommodation between Israel and the Arabs. Few episodes in modern history have been as well served by their major participants. Carter, Vance, Brzezinski, Kamel, Dayan and Ezer Weizman have published their accounts, while Quandt, himself a member of the American team, has written an informed analysis of what happened. Still, certain crucial exchanges may, like the secrets of the Gowrie Conspiracy, 'remain concealed till the end of time'. Success was not pre-ordained. The Egyptian and Israeli positions remained as they had been at Ismailia, and Sadat and Begin still disliked and distrusted each other. Despite every effort to provide relaxation and comfort the two delegations disliked the atmosphere of Camp David; nor, with the exception of Weizman, did they make any effort to mix socially. The Israelis distrusted Brzezinski, and probably Carter, which put a special responsibility on Vance, who had gained the goodwill of both sides.

These personal factors merely served to complicate the basic issues of what the three parties hoped to achieve and were trying to avoid. The Israeli position was the strongest. They were hoping to gain a bilateral peace treaty with Egypt which would secure their southern flank and remove their most powerful opponent from the military equation. They wanted to do so without having to surrender the Rafah settlements or their airbases in Sinai, Etzion and Etam. Interestingly, Sharm al-Sheikh, so long a focus of tension, does not seem to have figured prominently in their calculations. Above all, however, the Israelis wanted to give away nothing on the West Bank and Gaza beyond the limited autonomy formula Begin had earlier produced. They had little to fear from the conference's failure, only the need to avoid being blamed in a manner which would embarrass or offend their supporters in Congress. Their negotiating position was further strengthened by Carter's long-standing commitment not to threaten Israel. Compared with this, the Egyptian position was poor. It rested on Sadat's need for a success. But it had to be an outcome which would enable him to retain the support of his own population and regain what his initiative had so far cost him in the Arab world. The Arabs, knowing that a peace treaty with Israel would make her invulnerable, would judge Sadat by whether he had gained anything for the Palestinians. A total Israeli withdrawal from Sinai, including the settlements and airfields, hardly needed saying. Carter, too, needed something to show for putting his prestige so obviously behind a Middle East settlement. The Americans were now familiar with Begin's confrontational negotiating style but believed that Dayan and Weizman were more flexible, while they thought that Sadat was more open to persuasion than his advisers. Crucially, though Carter was still willing to fight over the West Bank and Gaza, he seems to have realised that Sadat would ultimately settle for a bilateral agreement with Israel, thus more or less guaranteeing that the summit would register some kind of success; 'the American electorate', Quandt argued, 'would not care much about the details of the agreement'.[22]

These issues formed the basis of seemingly intractable arguments over the first ten days of the summit. On 15 September, Vance came to Carter with the news that the Egyptians had ordered a helicopter and were preparing to leave. Carter's response was to appeal to Sadat that this would mean the end of the relationship between the two countries, probably the end of his presidency and the severing of their friendship.[23] The appeal worked, but it put further pressure on Carter to reach an acceptable formula. Although the final three days were far from easy, slowly the Americans were inching each side toward two 'Frameworks', the first of which would define the nature of peace between them and a timetable for Israel's withdrawal from Sinai, the second outlining progress toward a transitional arrangement for the West Bank and Gaza. Their priorities may be judged by the fact that Sadat was negotiating hard on the first, Begin on the second; 'Sadat was not particularly interested in the detailed language of the Framework for Peace, and with the exception of the settlements, Begin was not very interested in the details of the Sinai agreement', Carter recalled.[24]

The Camp David accords, signed in the White House by the three leaders on 17 September, earned Begin and Sadat, though not Carter or Vance, the Nobel Prize for Peace. By the first Framework, Egypt was promised the return of the entire Sinai, the primary aim of her foreign policy since 1967, the key Israeli concessions being abandonment of the airbases and a promise to put a motion to the Knesset on withdrawal from the Rafah settlements. As far as Egypt was concerned, this was the overdue return of her sovereign territory, which Israel had colonised illegally, in return for all the benefits of a peace treaty. Many Israelis, still distrustful of Sadat's intentions, saw it as the surrender of an area larger than the state itself in exchange for a treaty which might prove as fragile as its author's life. They could not have been reassured by the immediate resignation of Foreign Minister Kamel, who believed that Sadat had surrendered on all the essential points relating to the West Bank and Gaza, leaving Egypt isolated in the Arab world.[25] What Kamel was objecting to was the second Framework, where the Israelis had negotiated tenaciously on practically every word, not surprisingly since the future of the occupied territories lay at the heart of Begin's political credo. The central section laid down that '... there should be transitional arrangements for the West Bank and Gaza for a period not exceeding five years. In order to provide full autonomy to the inhabitants, under these arrangements the Israeli military government and its administration will be withdrawn as soon as a self-governing authority has been freely elected by the inhabitant of these areas to replace the existing military government.' It was also said that Jordan and 'the representatives of the Palestinian people' should take part in the negotiations.

What seemed at first reading to be Israeli concessions on the West Bank and Gaza proved to be nothing of the kind, for Begin had succeeded in defending the 'cultural autonomy' formula which he had unveiled to the Americans earlier in the year. Determined to yield nothing which might amount in time to a Palestinian state, the most he would concede was 'full autonomy' but this was not defined and when the time came to negotiate it the Israeli version fell far short of American expectations.[26] An immediate foretaste of the difficulties ahead was a dispute between the Americans and Begin over the length of time it had been agreed for a moratorium on further settlements in the West Bank and Gaza. Carter and Vance claimed that this could be for the five years of the transitional arrangements, while Begin and Dayan countered that they had only agreed to the three months it was envisaged that final peace negotiations with

Egypt would take.[27] Begin's belief that he had confirmed and consolidated Israel's position in the territories was shared by the Palestinians who regarded the likely outcome of Camp David with undisguised dismay. For them, the 'full autonomy' formula simply meant *de facto* Israeli annexation of the occupied territories with the willing support of the United States and Egypt. Hopes that, between them, Carter and Sadat might force a change in Israeli policy were confounded. Echoing Brzezinski's earlier fears, Edward Said, the Palestinians' foremost advocate in the USA, wrote that the effect of Camp David was 'to put the Palestinians under Israeli military authority forever in a Bantustan', certainly the view held in the territories for the next decade.[28]

There was widespread acclaim amongst the American public for what had been achieved but the Frameworks still had to be translated into reality and, once the three leaders emerged from their isolation to face domestic and international pressures, differences in emphasis were bound to emerge. Begin, criticised by many right-wingers who had long looked to him for inspiration, responded by pushing ahead with plans for more West Bank settlements, while Sadat was condemned by other Arab leaders who rallied around Syria. As the goodwill of Saudi Arabia and Jordan's participation in the negotiations were felt to be essential elements in success, Vance left as soon as possible to explain the nature of the accords. Both King Hussein and Prince Fahd left him in no doubt of their belief that Sadat had regained the Sinai at the expense of a comprehensive peace settlement. His attempt to reassure them that the autonomy formula could lead to self-determination for the Palestinians was belied by the statements coming out of Jerusalem. If anything, Vance's visit impeded progress, for Hussein asked for, and received, written answers to a series of questions on Camp David. Designed to encourage him to take a positive view of the accords, it was only to be expected that they would displease the Israelis, especially the reaffirmation of the view that Resolution 242 demanded 'withdrawal on all fronts'.[29] But to the Americans' dismay, Jordan and Saudi Arabia would make no public endorsement of the agreements. By November, they were amongst Sadat's critics.

It was, then, hardly surprising that when the Israeli and Egyptian delegations convened in Washington on 12 October to begin negotiating the details of the peace treaty, there was a sober awareness of the difficulties still ahead. Under mounting criticism in the Middle East, Sadat needed to keep the future of the West Bank and Gaza firmly linked to progress on the peace treaty, while the Israelis had their eyes fixed on the latter and seemed to the Americans to be constantly backing away from the commitments they had made over the territories. By 8 November, Carter, who understandably seems to have hoped that the treaty might be signed before the congressional elections, was forced to agree with Brzezinski's assessment that what the Israelis wanted was a separate treaty which would allow them a free hand in the West Bank and Gaza.[30] As the target date for the conclusion of the negotiations, 17 December, approached with no prospect of success, Vance returned to the Middle East, this time with clear instructions from Carter to be hard on the Israelis, no matter the ultimate political consequences. In an attempt to ensure progress on the West Bank and Gaza, Sadat was holding to the position that ambassadors would be exchanged only after the establishment of a self-governing authority. When Vance put this to the Israeli cabinet on 13 December the result was an angry confrontation, made no better when he acknowledged his basic agreement with the Egyptian position. The talks ended in mutual recrimination, with the Israelis rejecting the American interpretation and Vance blaming them for the impasse.[31]

Carter, now mid-way through his term, was confronted by a foreign policy disaster which deeply affected the fate of the Camp David accords. By November 1978, the Shah of Iran, in whom the USA had invested so much since Britain's departure from the Gulf, was in serious trouble. Confronted with widespread disturbances and growing internal chaos, the Shah vacillated and the Carter administration did not know what, if anything, it could do to save him. On 16 January, the Shah and his family flew to exile; on 1 February, Ayatollah Khomeini returned in trumph from his own banishment in France and the Iranian revolution had begun. It was a sobering experience for all the parties to Camp David. Israeli fears for the permanence of a peace agreement were reinforced by the apparent ease with which an autocratic ruler could be swept away. For Carter it made a successful conclusion to the Camp David process all the more pressing.[32] His determination to press ahead was not an easy one, for some advisers, including Brzezinski, were now of the belief that part of Israeli strategy was to prevent his re-election, and Carter himself had concluded that all that could now be achieved would be a peace treaty followed by negotiations on the West Bank and Gaza. Nevertheless, he was prepared to keep trying and a further visit to Washington by Begin in early March seemed at last to show that the

American and Israeli terms for a peace treaty were narrowing to a point where agreement seemed possible. The final issues appeared to be Israel's concern over the loss of oil wells in Sinai now that the Iranian revolution was threatening her supplies, the Egyptian idea that autonomy should be implemented first in Gaza, and the vexed issue of 'priority of obligations'. This was to be Article VI in the peace treaty where the Israelis hoped to commit Egypt to a declaration that the treaty overrode her agreements with other states.[33]

After months of fruitless negotiation, events now moved quickly to a conclusion. Carter decided to fly to the Middle East to secure final agreement, first sending Brzezinski to Cairo to show Sadat what had so far been agreed. On 5 March, the Israeli cabinet approved the terms Begin had discussed and Sadat sent Carter a message assuring him of success; the following day he also confirmed with Brzezinski that the agreement was acceptable. Hence, Carter's visit to Egypt on 7 March was largely ceremonial, though full of mutual assurances for the future, but his arrival in Israel three days later was characterised by the kind of acrimonious confrontation which had always been present in his relationship with Begin. The Israeli leader was no more ready for the easy compromise than he had been at the time of Sadat's visit to Jerusalem. Apparently unwilling to concede on any of the remaining points, Carter was moved to conclude that Begin would do anything to prevent the treaty and to avoid having to face the problem of the full autonomy he had promised to the inhabitants of the West Bank. Carter was particularly disappointed that the treaty would not be signed during his trip, as Begin insisted that its terms would have to be submitted to the Knesset. A Knesset session addressed by the two leaders and Shimon Peres, leader of the opposition, was not a success, Begin's speech being so vigorously heckled as to leave Dayan 'sorry and ashamed'. But Dayan and other ministers, 'dispirited' by what had happened, determined to rescue the President's mission on the eve of his departure. With Begin's agreement, Dayan met Vance, whom he had come to like and trust. Together, the two men composed the final differences between the two sides. Dayan convinced Vance not to press the 'Gaza first' issue nor to have Egyptian liaison officers there, arguing that once the treaty had been signed, any Egyptian would be able to travel there on an Israeli visa. They also agreed that the USA would guarantee Israel's oil supplies for the next fifteen years.[34] Carter's visit, and with it the peace treaty, had been saved.

On 26 March 1979, just over thirty years after the Rhodes Armistice agreement, the Treaty of Peace between the Arab Republic of Egypt and the State of Israel was signed in Washington with due ceremony. It represented months of commitment by the President, his Secretary of State and National Security Adviser, and would hardly have come about without their willingness to become so totally engaged or without the detailed drafting and negotiating of their aides. They had helped Egypt restore her territory and Israel to realise the hope that one day she would start to make peace with her neighbours. Few would dispute that at the end of the day the balance of advantage lay with Israel, whose leaders had never lost sight of what they wanted and refused to be swayed either by the emotion of Sadat's visit or the blandishments of an American President whose political capital was diminishing. Not only did they secure the treaty and guarantees over their oil supplies but an accompanying Memorandum of Understanding was signed assuring them of American support in the event of violations and a continuing commitment to be 'responsive' to Israel's military and economic requirements.[35] All of this had been secured without surrendering control over the West Bank and Gaza, an issue on which Begin had never wavered.

The talks on autonomy for the territories began but soon stalled. Vance has conceded that only a degree of American commitment equivalent to the effort which had been put behind Camp David and the peace treaty would have secured progress and that was not realistic. Too much time had already been taken up and the presidential election was now in sight, absorbing attention and limiting options. Above all, perhaps, came the crisis in Iran. At the end of October 1979, the exiled Shah arrived in the USA for a cancer operation; on 4 November, the embassy in Tehran was seized by a revolutionary crowd and sixty-nine Americans were held hostage. The 'hostage crisis', including a failed rescue mission, was to absorb the attention of the Carter administration throughout its final year, contributing in substantial measure to its defeat by Ronald Reagan. It was hardly surprising that the autonomy talks withered, leaving the inhabitants of the West Bank and Gaza under an Israeli occupation which seemed to assume ever more concrete expression. A new voice, that of militant Islam, inspired by Khomeini's Iran, was resonating throughout the Middle East. Its call was heard by the young soldiers who assassinated Sadat as he reviewed a military parade on 6 October 1981, in the Shi'ite quarters of south Beirut and, increasingly, in the refugee camps of Gaza and Nablus. Its message was uncompromising hostility to Israel and the United States. Much had happened in the four years of Carter's presidency and he took pride in the peace treaty which he had been instrumental in bringing about.

8 Reagan, Israel and Lebanon

It was inevitable that Ronald Reagan's inauguration would mark a distinct change in emphasis in American policy. Little was known about his attitudes to the Middle East beyond the fact that he was a warm supporter of Israel. Carter's policies had won him few plaudits amongst American Jews and in the 1980 election Reagan had sensibly made the most of his commitment to Israel's security, winning 39 per cent of the Jewish vote, a record for a Republican presidential contender. It is fair to say that the Jewish community had mixed expectations of him. Although they welcomed his warm commitment to Israel, an early hope that he would recognise Jerusalem as the capital failed to be realised and many Jews, strong supporters of the separation of church and state, were wary of the evangelical Christian nature of much of Reagan's support. From the Israeli perspective there was one clear improvement, however. Whereas, from the start of his presidency, Carter had tried to focus on the central Israeli–Palestinian impasse, the Reagan administration preferred to fit the Middle East into a much broader global framework of American foreign policy. The rhetoric of the election campaign had cast the record of the Carter administration as one of incompetence and failure. A formidable indictment was presented to a public baffled by the apparent impotence of power: the Soviet invasion of Afghanistan, the Sandinistas' success in Nicaragua, and, above all, the humiliation in Iran. Such decline was to be reversed by establishing new priorities, chief amongst which was containment of the Soviet Union. The appointment of Alexander Haig, former NATO Supreme Commander in Europe, as Secretary of State, seemed to show where the administration's interests lay. Secondly, recent events had left the public with a robust, if poorly defined, dislike of terrorism, soon powerfully reinforced by the attempt on the President's life. Carter's advocacy of human rights gave way to a desire to counter terrorism, a change in emphasis which did not bode well for any dialogue with the Palestinians, but was reassuring to Israel.

Early policies in the Middle East reflected these concerns. The administration was well aware of the area's strategic and economic importance. The establishment of Soviet bases in western Afghanistan, the loss of the West's major ally and the destabilising nature of militant Shi'a Islam argued for a reinforcement of America's military presence. An early aim was to increase the capability of the Rapid Deployment Force, which Carter had created, by negotiating a regional 'strategic consensus', which, at its most optimistic, would embrace Israel, Egypt, Saudi Arabia, Oman, Somalia and Kenya. The Camp David autonomy negotiations were not abandoned but did not appear to be a priority. The Republican agenda for the Middle East was not impressive. How the Soviet Union and terrorism were to be contained was unclear, as was the prospect of Israel and Saudi Arabia agreeing to combine in a strategic consensus, however loosely defined. The resulting policies not only failed to address the main issues in the Middle East but were to lead to America's dispiriting, and costly, involvement in Lebanon. Nixon, Kissinger and Carter had in their own way tried to resolve the key issues of the Middle East. In contrast, many in the Middle East came to view the Reagan administration's 'excessive partiality' for Israel as part of the problem itself.

In its first year, the administration seemed to be reacting to events rather than setting a clear course of action. As people in the Middle East were still trying to adjust to the changed circumstances in Iran and Afghanistan, and the Gulf War between Iran and Iraq, perhaps this was inevitable; but it dismayed those who looked to Washington for leadership, especially over the unresolved issues of Camp David. When Haig toured the region in April 1981 to explore the prospects for a strategic consensus, it was clear that only the Israelis had any enthusiasm for the idea. Israel could offer the Americans attractive possibilities, especially as NATO's south-eastern flank had been rendered almost meaningless because of the quarrel between Greece and Turkey over Cyprus. The striking power of her armed forces needed no emphasising. The Israelis argued, for example, that even if 20 per cent of their air force were to be committed against the Soviet fleet in the Mediterranean they could destroy it in four days. The stability of Israeli democracy meant that such co-operation could be guaranteed.[1] Although these were attractive arguments, the administration was not sure how to respond to them. While Haig strongly supported such a strategic arrangement, Defense Secretary Caspar Weinberger and his officials feared the effect this would have on Egypt, Saudi Arabia and the Gulf states whose attitudes they believed to be vital to the West's oil routes. Despite such reservations, the principle of co-operation was agreed when Begin visited

Washington in September and was confirmed at a ceremony on 30 November attended by Defence Minister Ariel Sharon and a reluctant Weinberger who would not permit photographs. This bilateral agreement fell far short of the strategic consensus concept and seemed to show that Israel had won an important battle for Washington's favour. In fact, relations between the two governments had been far from easy and the arrangement was to last less than three weeks.

For most of 1981, the initiative had appeared to rest with Jerusalem with the US administration constantly having to react. For some time, the Israelis had been watching the nuclear reactor the Iraqis were building at Osirak with French and Soviet help, fearing its capacity to manufacture weapons. Without consulting the Americans, on 7 June, F–16 aircraft of the Israeli air force destroyed the reactor which was on the verge of becoming active. The US administration was publicly embarrassed, though privately Haig agreed with Begin's assessment.[2] Nevertheless, as the raid had been carried out with American-supplied jets, contrary to the terms under which they had been sent, some reaction seemed called for. The administration showed its disapproval by suspending the delivery of four F–16s, but many in the Middle East saw the raid as confirmation of Israel's determination to maintain a total regional hegemony with Washington's support.

More serious was the Knesset vote on 14 December to approve the *de facto* annexation of the Golan Heights. Israel's determination to hold on to the area had been well known, both for security reasons and its effect on water supplies but the American position was that it would ultimately revert to Syria as part of a peace settlement. Israel's action seemed aimed at precluding this; it was clearly contrary to the wishes of its Druse inhabitants, who commenced a spirited campaign of civil disobedience, and it seemed to herald a similar move over the West Bank and Gaza. An acrimonious exchange between Washington and Jerusalem resulted in the suspension of the agreement on strategic co-operation. Weinberger's obvious reluctance over the agreement and the bitterness of the exchanges over the Golan were largely the result of the sustained battle Israel had waged in Congress earlier in the year to prevent the sale of AWACS to Saudi Arabia.

The origins of this controversy lay in the US administration's attempt to reinforce Western security in the Gulf after the fall of the Shah. While the Americans had never seen the Shah in simplistic terms as the West's 'policeman', the presence of a militant Islamic republic added to the problems of such an economically vital area. Iran's appeal to the Shi'ite minorities in the Gulf raised questions about America's willingness to defend its conservative regimes, and the Reagan administration was determined to provide this reassurance. In the final months of the Carter administration, the Saudis had submitted an arms request aimed at upgrading the range and capability of their F–15 jets, basic to the success of which was the provision of five sophisticated Airborne Warning and Control System (AWACS) aircraft. Weinberger and his defence experts strongly supported this request and within weeks of Reagan's inauguration things seemed to be well advanced. There would clearly be opposition from pro-Israeli groups in Congress but, like Eisenhower in February 1957, the incoming administration had no obvious reason to fear political repercussions. For the Saudis a successful outcome was the touchstone of American intentions.

But the provision of such sophisticated equipment to the Saudis was viewed very differently by Israel. Although the AWACS were vulnerable aircraft, the Israelis, knowing that air power was the key to military supremacy in the region, moved to head off the supply of a weapon which might give the qualitative edge to a potential Arab enemy. Realising that it was taking on a popular President at the start of his term, AIPAC mobilised a full campaign in the Senate against the sale. It proved a bitter battle with AIPAC pitted against their Saudi rivals and others interested in the deal's success. But at the end of the day, its campaign was only reversed by the personal intervention of the President and intense lobbying by his staff. It was an unequal contest but, even so, when the vote was taken in the Senate the sale was only approved by the margin of 52 votes to 48. The struggle had a mixed legacy. The fact that it had taken eight months of effort, latterly involving the authority of the President, to secure the sale seemingly confirmed AIPAC's influence on Capitol Hill. Clearly, it was not a battle the administration would want to repeat too often. But AIPAC, too, had a problem, for there had been disturbing signs that its campaign had stirred up anti-Semitism; there was also the unwelcome legacy that highly-placed members of the administration had greatly resented the episode and were in no mood to be pushed in future.[3]

The spring of 1982 confirmed the limitations of American power. Failure to prevent two of her closest allies going to war over the Falklands Islands did not bode well for her ability to control a potential conflict which officials knew was maturing on Israel's northern border. On 3 June, Israel's ambassador to London, Shlomo Argov, was seriously wounded by Palestinian gunmen. Despite information from London that this was the work of a group hostile to Arafat's PLO, it was clear that the shooting would provide the Israeli government with what it needed to justify an assault on Palestinian positions in Lebanon. Arguing that the attack breached a ceasefire agreement with the PLO which the American diplomat Philip Habib had worked out the previous July, on 6 June Israeli forces began major operations in southern Lebanon; by the following day it was clear that this was not another retaliatory raid but was a full-scale invasion with all that this implied for the fragile stability of the Middle East. 'Operation Peace for Galilee', in fact the fifth Arab–Israeli war, had begun.[4] Its declared purpose was to create a 24-mile security zone along Israel's northern border, but it soon became clear that its sponsors had more ambitious aims, which included the withdrawal of Syrian forces from the country and the establishment of a pro-Israeli government in Beirut which would sign a peace treaty. As the operation unfolded an even more ambitious agenda emerged; namely, the expulsion of the PLO from Beirut, which, it was suspected, would be the prelude to annexation of the West Bank.[5]

The invasion was no surprise to the Americans. They had felt that with Israel's withdrawal from the Sinai due to be completed by 25 April it was bound to be an anxious spring. The obvious next step was to revive the defunct autonomy talks on the future of the West Bank and Gaza. In May, Haig sent a special envoy to Cairo and Jerusalem to prepare the way for this. Begin was invited to come to Washington the following month when the question of renewing the negotiations would be raised. This was not a welcome development for the Israeli government which was divided in its approach. A well-informed article by Amos Perlmutter on 17 May explained that Begin, though loyal to his interpretation of Camp David and prepared to accept a form of Palestinian self-expression, believed that the territories were an integral part of Eretz Israel and was working towards *de facto* annexation. Sharon, on the other hand, was advocating a crushing blow against the Palestinians in Lebanon.[6] Officials were uneasily aware that the Falklands war might provide the necessary international diversion, just as the Israelis had chosen the day military rule was imposed in Poland to annex the Golan Heights.[7]

Attempts were made to urge restraint on the Israelis, and, through intermediaries, on the PLO. Haig later complained that his attempts to urge the seriousness of the situation were hampered by the 'incoherent' bureaucracy of the National Security Council, but the ambassador in Tel Aviv was instructed to warn Begin of the adverse effect such an action would have on relations. When Sharon came to Washington in late May, it became clear that Israel was awaiting the occasion to move. Haig hoped to use a major speech to the Chicago Council on Foreign Relations on 26 May to unveil his plans but, with the speed of events, these had to be signalled rather than spelled out. Arguing that 'we cannot allow the peace process to end in the desert', he warned the Israelis against annexation of the West Bank and Gaza and threw out the hope to the Arabs that autonomy would simply be a transitional stage. With his knowledge of what was maturing, he did issue a warning over Lebanon but it was to the PLO, not the Israelis: 'violations could escalate into major hostilities'. More generally, he argued that: 'The time has come to take concerted action in support of both Lebanon's territorial integrity within its internationally recognised borders and a strong central government capable of promoting a free, open, democratic and traditionally pluralistic society.' These were admirable sentiments which would haunt later policymakers. More to the point, there was no strong signal to the Israelis that they should not move into Lebanon, though Haig could not have anticipated the Argov attack. Although Haig has argued that the invasion took place despite the 'strongest possible warnings' by the United States, there is no doubt that the Israeli government regarded what was said as mere ritual.[8]

Lack of a clear lead, which many misinterpreted as American support for the invasion, was compounded by administrative disarray. Key State Department and National Security Council officials were absent from Washington. Reagan and Haig were in Versailles attending a delicate summit of industrialised nations, and it proved difficult to co-ordinate their reaction with those of their crisis management team in Washington under Vice-President George Bush. To expect leadership in such circumstances, observed Anthony Lewis in the *New York Times* was 'comic', but it reflected the President's apparent lack of interest in the Middle East.[9] A letter from Reagan in the early morning of 6 June was too late to stop the invasion but produced a reply defining Israel's aim as the creation of a 24-mile security belt along her northern border. While other Western leaders at Versailles held press conferences condemning Israel's action, Reagan was silent, confirming the belief that the administration tacitly supported the Israeli strategy. Observers could not but contrast this with the reaction to the Osirak raid or the annexation of the Golan Heights, and the identification with Israel seemed complete when Haig used the term 'we' in referring to Israeli air losses.[10] Support for Israel was also reflected in the Security Council. On 6 June, the Americans supported a resolution demanding 'that Israel withdraw all its military forces forthwith and unconditionally to the internationally recognized boundaries of Lebanon'. Two days later, Reagan agreed to support a draft resolution condemning Israel's non-compliance with this and implying the use of sanctions. But Haig was unwilling to endorse a step so clearly identifying the United States with condemnation of Israel, hence jeopardising whatever leverage he possessed, and he persuaded the President to reverse his position.[11] Faced with this abrupt reversal, Ambassador Jeane Kirkpatrick justified her veto of the draft resolution on the grounds that it was not 'sufficiently balanced'. As casualties in Lebanon mounted into the thousands, her apparent equation of this with the attack on Shlomo Argov caused widespread anger in the Middle East, reinforcing the view that Israel's invasion had the blessing of Washington.

With the invasion five days old, it was clear that this was not the three-day affair many Americans had imagined; by 10 June Israeli columns were reported to be in sight of Beirut. Three days later, they dominated the approaches to west Beirut with its largely Muslim population of 500 000, its Palestinian refugee camps and an estimated 5000–6000 PLO guerrillas. Though outnumbered by the most powerful armed forces in the Middle East, the PLO had bitterly contested the Israeli advance to the city, with tragic consequences for southern Lebanon. The major towns along the way, Tyre, Nabatiyeh and Sidon, had suffered widespread destruction, while the poorly-built Palestinian camps were rendered almost, or totally, uninhabitable. American television viewers could see that this was going far beyond anything implied by 'Peace for Galilee'. By 14 June, the State Department was estimating that 10 000 had been killed or wounded in Beirut alone.[12] Inevitably, as Israeli troops approached the southern end of the Syrian-controlled Bekaa valley fighting developed. By 9 June, major air battles were in progress and, as officials in Washington were well aware, Syria had a treaty of friendship with the Soviet Union which required consultation in the event of war. Israel's relentless advance threatened to change the map of the region and if the US administration hoped to have any say in what might emerge then it would have to define its policies quickly and effectively.

Instead, the following weeks saw the depressing spectacle of an administration at odds with itself. Displeased that the Israelis had advanced far beyond the 24-mile limit which he had announced at Versailles, Reagan wrote again to Begin on 10 June pointing out that the invasion had exceeded what was needed to secure the northern border. [13] It was the first real sign of a presidential displeasure that was to grow in the coming weeks. Philip Habib was sent back to the Middle East to negotiate a series of temporary ceasefires. Beyond that, it was an open secret that the administration was badly split, with Bush and Weinberger advocating a 'hard' line with Israel. [14] But Haig now believed that the scale of Israel's victory offered a way forward which would be in America's best interest. With Israel poised outside Beirut, he argued that Syria and the PLO, whom he believed had been instrumental in undermining the stability of Lebanon, could be persuaded to evacuate. This would restore Lebanon's integrity and secure Israel's northern border. [15]

Haig's idea suffered from several flaws, most obviously because of the hazy line it drew between 'the PLO' and the mass of Palestinians in the country. Tactically, it could only have succeeded if the PLO men in Beirut were convinced that they were facing an imminent overwhelming attack while relying on the fact that Israeli commanders wanted to avoid bitter street-fighting. Such a delicate act would need clear directives and too many members of the administration were opposed to Haig's policy for this to happen. In fact, influential opinion was increasingly unhappy over events in Lebanon. The *New York Times* ran a series of articles sharply critical of any attempt to make capital out of the 'hell of Beirut' and warning against endangering links with Arab governments. These sentiments were shared by leading politicians. As early as 9 June, Representative Clement J. Zablocki (Democrat, Wisconsin), Chairman of the House Committee on Foreign Affairs, voiced disquiet over Israel's use of American weapons, the first of many such statements. [16] Four days later, the Chairman of the Senate Foreign Relations Committee, Charles Percy (Republican, Illinois), publicly dissociated himself from the Haig strategy. Condemning Israel's actions and expressing support for some kind of Palestinian entity, he hinted at possible moves against aid to Israel. [17]

These views inevitably surfaced during Begin's American visit. Aware that it would be contentious, the Prime Minister had told his cabinet to ignore American 'threats'. [18] His meeting with Reagan on 21 June, officially described as 'blunt', was distinguished by none of the pleasantries usual in such exchanges. A development of great significance for the future was Begin's suggestion that United Nations troops in Lebanon be replaced by a force including Americans. Reagan was unenthusiastic, but he did not totally rule it out. Otherwise, it was an unhappy meeting at which a row developed between Begin and Weinberger, who had already broken publicly with Haig.[19] A subsequent meeting with a closed session of the Senate Foreign Relations Committee was described by Paul Tsongas (Democrat, Massachusetts) as the angriest with a foreign leader he had ever seen.[20]

Isolated as he was, Haig could not put sufficient authority behind his plan. Its success would have rested on a PLO belief that they faced annihilation but this was undermined by a White House announcement on 24 June that Begin had promised that his troops would not enter Beirut. As he complained that lack of discipline in the US administration was undermining his policy, the following day his resignation was announced by the President. Contributing to Haig's downfall was the feeling that even if his plan succeeded in removing PLO and Syrian troops from Lebanon, it would not be matched by any generous Israeli response over the West Bank and Gaza.[21] His abrupt departure marked the end of a distinct phase in the administration's handling of the crisis, for he was its most pro-Israeli member. His view that the best way forward was to avoid confrontation with Begin's government and seek to build on its military successes changed over the next few weeks as the direction of foreign policy was assumed by George P. Shultz.

In the days that followed, the Israelis tightened their siege of west Beirut. By 5 July, their artillery was reported to be bombarding residential areas and Palestinian camps which were running short of food, water, electricity and medical supplies. Despite this pressure, the PLO men appeared undaunted. Touring south Beirut, the *New York Times*'s Thomas Friedmann noted that every building held five or six well-armed Palestinians, supported by concealed anti-aircraft guns.[22] If a final showdown were about to take place, no one doubted that it would be a bloody affair, with the city's civilians as its principal victims. As the crisis deepened, a tight-lipped President Reagan fended off questions at his 30 June news conference. Alluding to little more than the delicacy of the negotiations, he left for his Californian vacation.[23]

He was effectively concealing intricate diplomatic moves through which Habib was trying to find an acceptable way out of the impasse.

Neither side wanted a battle in the labyrinthine warrens of west Beirut. The PLO had the determination to make a bloody stand but knew that they were outnumbered and outgunned. Although the Israelis had the military advantage on the ground, this was not the case on the wider perspective. Israel was isolated diplomatically, the USA now her sole supporter in the United Nations. Perhaps worse was the deep division being exposed in Israeli society, as concerned voices questioned the morality of what was being done and the political wisdom of a strategy which appeared to equate a military defeat of the PLO with a solution to the problem of the Palestinians. The army, which was admitting 270 dead including a senior general, could not be happy at the thought of further heavy casualties. In these circumstances, Habib's chances of averting an all-out assault were greater than the events dominating the world's headlines appeared to suggest.

The key element in his negotiations was the possibility of using American troops to oversee a disengagement agreement, possibly involving the evacuation of PLO fighters. With recent memories of Vietnam, the commitment of troops to such an unpromising location as Lebanon was bound to be controversial, but a short-term mission would mask the military defeat of the PLO and the political defeat of the Israelis, extricating each from its current dilemmas. Any longer-term deployment would imply a political role to help rehabilitate the Lebanese state.

Despite the possible dangers, Habib felt that a military contribution would provide the parties, especially the Palestinians, with the reassurances they needed. If this would break the deadlock, the President agreed to include it as part of the bargaining.[24] The possibility had been raised by Begin during his Washington visit and the Israelis had since returned to the theme, though more in the context of the Americans supervising a multinational force in southern Lebanon rather than being sent to Beirut. The PLO, too, had suggested a multinational force. This involved an Israeli withdrawal from the city's outskirts together with their own withdrawal into the refugee camps, creating a buffer zone. Their men would then be withdrawn from Beirut, to be re-organised under Lebanese command in the north of the country and the Bekaa valley. Their headquarters would be transferred to another Arab capital, leaving a diplomatic mission and information office in Beirut. Concerned that this would leave the refugee camps at the mercy of the Christian militias, they saw American troops as the guarantor of their safety. Arafat could also see that this opened lines to Washington, a prospect officials did not entirely discourage. Nor was it forgotten that after the assassination of the ambassador to Lebanon in 1976, the PLO had helped to guard American diplomats and assist Americans escape from the civil war. Their proposal left them too large a presence in Lebanon from Israel's perspective but offered Habib a way forward.

On 6 July, as reports of what was being negotiated appeared on Israeli and Lebanese radio, Reagan confirmed that he had agreed in principle to the contribution of a small contingent for 'temporary peacekeeping' in Beirut. It would be assisted by the French and only deployed once agreement had been secured among the parties. The nature and purpose of the force were amplified by his spokesman, Larry Speakes, who explained that what was envisaged was the equivalent of a battalion of marines drawn from the Sixth Fleet who would supervise the 'orderly and safe' evacuation of PLO fighters from Beirut. But even at this early stage there was more than a hint that the US administration might have more ambitious goals, as Speakes alluded to the possibility that the peacekeeping force might restore the authority of the Lebanese government, implying a prolonged commitment only possible under the War Powers Act.[25] Events were to show just what a hostage to fortune this was, for Lebanon had enjoyed no government worth the name since 1975.

Initial political reaction reflected these fears. Some support came from two leading Democrats on the Senate Foreign Relations Committee, Alan Cranston and Claiborne Pell, but Clement Zablocki felt that the administration's assurances were too vague. More worrying was the opposition of senior Republicans like Charles Mathias and Senate majority leader Howard Baker, who told the President that he believed most Congressmen opposed the commitment of troops. Clearly, what was uppermost was the fear that American lives would be lost. As Senator John Glenn remarked, 'we're going to be attending some funerals over in Arlington with marines coming back in body bags one of these days'.[26]

As this crucial new element in the US administration's thinking was emerging, Shultz was assuming the direction of foreign policy. A former marine and professional economist, he had served as Nixon's Treasury Secretary, earning respect for his level-headed approach to public affairs. Annoyed by the loss of Haig, the Israelis were inclined to be suspicious of him, noting his presidency of the Bechtel Group with its extensive interests in Saudi Arabia and other Arab countries. Knowing that this would be aired at the confirmation hearings, Shultz severed all connexions with the Group and made sure that his attitude toward the Arab–Israeli conflict was a matter of public record. He made clear his belief that the use of troops as part of a multinational force could ensure the safe departure of the PLO fighters and avoid an Israeli assault on west Beirut, opening the way for the withdrawal of all foreign troops and the chance to rebuild Lebanon. But he also wanted to express sentiments about the Arab–Israeli conflict hitherto absent from the Reagan administration. The central reality, he reminded the confirmation hearing, was that the 'legitimate needs and problems of the Palestinian people must be addressed and resolved – urgently and in all their dimensions'. The 'full autonomy' formula could only be a first step toward that and the Palestinians would have to be represented in any talks. When pressed about the implications of this for his attitude toward the PLO, he indicated that if it were to abandon violence and accept Resolutions 242 and 338 then the administration would consider its position. He also expressed disapproval of the Israeli dismissal of West Bank mayors. In short, he appeared to be preparing to move from the management of the immediate crisis to a major peace initiative, with aims very different to those the Israeli government had intended.[27] Once confirmed on 15 July, Shultz set his specialists to work on a plan which would amplify what America believed the Camp David formula had held out for the West Bank and Gaza. As the crisis showed no signs of abating, the President took an increasingly personal interest in what was being formulated, even if little could be done until the immediate problem in Lebanon was defused.

That arduous task lay with Habib and his assistant Morris Draper in Beirut. By the first week in July, the broad outline of what they wanted was common knowledge – an evacuation of the PLO under the supervision of a multinational force which would include American troops – but the obstacles in the way of this remained stubbornly in place. Part of Habib's problem was that the terms of Kissinger's 1975 commitment to the Israelis impeded communication with the party at the centre of the storm. His main line to Arafat was through the Lebanese Prime Minister Shafik al-Wazzan and former Prime Minister Saeb Salam, but even once the PLO's position became known it could only be communicated to Begin's government through the embassy in Tel Aviv. The possibilities for delay and misunderstanding were infinite.

Even more difficult was the position of Syria, whose acquiescence in any plan was essential. With 60 000 troops in the country, the

Syrians knew that they would have to be fully consulted. Publicly at least, they took the view that, as the invaders, the only evacuation that needed to be discussed was that of the Israelis.[28] Nothing, of course, could have been further from the Israelis' intention, but equally there was uncertainty over how to proceed. While there would have been a national consensus on establishing a security zone in southern Lebanon, this had been broken by the advance to Beirut. Having committed themselves to ambitious goals, the Israeli government could not now easily retreat. It was never likely to be easy to withdraw a victorious army back from positions where it had its enemy trapped, but Begin's analogy of directing his armies on Arafat's positions like the assault on Hitler's bunker left world opinion unimpressed. What worried many Israelis was the opposite; namely, that the PLO and the Palestinian cause could only benefit from the image of outnumbered fighters defying the most powerful military machine in the Middle East as it created havoc among the hapless Lebanese. 'The tenacity with which Jerusalem refused to see this simple fact', wrote two of Israel's most respected journalists, 'was one of the wonders of the war in Lebanon.'[29]

Arafat understood perfectly well that wars are fought for political objectives and that his position was far more promising than his military situation warranted. In July, a number of carefully placed statements attempted to raise the PLO's profile as a moderate body. At a meeting with five American politicians, Arafat appeared to accept Resolutions 242 and 338, subject to the qualification of Palestinian statehood. His prime aim in the negotiations with Habib was to ensure the departure of his men in such a manner as to leave its organisation intact and its dignity unimpaired, denying the Israelis the principal objective of their costly invasion.

With each side conscious of what was at stake, it was inevitable that Habib's search for an acceptable formula would be elusive; but during this process the situation on the ground deteriorated sharply. PLO suspicion of a purely American force was eased by the French and Italian announcements that they would take part in a multi-national force.[30] It was emerging that the possibility of an agreement turned on three considerations: the destination of the PLO contingents, the nature of their withdrawal, and what kind of presence, if any, the PLO would be permitted to retain in Beirut. By late July, Habib still had no agreement on his outline plan, which envisaged the withdrawal of PLO leaders to Syria, Egypt and Jordan, to be followed by the evacuation of the main force to what was an

uncertain destination. This stalemate was only broken when renewed
Israeli militancy roused the Reagan administration into an unprecedented display of public anger.

On 1 August, the Israelis began a concerted land, sea and air
assault on west Beirut. Their forces were now in close contact with
Palestinian areas in the south of the city, capture of Beirut International Airport meant that the PLO could not now be evacuated by
air, and 127 air sorties marked the heaviest raids the city had yet
endured. Thomas Friedmann reported that whole areas of the city
where there were no Palestinians had been devastated by the bombardment.[31] Faced with this, and responding to messages from Habib
that the Israelis were the main obstacle to the success of his
negotiations, the US administration felt that the time had come to
move to public diplomacy. Reagan's initial reaction to the renewed
attack was to confide in reporters that he had lost patience a long time
ago. This ushered in a frosty meeting the next day with Foreign
Minister Yitzhak Shamir, which produced the terse communiqué that
'The world can no longer accept a situation of constantly escalating
violence'. Privately, the President tried to drive home his opposition
to an assault on west Beirut.[32]

But the attacks went on. By 4 August, Israeli bombardment was
hitting government offices, including that of the Prime Minister and
the hotels from which the world's press corps was reporting the city's
misery. Habib's negotiations had come to a halt at the very time when
the PLO was making important concessions and officials no longer
bothered to conceal their belief that the Israeli actions were designed
to destroy his mission. Reagan's response was an unequivocal
message to Begin that a ceasefire must be observed, making it clear
that sanctions through the Security Council might become a possibility. The American delegation to the United Nations abstained on a
motion censuring Israel for her actions and opening up the question
of sanctions. The reality, however, was that the Americans feared
that any sanctions would simply push the Israelis into even more
extreme actions, forfeiting whatever influence they possessed
through the special relationship: Begin chose to remind a group from
the United Jewish Appeal that Jews knelt only to God.[33] More
formally, on 6 August his government rejected Reagan's approach,
with Sharon making it clear that he would not be diverted by threats
of an American arms embargo.[34] Reagan's well-publicised 'anger'
seemed to reflect little more than his administration's impotence.

Clearly, events were rapidly moving toward a crisis. On 9 August, the Israeli air force renewed its attacks, initiating four days of sustained aerial bombardment which were widely believed to be the prelude to a full-scale assault. That day, fearing that the Americans might be about to land French troops of the proposed multinational force, Israeli fighters harassed helicopters from the USS *Forrestal* carrying a military liaison team, and army jeeps subsequently tried to prevent them landing at Junieh north of Beirut, itself an indication of how tight the grip around the city had become.[35] Two days later, an Israeli armoured column passed beyond Junieh to Jubeil, threatening to turn the Syrian positions in the Bekaa valley.

On 12 August, as the Israeli air force mounted eleven hours of unrelenting raids on west Beirut and the prospect of new fighting with Syria was opening up, Reagan intervened directly and decisively. He had little alternative, as the outraged Lebanese had already ordered Habib to leave. His words with Jerusalem were blunt. In a message and a well-publicised telephone call to the Israeli leader, 'The President expressed his outrage over this latest round of massive military action. He emphasized that Israel's action halted ambassador Habib's negotiations for the peaceful resolution of the Beirut crisis when they were at the point of success. The result has been more needless destruction and bloodshed.' Begin was particularly cut when Reagan referred to the events in Beirut as a 'holocaust'.[36] His action coincided with a cabinet revolt in Jerusalem which in effect removed Sharon's authority to order air strikes. By the late afternoon, Begin was able to assure Reagan that a ceasefire was in place.[37] It had been the lowest point in American–Israeli relations for many years; much would now rest on Habib's ability to make use of the lull which had been achieved.

Behind the American anger lay the belief that the Israeli actions had been aimed at preventing a peaceful evacuation of the PLO.[38] Even as the battle was going on, the key concessions were coming. On 10 August, the Syrians at last announced their willingness to accept evacuated PLO men and the Israeli cabinet accepted the main principles of the Habib plan. With the destruction of large areas of Beirut, Arafat, too, was under intense pressure from Lebanese politicians and Arab leaders to agree to an evacuation. On 13 August he submitted to Habib a list of 7100 guerrillas with a detailed timetable for their land and sea evacuation to Algeria, Tunisia, Jordan, Iraq, South Yemen and the Sudan.[39] This was followed by a formal request from the Lebanese government that the United States, France and Italy contribute to a multinational force to assist their army in assuring 'the withdrawal from Lebanese territory of the Palestinian leaders, officers and combatants'. A detailed schedule had already been prepared for a thirty-day operation, beginning on 21 August when French Foreign Legion paratroopers would arrive in Beirut and deploy in the port area to supervise the embarkation of PLO men to Tunisia and Yemen. By 26 August, they would be re-deployed on the Beirut–Damascus road to guard a further PLO departure to Syria. By then, they would be joined by the Italians and the rest of the French contingent, leaving the port area to marines of the Sixth Fleet. Their objective was defined as assuring 'the safety of such departing PLO personnel'; guaranteeing 'the safety of other persons in the Beirut area'; and 'the restoration of the sovereignty and authority of the Government of Lebanon over the Beirut area'. While the first of these was to be achieved in such a manner as to reflect great credit on the arrangements Habib and his team had made in the most difficult circumstances, the other two were more problematic. How 2000 foreign troops could, in thirty days, do much to restore the sovereignty of a government which had virtually ceased to exist was not clear; nor was the means of guaranteeing the safety of the thousands of Palestinian civilians after their own men and the multinational force were no longer there to defend them. These issues largely escaped the notice of a world caught by the spectacle of the PLO's noisy and often exuberant departure from Beirut, but both would come to haunt American policymakers.[40]

But the tragedy of the Palestinians and America's subsequent ordeal in Lebanon were to be triggered by an unforeseen event, and they should not be allowed to detract from Habib's real achievement in negotiating a means of avoiding a full-scale battle in the crowded suburbs of south and west Beirut. Instead, by 9 September the multinational force had supervised the evacuation of 8144 PLO men by sea and 6254 Syrians and Palestine Liberation Army men overland to Syria. It was a tribute to the good sense and steady nerves of everyone involved, not least the French, Italian and American servicemen. But the evacuation was only one element in the problem. As the Israelis tried to assess what they had gained, only the removal of the PLO from the northern border stood out. Although official spokesmen tried to claim that the PLO had been dealt a mortal blow, it had a hollow ring. The nature of its stand and departure from Beirut ensured that it remained a major political force, precisely what the Israelis had been most anxious to destroy. If part of the 'hidden agenda' of the war was to prepare the way for *de facto* annexation of the West Bank, then that was likely to be affected by moves on the area's autonomy which were maturing in the State Department under Shultz's direction and with Reagan's personal interest.

Almost as worrying for the Israelis were signs that the anticipated peace treaty with Lebanon might be slow in coming. On 23 August, the rump of the Lebanese parliament elected Israel's ally Bashir Gemayel to succeed President Sarkis. Begin's government confidently expected him to move quickly toward signing a peace treaty, but Gemayel was too conscious of the need to reach out to his Muslim fellow-countrymen to make any hasty move. An angry meeting with Begin at Nahariya on 30 August delivered the nasty jolt to the Israelis that the man they regarded as a prime beneficiary of their invasion was not prepared to deliver an immediate peace treaty. The Israelis' temper on the occasion was not improved by the fact that the American ambassador had just given them the unwelcome details of the peace plan which Reagan was about to announce.[41] Major battles on issues believed fundamental to the country's future clearly lay ahead. Even before the last PLO men had left Beirut, Israel's failure to achieve her aims was becoming clear.

Parallel with Habib's negotiations, Shultz had been directing a wide-ranging review of policy options, involving discussions with experienced politicians and officials to find out what was realistic domestically and in the region. Jordan was believed to hold the key. A 'Jordanian option' had become the preferred solution for the West Bank and Gaza of the Labour leader, Shimon Peres, and contacts had long subsisted between his party and King Hussein. In order to test Arab reactions to the new ideas, Assistant Secretary of State for Near Eastern and South Asian Affairs, Nicholas Veliotis, was secretly sent to Amman; Hussein then relayed the details to King Fahd in Saudi Arabia.[42] Knowing that the Israeli government would almost certainly try to mobilise its forces in Washington to stifle any move on autonomy, it was excluded from these consultations. The resulting frustration in Jerusalem did not enhance the plan's prospects.

Reagan timed his move to the best advantage, with the final departure of the PLO and just before the Arab summit in Fez, from which it was hoped encouraging signals would come. Personal backing for the plan was to come from Weinberger who flew into Israel for a two-day visit just as the letter detailing the proposals was delivered to the surprised government. As leaked to the Israeli press, the plan was constructed around the West Bank and Gaza linked with

Jordan. Israel was to be reassured that the Americans did not consider the PLO a possible negotiating partner, nor were they seeking a Palestinian state. But the Arabs were to be encouraged to join the negotiations by a total freeze on settlement in the West Bank and Gaza, the Arabs of east Jerusalem were to be allowed to vote for the envisaged West Bank council, and the West Bank Arabs were to become responsible for their own security. The tone of the government's response was set by spokesmen who described the proposals as a 'grave deviation from Camp David'. For many Knesset members it was a revival of the 'infamous' Rogers Plan and the ambassador to Washington, Moshe Arens, counselled his countrymen not to panic in the face of American pressure.[43]

When the President broadcast on 1 September, some of the more contentious issues revealed in the Israeli press were notably absent, but his overall thrust was clear. Emphasising his strong personal commitment to Israel, which he had personally inserted into the State Department text, he continued: 'The departure of the Palestinians from Beirut dramatises more than ever the homelessness of the Palestinian people. Palestinians feel strongly that their cause is more than a question of refugees. I agree.' The key to the situation lay with the autonomy talks which, he argued, he had been trying to revive when 'pre-empted' by the invasion of Lebanon. Ruling out both a Palestinian state and annexation by Israel, he said 'it is the firm view of the United States that only self-government by the Palestinians of the West Bank and Gaza in association with Jordan offers the best chance for a durable, just and lasting peace'. Finally, he warned that the United States would not support further Israeli settlements in the territories and that the status of Jerusalem had still to be decided.[44]

Begin's reported reaction that the proposals were 'worse than Rogers' reflected his government's indignation at a plan which promised to rob them of the benefits of their campaign and which had been discussed in Arab capitals. Arguing that it was a deviation from Camp David, the government issued a detailed rebuttal. The agreement had nowhere mentioned that the Arabs of east Jerusalem should be allowed to vote for a West Bank–Gaza authority; to allow this would amount to the city's re-partition. If the Arabs took over the internal security of the territories, they would become a base for terrorism. The Prime Minister had only consented to a three-month freeze on settlements at Camp David; otherwise, such settlements were a 'Jewish inalienable right', and would be continued without evicting existing inhabitants. On the question of autonomy, the government reiterated its familiar position that this referred to the inhabitants not the territories. Further, the agreements made no reference to a possible link between the territories and Jordan, nor did they preclude Israeli sovereignty. As there would be nothing to inhibit King Hussein from handing over the territories to Arafat, the President's rejection of a Palestinian state, it was argued, was hollow.[45]

This rejection, confirmed by the Knesset a week later, came as no surprise in Washington, where officials pointed out that the two governments had never agreed on an interpretation of Camp David and that the elements in the plan had all featured in the lengthy autonomy negotiations. Knowing that there was no 'right' time to launch such far-reaching proposals, they hoped that with full presidential approval they could start the long process of negotiation. Initial signs were not too discouraging. Labour leader Peres openly welcomed the 'Jordanian option', leading to the inevitable riposte that Washington was interfering in Israeli politics. Nor could Begin's government rely on American Jews to attack the plan, for they were very uneasy about events in Lebanon. Hence, the prospect of a return to peace talks was welcomed by the Conference of Presidents of Major American Jewish Organizations and B'nai B'rith. Even more significant was the open breach with Begin's government by AIPAC's Thomas Dine who saw the plan as constructive.[46]

The Americans hoped that by attracting Arab, especially Jordanian, support for the plan they could give it a decent start, but the results of the Fez summit were not very encouraging. Confirmation of the PLO as the legitimate representative of the Palestinian people apparently left little place for King Hussein. The best that could be found was a clear indication that all the Arab states wished to settle their differences with Israel through negotiation and a rather Delphic statement which seemed to acknowledge her right to exist. Given the passions aroused over events in Lebanon perhaps it had been fanciful to expect anything more. Privately, Arab leaders argued that they had gone far toward recognising Israel and supporting the Reagan Plan, but the US administration felt it was all too hesitant and, in a speech, George Bush spelled out their feeling that the time had come for the Arabs to stop speaking in allusions and codes.[47]

Progress on the Reagan Plan was clearly going to involve a long haul. The Americans were prepared for this, but not for the murderous events in Beirut which were first to deflect and then sap their efforts. Bashir Gemayel was the hero of the Maronites but had a long history in his country's civil war. On 14 September, he was assassinated by a bomb at a Phalange party meeting in Beirut. Events moved very quickly. The following morning, Israeli troops began to take over west Beirut, avowedly to prevent chaos and bloodshed. Condemning this as a 'clear violation' of Habib's agreements, the Americans demanded that the troops be withdrawn. On 17 September Colin Campbell of the *New York Times* filed an ominous report that 'With Israeli tanks standing guard outside, Israeli-backed Phalangist militiamen moved by foot and jeep into the battered Sabra and Shatila camps. Automatic fire could be heard from within, and women weeping hysterically began appearing in downtown west Beirut saying that their husbands and sons had been taken away by armed Phalangists.'[48] He was witnessing the start of the Sabra and Shatila massacres which Israeli intelligence later estimated left 800 Palestinian men, women and children dead. During Habib's negotiations, many had feared for the fate of the camps' inhabitants if the Phalangists were able to take retribution for events in the civil war. That they now avenged the death of their leader proved to be the watershed of the Lebanese crisis. Israel could not escape guilt by association. Yielding to the insistence of its citizens and international opinion, the government appointed a commission of inquiry under Chief Justice Yitzhak Kahan. Its report and recommendations in February 1983 helped repair the damage the massacre had done to the country's image in the United States.

More immediately, Sabra and Shatila brought American troops back into Lebanon. It was an open secret that the French and Italians believed that the United States had withdrawn the marines too quickly after the PLO's departure and the tragic events which followed appeared to have borne out their fears. The Italian government's reaction was to suggest that the multinational force be reconstituted. It seemed the obvious way to ensure the safety of civilians in west Beirut. The reactions coming from Washington were mixed. While Reagan was reported to be 'aghast' at what had happened, especially as the Israelis had assured Habib that they would not enter west Beirut, officials made it clear that he remained a strong supporter of Israel. Proof of this came on 23 September when the Senate Appropriations Committee voted aid to Israel at the level of $2.2 billion a year, no question having arisen of reducing the level of assistance.[49] But along with the indication of presidential support and the notable absence of sanctions, came a categorical demand that the Israeli army evacuate west Beirut. Despite a show of reluctance, by 22 September the State Department was able to report that Israeli units were beginning to pull out of sections of the city. By that date marines of the Sixth Fleet were sailing towards Beirut to join once more with the French and Italians in a multinational force, MNF II as it came to be termed.[50]

Its predecessor had gone into Beirut with a difficult but carefully prepared and precisely defined mission; MNF II was a hastily improvised reaction to unforeseen events. From the start, there were doubts and ambiguities about the nature and duration of its task. In announcing its formation on 20 September, Reagan spoke of its 'mission of enabling the Lebanese Government to resume full sovereignty over its capital, the essential precondition for extending its control over the entire country'. On 28 September, however, he appeared to amplify this by saying that the force would remain until Israeli and Syrian troops had left the country, leaving his officials to explain that he was voicing an 'expectation' that this would be accomplished by the time the authority of the Lebanese government was restored.[51] It was not a promising start to an enterprise which many inevitably compared with the early commitment to Vietnam. The force's deployment reflected what were felt to be the sympathies of its contingents: 1500 French held the northern port area close to Christian east Beirut, while 1400 Italians covered the central sector containing the Palestinian camps. The American contingent of 1400 marines was given the critical southern sector next to the Israelis. A token British force, which was added in February 1983, was placed next to the Americans. The marine area was a critical one as it contained the airport but was, as it turned out, fatally vulnerable to bombardment from the nearby Chouf mountains and to attack from the ardently Shi'ite southern suburbs of the city. But at least the Israeli army was out of the city and as the multinational force began its patrols the French and Americans could begin the task of helping to rebuild the Lebanese army.

But American diplomacy, which had seemingly been set a clear, if difficult, path in early September, now had to advance on two fronts. With the marines now patrolling in Beirut it was inevitable that the Lebanese involvement would take priority over the pursuit of the Reagan Plan, which conspicuously failed to develop any momentum. From the start, officials had known that the only way to induce the Israeli government to make any positive response would be the full involvement of King Hussein. The King's problem, however, was that he was bound by the Rabat summit decision of 1974 recognising the PLO as the legitimate spokesman for the Palestinians and the fact that, despite all that had happened in Beirut, Arafat still presided over a viable organisation. Months of negotiations between Hussein and Arafat culminated in three days of discussions in early April 1983. Strong efforts by the Americans to stiffen the King's resolve, including a personal telephone call from the President and a public pledge that the administration would try to halt the Israeli settlements in the West Bank, failed. On 10 April, the Jordanian government announced that as it had failed to reach agreement on a negotiating formula, it was leaving the future of the Palestinians to the PLO. As the Americans were still bound by Kissinger's pledge over negotiations with the PLO, the outlook seemed bleak; as if to confirm this, the Jordanian announcement coincided with the assassination in Portugal of the leading PLO moderate and Arafat adviser, Dr Issam Sartawi, by Palestinians determined to oppose any accommodation with Israel.[52]

These setbacks, viewed by many as fatal to the Reagan Plan, were soon eclipsed by events in Beirut which had incalculable effects on American policy. On 15 March, the multinational force sustained its first casualty with the death of an Italian soldier at the hands of Islamic Jihad, a little-known Shi'ite group with pro-Iranian loyalties; the following day, five American marines were wounded. These attacks were the prelude to the shattering car bomb at the Beirut embassy on 18 April. Among the forty dead were seventeen Americans. By any reckoning it would have been a cruel blow for an administration pledged to the opposition of terrorism, but among those killed were the CIA's station chief in Beirut and seven of his operatives, working under diplomatic cover. They were meeting with one of the administration's key figures in policy formation, the CIA's chief Middle East analyst, Robert C. Ames. Not only did Ames possess an unrivalled knowledge of the area's networks but he had been a major influence with Shultz in the formulation of the Reagan initiative. His death compounded the tragedy for the Americans.[53]

Faced with this succession of blows, Shultz decided it was time to make his first trip to the Middle East in an attempt to negotiate the withdrawal of Israeli and Syrian forces from Lebanon. Previously, he had maintained that such a mission would only be undertaken once success was assured; he now no longer had that luxury, not least because congressional and media opinion was beginning to voice unease over the marines' vulnerability and to question whether there was any real sense of commitment to the Reagan initiative.

Shultz arrived in the Middle East on 25 April with very mixed prospects. He knew that Syria had already agreed in principle to withdraw her 40 000 troops from Lebanon, but only on condition that Israel did so in a manner which left Lebanese sovereignty intact. With his armed forces powerfully re-equipped by the Soviets, Assad was in a strong bargaining position. Faced with the expense of sustaining over 30 000 soldiers in the country and continuing casualties, the Israeli government had every incentive to withdraw from Lebanon, but they needed something to show for the 500 dead and 2700 wounded in a war which had provoked widespread opposition and anxiety. Their aim was to secure agreement ending the state of war with Lebanon, and security arrangements which would allow them a continuing presence in the south of the country linked with Major Saad Haddad's pro-Israeli militia. The Lebanese, conscious of their position in the Arab world, were not willing to concede anything approaching a peace treaty and regarded Haddad as a deserter whom they did not wish to see integrated into their army. Shultz could offer inducements to the Lebanese and the Israelis to reach an agreement, the former clearly being attracted by the continuing American commitment to the restoration of stability and the reconstruction of their armed forces. Seeking to counteract the tensions of the past year, he went out of his way to nurture good relations with Begin and his government, with considerable success. Shultz's technique was to avoid the appearance of threat, but to hold out the prospect of tangible reward in three areas the Israelis considered important: the delivery of seventy-five F–16 aircraft embargoed since the start of the invasion, the supply of vital components to Israel's projected Lavi fighter, and the re-activation of the agreement on strategic co-operation which had been languishing since the annexation of the Golan Heights.[54] His problem was that he had nothing to offer the Syrians.

Inevitably, then, the agreement of 17 May negotiated by Shultz and his team, and signed by the Israelis and Lebanese, lacked the ingredient vital to its success: the acquiescence of Syria. Israel would evacuate her armed forces in return for a continuing security presence in southern Lebanon. This envisaged close liaison with a 'southern brigade' of the Lebanese army in which Haddad was to have an important role and eight joint Lebanese–Israeli 'verification patrols' which would have the right of self-defence. As part of the agreement, Israel was assured that she would not have to withdraw until this had been done by the Syrians and PLO forces in the Bekaa valley.[55] But Shultz's meetings with Assad had established no rapport; Syria and the PLO, with strong Soviet backing, rejected the agreement, which seemed merely to confirm an Israeli–American hegemony they were determined to resist.

The Middle East was proving barren ground for an American administration which was now starting to think of the next presidential election and was only too aware of the effect of the Iranian débâcle on Carter's fortunes. Discouraged by the joint failure of the Reagan Plan and his Lebanese agreement, Shultz was inclined to blame the Arabs for his inability to show any progress.[56] As a result, relations with the Israelis steadily improved. This new warmth between Washington and Jerusalem came at a time when the position of the multinational force in Beirut was becoming increasingly perilous and its ill-defined mission open to question. The marines' positions at Beirut International had always been potentially vulnerable. On 3 September, however, the Israelis, under pressure from public opinion, suddenly pulled their troops well to the south of the city. Their positions in the Chouf mountains overlooking the airport were occupied by the Druse militia who began bombarding the Americans. As the first fatalities occurred, the US administration came under pressure to push the marines into the Chouf, a move which Shultz and Weinberger opposed. Even so, the degree of American commitment apeared to be increasing in a way which seemed all too reminiscent of the early days in Vietnam. Warships of the Sixth Fleet off Beirut began shelling Druse positions in the mountains; they were reinforced by the battleship *New Jersey*, whose sixteen-inch guns could reach far into the interior.

With the United States apparently becoming a protagonist in the Lebanese conflict, it was inevitable that the commitment would come under the scrutiny of the War Powers legislation, the White House and leading congressmen reaching a compromise on 29 September that the marines could be deployed for eighteen months. This seemed to signal the end of their mission, for it was unclear what they could achieve in such a time. In Beirut itself, the multinational force, far from contributing to stability, was fast becoming the focus of anti-government and anti-Western groups, of which there was no lack. The fatal blow came on 23 October when suicide car bombs from Shi'ite south Beirut were driven into the marine compound and the French headquarters, resulting in the death of 58 French servicemen and 241 marines. Brave words from the US administration could not disguise the fact that the marines' role was now largely reduced to maintaining their perimeter. American public support, confused by the nuances of the Lebanese situation, was fast eroding; an opinion poll in January 1984 put support for a continuing marine presence at 38 per cent. As the Democratic contenders for the presidential nomination called for a withdrawal, leading Republicans were warning of the electoral consequences of an increasingly unpopular, and ultimately fruitless, commitment. Some, like Howard Baker and Barry Goldwater, had been opposed from the start. With no clear end in sight, Reagan announced on 7 February that the marines would be 'redeployed' to ships off shore. MNF II had run its course, for the French, Italians and British knew that the American role had come to an end.[57] As the marines were evacuated in the course of February under the guns of the Sixth Fleet, what remained of American policy in Lebanon quickly fell apart. On 5 March, the Lebanese government, now beholden to the Syrians, abrogated its agreement with Israel, the only thing the Reagan administration had to show for its Middle East policy.

The abrupt reversal of policy left America's friends in Lebanon with a sense of betrayal, and pro-Western governments in the Middle East wondering about her resolve. The fundamental cause of America's failure was an inability to appreciate the extent to which the Lebanese state and its armed forces had disintegrated under the strain of events. The only clear winner from the Lebanese involvement was Syria, which the Americans had failed to cultivate and which had demonstrated its ability to dictate events. In almost every other respect, the Israelis had set the agenda, with the Americans following behind. As the US administration became disillusioned with the Arabs, the Israelis, despite all the tensions of the Lebanese war, regained their favoured status, the symbol of which was renewed strategic co-operation between the two countries. 'Since I took office', Reagan assured the Young Leadership Cabinet of the United Jewish Appeal in March 1984, 'the US–Israel relationship had grown closer than before.'

The truth of that was plain to see. Recriminations over Israel's actions in Lebanon were in the past; little more was heard of the Reagan Plan; and, as nothing was done to advance discussion of the West Bank and Gaza, the sullen alienation of their inhabitants turned into violence bred of hopelessness. With the second Reagan administration, the wheel had come full circle, for America's priorities were once again terrorism and the security of the Gulf, where, by the summer of 1987, her ships were deployed in support of Kuwaiti tanker traffic against threatened Iranian attack. The former concern led to the air strike on Tripoli and Benghazi in Libya in April 1986, while in May 1987, in an incident eerily reminiscent of the *Liberty* twenty years before, the USS *Stark* was attacked by an Iraqi aircraft leaving thirty-seven dead. The possibility that the country might be sucked into the Iran–Iraq war brought the Middle East once again to the forefront of discussion. But the region's central issue appeared to have been cast into limbo.

On 8 December 1987, the tensions long felt in the occupied territories burst out in the *intifada* which left over 300 Palestinians dead. The initial American reaction was to begin talking again in an attempt to keep diplomacy alive until the new administration could attempt to address the situation. But such a policy came under increasing pressure, not least from America's European allies and friends in the Middle East, who believed that the *intifada* demanded a more imaginative response. In July 1988, King Hussein abruptly severed his connexion with the West Bank, wrecking the hope, sustained under Kissinger, Carter and Reagan, that he would serve as the spokesman for the Palestinians. Accepting this, and determined to show political gain from the *intifada*, on 15 November the PLO national council proclaimed an independent Palestinian state on the West Bank and Gaza, implying recognition of Israel. A month of intense activity, involving public acrimony between Schultz and Arafat but also crucial 'back channel' negotiations involving the Egyptians, the Saudis, a group of American Jews and, on the fortieth anniversary of Bernadotte's assassination, the Swedes, brought the promise of 'substantive dialogue' if the PLO would renounce terrorism and accept Israel's right to exist. Although Arafat's speech to the United Nations in Geneva on 13 December seemed to fall short of Schultz's conditions, Swedish mediation resulted in a press conference the following day at which the PLO leader appeared to give an unequivocal renunciation of terrorism and acceptance of Resolutions 242 and 338. Ambiguities remained, but it enabled Robert Pelletreau, ambassador to Tunisia, to meet members of the PLO executive council, beginning the 'substantive dialogue' Schultz had promised.

Conclusion

As Roosevelt had known it would, the Middle East became a major preoccupation of post-war foreign policy, with Palestine the issue which eclipsed all others. Once the Cold War started, it was certain that the region would feature prominently in what most Americans saw as a global competition for influence and security. As British power declined, the United States was forced to assume the leadership of Western interests. Although Britain's decision to refer Palestine to the United Nations in 1947 signalled the weakness of her position, the Americans needed time to adjust to what became a prolonged period of withdrawal. The year 1956 proved decisive, when an irate Eisenhower forced the end of the Suez adventure, ending any lingering pretension to imperial greatness.

Eisenhower's handling of that crisis was dictated by a broad view of Western interests at a time of acute international tension. Israel was simply one element in the regional situation. The view, which started under Acheson but developed under Eisenhower and Dulles, was that Israel's search for security, still less her economic problems, could not be allowed to distort the pattern of American interests. In short, Acheson and Dulles believed that Israel had no special claim on their affections, a view which her actions in the early 1950s, especially over Jerusalem, did little to change. Between 1952 and 1955, the State Department and the CIA made serious efforts to reach a working arrangement with revolutionary Egypt, but ultimately could not come to terms with Nasser's desire for genuine neutrality. Nasser remained a difficult figure for Americans, who recognised his claims to leadership, while feeling frustrated by the contrast between his private assurances and public rhetoric. George Shultz was not the first to become discouraged by the nature of Arab attitudes.

Such policies contrasted with what had happened under Truman, at least during his first administration. Starting from a feeling of sympathy with the Jewish Displaced Persons, Truman moved unsteadily toward support for the Zionists. While resenting Zionist pressure, he was receptive to the degree of concern felt by his Jewish fellow-countrymen and alert to the danger of this being tapped by his political opponents. If there were benefit to be gained by acting over Palestine, then it should accrue to him and not to Dewey or Wallace, and it is foolish to ignore the electoral factors behind what he did. When he intervened, he did so with telling effect, for he was instrumental in securing the partition vote and the subsequent recognition of Israel. He was susceptible to influence, whether from aides he valued like Niles and Clifford, from his trusted friend Jacobson, or from the consummate diplomacy of Weizmann; but the decisions were his and his successors' policies had to adapt to what he had done.

The decision-making process was, and remains, complex. The 1970s saw attempts in Congress to assert a more positive role in the evolution of policy but while congressional attitudes had to be attended to, the President with his advisers still set the basic agenda. Just as Truman and Eisenhower had marked out distinctive policies, so did Nixon, Ford, Carter and Reagan. All were vulnerable to the domestic political cycle, Carter complaining that he would have been a better President had he not also been a candidate.[1] Few have been as willing as Carter to immerse themselves so completely in the Middle East as he did between 1977 and 1979. His achievement, while substantial, was bought at a price which some thought too high. His bid for a comprehensive settlement came after Kissinger had shown the degree of effort needed to produce results. Kissinger made it his business to reduce tension and secure American interests. By rigorously confining himself to what seemed possible, he succeeded in easing the degree of enmity between Egypt and Israel while building bridges to Syria which were to be sadly neglected under his successors. The practical effect of his diplomacy was to tie the United States and Israel firmly together, secure Sadat as a partner for the West and exclude the PLO from the mainstream of diplomacy.

That no President proved able to avert the wars of 1948, 1956, 1967, 1973 and 1982, confirmed the limits of power and the need for active involvement. Crisis management proved possible. Eisenhower's actions have already been referred to; both Carter and Reagan succeeded, ultimately, in curbing Israel's actions in Lebanon, while Kissinger's reactions to the 1973 war showed skill and confidence. But much of the history of American policy has been one of reacting to events rather than dictating them. Given the extent of American influence, not least financial, this may seem surprising but it is nothing less than a measure of the passions involved.

The Palestinians have come to feel themselves the principal victims of American policy. Largely discounted under Truman, as the loss of

their homes, land and political hopes then hardened into permanence, the Americans assumed the principal burden of providing
assistance for the Palestinian refugees through UNRWA. But it was
hardly enough and Israel's success in freezing the Palestinians out of
American policy materially contributed to continuing tension. Brief
attempts at dialogue proved unsatisfactory, partly through the
vigilance of Israel's supporters and partly through the inability of
Palestinian leaders to present a formula with regard to Israel which
Washington could accept. Pushed to the edge of diplomacy, the need
to remind the world of their frustration contributed in no small part
to the violent protests which broke out amongst the inhabitants of the
West Bank and Gaza in December 1987.[2]

Israel has come to dominate America's Middle East policies to a
degree which would have seemed unlikely in the 1950s. The Reagan
administration saw Israel's influence in Washington at its zenith and
apparently secured into the future. The simplistic explanation for this
would be the strength of the Israeli lobby and the activity of its
supporters throughout the country. That AIPAC exerts power on
Capitol Hill and that pro-Israeli groups have affected the fortunes of
certain politicians are truisms of American politics. But the lobby is
not all-powerful, as Kissinger showed in 1975. The earlier lobbying
on Truman was very nearly self-defeating. Some Israeli commenta-
tors have questioned the lobby's wisdom in trying to prevent or delay
arms sales to Arab countries which inevitably turn to alternative
sources over which Washington has no control. AIPAC's most
conspicuous success has been in helping to ensure that Congress
approves continuing aid to Israel. It is not surprising that Israel has
bent every effort to ensure continuing support, for the state is
financially, militarily and diplomatically dependent on the United
States to a degree that many of her citizens find frightening. Israelis
can take comfort from the broad feeling amongst Americans that
Israel deserves that support. American Jews, whatever else may
divide them, are overwhelmingly dedicated to Israel's survival and
success; in the light of the Jewish experience it could not be
otherwise. It was cause for concern when events in Beirut led many to
question what the nationalism of the 1970s and 1980s had in common
with the humanistic Zionism of Wise, Goldmann and Weizmann
which had attracted Truman.

By 1987, the State Department could do little more than resort to
Churchill's wise maxim that 'jaw, jaw' was preferable to 'war, war',
encouraging dialogue between those Israelis and Palestinians who

were willing to explore each other's positions. It was a far cry from the heady days of shuttle diplomacy and Camp David but it kept alive hope that, if Arabs and Jews could be brought to acknowledge each other's tragedy, then something positive might be introduced into the bitter world of Middle East politics.[3]

By the end of 1988, this unobtrusive 'holding operation' had succeeded in keeping the diplomatic process in play. Then, in the final weeks of the Reagan administration, the pace of events quickened as a result of events in the West Bank and Gaza. Despite, or perhaps because of, their strong links with Israel, Reagan and Schultz opened up the possibility of a new relationship with the PLO. It was a move which Israelis had long feared and it left them with mixed feelings of hurt, defiance and apprehension. But America's commitment to Israel's survival had never been in doubt from the moment of Truman's recognition. The continuing levels of aid and support in the United Nations were testimony to that central reality. But in its dying weeks, the Reagan administration had allowed its successor, under George Bush, the flexibility to try new directions in the Arab–Israeli dispute which had engaged American attentions ever since Franklin Roosevelt had first grasped the significance of the Middle East for his country's post-war foreign policy.

Notes

ABBREVIATIONS

DSB   *Department of State Bulletin*
FRUS   *Foreign Relations of the United States*
HSTL   Harry S. Truman Library, Independence, Missouri
NA   National Archives, Washington, DC
NYT   *New York Times*
UNO   United Nations Organisation

The principal sources for this book are indicated in the Notes. Useful studies which cover American policy in the Middle East, from different standpoints, are: N. Safran, *Israel, the Embattled Ally* (Cambridge, Massachusetts, 1978); S. P. Tillman, *The United States in the Middle East: Interests and Obstacles* (Bloomington, 1982); N. Chomsky, *The Fateful Triangle* (Boston, 1983); S. L. Spiegel, *The Other Arab–Israeli Conflict* (Chicago, 1985); B. Reich, *The United States and Israel* (New York, 1984); C. A. Rubenberg, *Israel and the American National Interest* (Urbana, 1986); S. Green, *Taking Sides* (London, 1984); M. K. Shadid, *The United States and the Palestinians* (London, 1981); H. H. Saunders, *The Other Walls* (Washington, 1985).

INTRODUCTION

1. Roosevelt to Wagner, 15 October 1944, *FRUS* 1944, vol. V, pp. 615–16.
2. Roosevelt to Ibn Saud, 26 May 1943, *FRUS* 1943, vol. IV, pp. 786–7.
3. Conversations between Ibn Saud and Roosevelt, 13–14 February 1945, *FRUS* 1945, vol. VIII, pp. 1–9.
4. Roosevelt to Ibn Saud, 5 April 1945, *FRUS* 1945, vol. VIII, pp. 696–9.

CHAPTER 1: TRUMAN'S SEARCH FOR A MIDDLE EAST POLICY

1. J. Snetsinger, *Truman, The Jewish Vote and the Creation of Israel* (Stanford, 1974) initiated this line of enquiry. It was countered in Clark M. Clifford. 'Recognizing Israel: The Behind-the-Scenes Struggle in 1948 Between the President and the State Department', *American Heritage*, April 1977, pp. 4–14. Truman's relationship with American Zionism is extensively covered in Z. Ganin, *Truman, American Jewry, and Israel, 1945–1948* (New York, 1979). A useful collection of essays is A. Weinstein and M. Ma'oz (eds), *Truman and the American Commitment to Israel* (Jerusalem, 1981). M. J. Cohen,

Palestine and the Great Powers, 1945–1948 (Princeton, 1982) should also be consulted.

2. M. Davis, 'Reflections on Harry S. Truman and the State of Israel', in Weinstein and Ma'oz (eds), *Truman and the American Commitment to Israel*, p. 83; M. Miller, *Plain Speaking, An Oral Biography of Harry S. Truman* (London, 1974) p. 218.

3. I am grateful to Professor John Grenville for this observation.

4. Truman to Rep. A. Klein, 5 May 1948, OF 204 Misc (May 1948), HSTL.

5. M. G. Baron to C. Ross, 28 February 1948, McGrath Papers, 63, 'Palestine, DNC Chairman', HSTL.

6. J. Daniels, *The Man of Independence* (London, 1951) pp. 186–7.

7. Truman to S. Wise, 6 August 1947, OF 204 Misc (June–August 1947), HSTL.

8. Syrian Minister for Foreign Affairs to US Legation, nd, *FRUS* 1945, vol. VIII, pp. 767–8.

9. Joint Chiefs of Staff to State-War-Navy Coordinating Committee, 21 June 1946, *FRUS* 1946, vol. VII, pp. 631–3.

10. Private correspondence. See Loy Henderson's Oral History in HSTL.

11. Jacobson's role is best studied with reference to a handwritten 'Chronology' amongst his papers in HSTL, attached to which are useful notes by Frank J. Adler of Kansas City.

12. Clark M. Clifford, Oral History, HSTL.

13. Niles's background and early career are described in notes compiled by Elliott A. Niles in 1955 and included with his papers in HSTL. See also Abram L. Sachar, *The Redemption of the Unwanted* (New York, 1983).

14. Niles to Truman, 27 May 1946, Niles Papers, N5.196, HSTL.

15. Niles to G. Riesman, 19 October 1949, Niles Papers, N5.99(2), HSTL.

16. Stettinius to Truman, 18 April 1945, *FRUS* 1945, vol. VIII, pp. 704–5.

17. Truman to Amir Abdullah *et al.*, 17 May 1945, *FRUS* 1945, Vol. VIII, pp. 707–9.

18. E. M. Wilson, *Decision on Palestine* (Princeton, 1979) p. 60.

19. Memoranda of Conversation, 20 and 27 June 1945, *FRUS* 1945, vol. VIII, pp. 710–15.

20. Truman to Churchill, 24 July 1945, and Attlee to Truman, 31 July 1945, *FRUS* 1945, vol. VIII, pp. 716–19.

21. H. Cantril to Niles, 'Public Opinion Toward Creation of Jewish State in Palestine', 4 April 1945, Niles Papers, N5.195, HSTL.

22. Jacobson, 'Chronology', June 1945, Jacobson Papers, HSTL.

23. Harry S. Truman, *Years of Trial and Hope* (New York, 1956) pp. 145–6.

24. Attlee to Truman, 14 and 16 September 1945, *FRUS* 1945, vol. VIII, pp. 739–41.

25. Dean Acheson, *Present at the Creation* (New York, 1969; p. 169.

26. Memo by Henderson, 24 August 1945, *FRUS* 1945, vol. VIIII, pp. 727–33.

27. Private information from a senior British diplomat.

28. Acheson to Truman, 2 October 1945, *FRUS* 1945, vol. VIII, pp. 753–5.
29. War Department to Department of State, 19 September 1945, and Henderson to Byrnes, 9 October 1945, *FRUS* 1945, Vol. VIII, pp. 742–3 and 762.
30. Memoranda of Conversation, Henderson, 12 October 1945, *FRUS* 1945, vol. VIII, pp. 766–7.
31. Department of State Press Release, 18 October 1945, *FRUS* 1945, vol. VIII, pp. 770–1.
32. Memorandum of Conversation between Byrnes and Lord Halifax, 19 October 1945, *FRUS* 1945, vol. VIII, pp. 777–9.
33. Memorandum to Truman, 24 October 1945, PSF Subject Files, Pol. 1945–47, HSTL.
34. Truman to Senator Joseph H. Ball, 24 November 1945 (not sent), PSF Subject Files, Palestine, 1945–47, HSTL.
35. Halifax to Byrnes, n.d., *FRUS* 1945, vol. VIII, pp. 771–5.
36. Byrnes to Winant, 13 November 1945, *FRUS* 1945, vol. VIII, pp. 819–20.
37. For a full discussion of the Committee's work see A. Nachmani, *Great Power Discord in Palestine* (London, 1987).
38. Truman to Byrnes, 27 November 1945, PSF Subject Files, Palestine 1945–47, HSTL; Niles to Crum, 20 February 1946, Niles Papers, N5.183(2), HSTL.
39. Kennan to Byrnes, 19 February 1946, Minister in Egypt to Byrnes, 1 March 1946, *FRUS* 1946, vol. VII, pp. 581–2.
40. Nachmani, *Great Power Discord*, p. 185.
41. W. Phillips, *Ventures in Diplomacy* (London, 1955) p. 293.
42. Summary of the Anglo–American Committee of Inquiry, 25 April 1946, *FRUS* 1946, vol. VII, pp. 585–6.
43. Trusteeship was consistently seen as the most viable option by British officials and their American counterparts. Information from a senior British diplomat.
44. Wilson, *Decision on Palestine*, p. 87.
45. Niles to Henderson and Crum, 20 February 1946, Niles Papers, N5.183(2), HSTL.
46. Henderson, Oral History, HSTL.
47. Pinkerton, Jerusalem, to Byrnes, 2 May 1946, *FRUS* 1946, vol. VII, pp. 590–1.
48. Memorandum of Conversation by the Director of the Office of European Affairs, 27 April 1946, Byrnes to Truman, 9 May 1946, *FRUS* 1946, vol. VII, pp. 587–8 and 601–3.
49. Truman to Senator Carl A. Hatch, 10 February 1948, OF 204 Misc (February 1948–Folder 1), HSTL.
50. Truman to Dean Alfange, 18 May 1948, PSF, Box 184, HSTL.
51. Truman to Kaufmann, 11 May 1946, OF 204, Misc (November 1945–May 1946), HSTL.
52. Jewish Agency to Truman, 2 May 1946, and Henry J. Latham to Truman, 23 May 1946, OF 204, Misc (November 1945–May 1946), HSTL.

53. The correspondence about the New York delegation is in OF 204, Misc, (June 1946), HSTL.
54. See note 9.
55. Acheson to Truman, 6 May 1946, *FRUS* 1946, vol. VII, pp. 595–7.
56. Niles to Truman, 7 May 1946, PSF, Palestine 1945–1947, HSTL.
57. Crum to Niles, 7 May 1946, Niles Papers, N5.183(2), HSTL.
58. Byrnes to Truman, 9 May 1946, *FRUS* 1946, vol. VII, pp. 601–3.
59. Ganin, *Truman, American Jewry and Israel*, pp. 71–3.
60. Memorandum of Conversation, 26 February 1946, Niles Papers, Israeli Affairs, 1943–1947, HSTL.
61. Niles to Charles Ross, 13 June 1946, Niles Papers, N5.196, HSTL.
62. Truman to Attlee, 1 and 2 July 1946, White House Press Release, 2 July 1946, *FRUS* 1946, Vol. VII, pp. 641–3.
63. Harriman to Byrnes, 19 July 1946, *FRUS* 1946, vol. VII, pp. 646–7.
64. W. Millis (ed.), *The Forrestal Diaries* (New York, 1951) pp. 346–7.
65. Acheson, *Present at the Creation*, p. 175.
66. See note 53.
67. Truman to McDonald, 31 July 1946, OF 204, Misc (July 1946), HSTL.
68. Truman to Attlee, 7 August 1946, *FRUS* 1946, vol. VII, p. 677.
69. See Ganin, *Truman, American Jewry and Israel*, chapter VII.
70. Truman to Attlee, 3 October 1946, *FRUS* 1946, vol. VII, pp. 701–3.
71. Celler to Truman, 7 October 1946 and Truman to Celler, 10 October 1946, OF 204 Misc (October 1946), HSTL.
72. Truman to Edwin W. Pauley, 22 October 1946, PSF Subject Files (Palestine–Jewish Immigration), HSTL.

CHAPTER 2: THE USA AND THE BIRTH OF ISRAEL

1. Gordon Merriam to Henderson, 27 December 1946, *FRUS* 1946, vol. VII, pp. 732–5.
2. Private information from a senior British diplomat.
3. Department of State to British Embassy, nd, *FRUS* 1947, vol. V, pp. 1014–15.
4. Henderson, Oral History, HSTL.
5. See UNSCOP, *Report*, vol. 1, chapter VI, part I, Plan of partition with economic union.
6. Memorandum Prepared in the Department of State, 4 June 1947, *FRUS* 1947, vol. V, 1096–101.
7. Henderson, Oral History, HSTL.
8. Statement by Truman, 5 June 1947, *FRUS* 1947, vol. V, pp. 1101–2.
9. Truman to Niles, 13 May 1947, PSF Subject Files (Palestine 1945–1947), HSTL.
10. Truman to Wise, 6 August 1947, OF 204 Misc (June–August 1947), HSTL.
11. Niles to Truman, 29 July 1947, Niles Papers, N5.198, HSTL.
12. Minutes of the meeting of the US Delegation, 15 September 1947, *FRUS* 1947, vol. V, pp. 1147–51.

13. Henderson to Marshall, 22 September 1947, *FRUS* 1947, vol. V, pp. 1153–8.
14. W. Millis (ed.), *The Forrestal Diaries* (New York, 1851) pp. 323–24.
15. Hilldring to Herschel Johnson, 24 September 1947, *FRUS* 1947, vol. V, pp. 1162–3.
16. Jacobson to Truman, 3 October 1947, Jacobson Corres. File, Corres. Harry S. Truman, 1945–47, HSTL.
17. These documents, and others, are in OF 204 Misc (October–November 1947), HSTL.
18. Fitzpatrick to Truman, 6 October 1947, OF 204 Misc (October–November 1947), HSTL.
19. Millis, *Forrestal Diaries*, p. 323.
20. Truman to Fitzpatrick, 8 October 1947, OF 204 Misc (October–November 1947), HSTL.
21. Truman to Wagner, 1 October 1947, OF 204 Misc (October–November 1947), HSTL.
22. 'US Initial Statement on Palestine', R. R. Nathan, 7 October 1947, Niles Papers, N5.198, HSTL.
23. Harry S. Truman, *Years of Trial and Hope* (New York, 1956) p. 165.
24. Jacobson to Connolly, 18 February 1948, OF 204 Misc (February 1948 Folder 2), HSTL; C. Weizmann, *Trial and Error* (London, 1949) pp. 561–3.
25. Memorandum by Wilkins, 7 November 1947, *FRUS* 1947, vol. V, pp. 1244–6.
26. Speech by Cadogan, 20 November 1947, UNO GAOR *Ad Hoc* Committee Annex 19, Report of Subcommittee 1.
27. Private information.
28. Memorandum for the President, M. J. Connolly, 22 November 1947, OF 204 Misc (October–November 1947), HSTL.
29. Jacobson, Chronology, 1947, Jacobson Papers, HSTL.
30. Henderson, Oral History, HSTL.
31. See note 29.
32. Connolly to Truman, 25 November 1947, PSF Subject Files (Palestine–Jewish Immigration), HSTL.
33. Celler to Truman, 26 November 1947, and Proskauer to Truman, 27 November 1947, OF 204 Misc (October–November 1947); Truman to Proskauer, n.d. (not sent), PSF Subject Files, Palestine 1945–47, HSTL.
34. Private information.
35. Information from two senior British diplomats.
36. Diary of Eben A. Ayers, staff conference, 28 November 1947, Ayers Papers, HSTL; Marshall to Truman, 10 December 1947, Truman to Marshall, 11 December 1947, *FRUS* 1947, vol. V, pp. 1305–6 and 1309.
37. Truman, *Years of Trial and Hope*, pp. 168–9.
38. Truman to Weizmann, 1 December 1947 (not sent), PSF Subject Files, Palestine 1945–47, HSTL.
39. Truman to Celler, 1 December 1947, PSF Subject Files, Palestine 1945–47, HSTL.

40. Truman to Marshall, 11 December 1947, *FRUS* 1947, vol. V, p. 1309.
41. Ayers Diary, 2 December 1947, Ayers Papers, HSTL.
42. The messages to Niles are in Niles Papers, Box 30, N5.137(2), HSTL.
43. Private information.
44. T. G. Fraser, *Partition in Ireland, India and Palestine: Theory and Practice* (London, 1984), pp. 181–3.
45. Information from a senior British diplomat.
46. Private information.
47. Truman to Morgenthau, 2 December 1947, OF 204 Misc (December 1947–January 1948), HSTL.
48. Private information.
49. Memorandum, 1 December 1947, OF 204 Misc (December 1947–January 1948), HSTL.
50. Kennan to Marshall, 20 January 1948, *FRUS* 1948, vol. V pt. 2, pp. 545–54.
51. Rusk to Lovett, 26 January 1948, *FRUS* 1948, vol. V pt. 2, pp. 556–62.
52. Millis, *Forrestal Diaries*, pp. 344–65.
53. Draft Report Prepared by the Staff of the National Security Council, 17 February 1948, *FRUS* 1948, vol. V pt. 2, pp. 631–2.
54. Department of State to Truman, n.d. (21 February 1948), *FRUS* 1948, vol. V pt. 2, pp. 637–40.
55. Truman to Marshall, 22 February 1948, *FRUS* 1948, vol. V pt. 2, p. 645; Statement by Austin to Security Council, 24 February 1948, *FRUS* 1948, vol. V, pt. 2, pp. 651–4.
56. Weizmann to Truman, 9 December 1948, OF 204 Misc (December 1947–January 1948), HSTL.
57. Rabbi Baruch Korff to McGrath, 12 February 1948, McGrath Papers, Box 63, Palestine DNC Chairman, HSTL.
58. Note, 12 February 1948, OF 204 Misc (February 1948–Folder 1), HSTL.
59. See report by T. Coffin, ABC, Niles Papers, Israeli Affairs, 1948, HSTL.
60. Jacobson, Chronology, 20 February 1948, Jacobson Papers, HSTL.
61. Weizmann to Niles, 23 February 1948, Niles Papers, Israeli Affairs, 1948, HSTL.
62. R. H. Ferrell, *Off The Record* (New York, 1980) p. 127.
63. Ayers Diary, 20 March 1948, Ayers Papers, HSTL.
64. Abba Eban, 'Dewey David Stone: Prototype of an American Zionist', *American Jewish History*, vol. 69, no. 1 (1979) pp. 5–14.
65. Jacobson, Chronology, 17–19 March 1948, Jacobson Papers, HSTL; Truman, *Years of Trial and Hope*, pp. 170–1; Clark M. Clifford, 'Recognizing Israel: The Behind-the-Scenes Struggle in 1948 Between the President and the State Department', *American Heritage*, April 1977, pp. 4–14; Abba Eban, *An Autobiography* (New York, 1977) p. 103.
66. Ayers Diary, 22 March 1958, Ayers Papers, HSTL.
67. Carlisle Humelsine to Marshall, 22 March 1948, forwarding report by Lovett, *FRUS* 1948, vol. V pt. 2, pp. 749–50.
68. Notes by Clifford, Clifford Papers, Palestine: corres. misc. folder 3, HSTL.

69. Marshall to Bohlen, 22 March 1948, *FRUS* 1948, vol. V pt. 2, p. 750.
70. See note 62.
71. Ayers Diary, 25 March 1948, Ayers Papers, HSTL.
72. Discussion between Truman and Rusk, 30 April 1948, *FRUS* 1948, vol. V pt. 2, pp. 877–9.
73. Weizmann to Truman, 9 April 1948, OF 204 Misc, Box 774, HSTL.
74. Ayers Diary, 24 March 1948, Ayers Papers, HSTL.
75. Ross to McGrath, 11 March 1948, McGrath to Ross, 3 April 1948, McGrath Papers, Box 63, Palestine DNC Chairman, HSTL.
76. Alfange to Vaughan, 5 May 1948, Truman to Alfange, 18 May 1948, PSF, Box 184, HSTL.
77. Truman to Klein, 5 May 1948, OF 204 Misc (May 1948), HSTL.
78. Clifford, Oral History, HSTL, and 'Recognizing Israel'.
79. 'Statement', 9 May 1948, Clifford Papers, no. 20, HSTL.
80. Memorandum of Conversation by the Secretary of State, 12 May 1948, *FRUS* 1948, vol. V pt. 2, pp. 972–7.
81. Truman, *Years of Trial and Hope*, p. 175; Report by Coffin, ABC, Niles Papers, Israeli Affairs, 1948, HSTL.
82. Clifford, Oral History, HSTL, and 'Recognizing Israel'; Note by Clifford, Clifford Papers, Palestine: corres. misc. folder 3, HSTL; Nathan to Connolly, 14 May 1948, PSF Subject Files, Palestine 1948–52, HSTL; Memorandum of Conversation by Lovett, 17 May 1948, *FRUS* 1948, vol. V pt. 2, pp. 1005–7.
83. Private information.

CHAPTER 3: POLICY IN THE COLD WAR ERA

1. The outstanding analysis of this is W. R. Louis, *The British Empire in the Middle East 1945–1951* (Oxford, 1984). G. Kirk, *The Middle East 1945–1950* (Oxford, 1954) and J. C. Hurewitz, *Middle East Dilemmas* (New York, 1953) remain invaluable.
2. *Chargé* in Egypt to Marshall, 7 August 1948, *FRUS* 1948, vol. V pt. 2, pp. 1295–6.
3. C. Weizmann, *Trial and Error* (London, 1949) pp. 587–8; Weizmann to Truman, 25 and 26 May 1948, *FRUS* 1948, vol. V pt. 2, pp. 1042–3 and 1050–1.
4. J. G. McDonald, *My Mission in Israel 1948–1951* (London, 1951) pp. 3–17; Telephone Conversation by Lovett, 22 June 1948, *FRUS* 1948, vol. V pt. 2, pp. 1131–2.
5. Private information.
6. Marshall to Embassy, London, 22 June 1948; Memorandum by McClintock, 23 June 1948; McDonald to Clifford, 24 August 1948, *FRUS* 1948, vol. V pt. 2, pp. 1133–7 and 1339–40.
7. Memorandum by McClintock, 30 September 1948, *FRUS* 1948, vol. V pt. 2, pp. 1437–8.
8. Jacobson, Chronology, 28 September 1948, Jacobson Papers, HSTL; Clifford to Lovett, 29 September 1948 and Memorandum by McClintock, 30 September 1948, *FRUS* 1948, vol. V pt. 2, pp. 1430–1 and

1437–8; Truman to Marshall, 17 October 1948, PSF Box 181, Foreign Affairs–Israel, HSTL.

9. Lovett to Marshall, 10 November 1948, *FRUS* 1948, vol. V pt. 2, pp. 1565–7.
10. Truman to Weizmann, 29 November 1948, *FRUS* 1948, vol. V pt. 2, pp. 1633–4.
11. Memorandum of Conversation by Lovett, 12 January 1949, *FRUS* 1949, vol. VI, pp. 645–7; J. and D. Kimche, *Both Sides of the Hill* (London, 1960) p. 263.
12. Lovett to Ethridge, 19 January 1949, *FRUS* 1949, vol. VI, pp. 681–3.
13. W. J. Hopkins to Niles, 31 January 1949, Niles Papers, N5.100(2), HSTL; Meeting with the President, 27 January 1949, Acheson Papers, Box 64, HSTL.
14. W. Eytan, *The First Ten Years* (London, 1958) p. 69.
15. Lovett to Truman, 27 May 1948, *FRUS* 1948, vol. V pt. 2, pp. 1058–60.
16. Satterthwaite to Acheson, 9 February 1949, *FRUS* 1949, vol. VI, pp. 739–41.
17. Acheson to Tel Aviv, 4 January 1950, NA 784A. 02/1–450.
18. Acheson to Tel Aviv, 26 January 1950, NA 784A. 02/1–2050.
19. Eytan, *First Ten Years*, pp. 72–3.
20. Davis to Acheson, 11 August 1952, NA 784A. 02/8–1152.
21. McDonald to Truman, 17 October 1948, *FRUS* 1948, vol. V pt. 2, pp. 1486–7.
22. UNO GAOR, Fourth Session, *Ad Hoc* Political Committee, Annex to the summary records of meetings, vol. 1, 1949, doc. A/1106, First Interim Report of the UN Economic Survey Mission for the Middle East.
23. Statement by the President, 3 April 1949, *FRUS* 1949, vol. VI, p. 862.
24. See Mark Ethridge, Oral History, HSTL; G. McGhee, *Envoy to the Middle World* (New York, 1983).
25. Memorandum by McGhee, 15 March 1949, *FRUS* 1949, vol. VI, pp. 827–43.
26. Memorandum of Conversation by Acheson, 5 April 1949, *FRUS* 1949, vol. VI, pp. 890–4.
27. Weizmann to Truman, 26 April 1949, *FRUS* 1949, vol. VI, pp. 947–8.
28. Webb to Embassy, Tel Aviv, 28 May 1949, *FRUS* 1949, vol. VI, pp. 1072–4.
29. McGhee, *Envoy to the Middle World*, p. 37.
30. Memorandum by W. J. McWilliams, 26 August 1949, *FRUS* 1949, vol. VI, p. 1332.
31. Ethridge, Oral History, HSTL.
32. M. K. Shadid, *The United States and the Palestinians* (London, 1981) pp. 56–61.
33. I am grateful to the staff of UNRWA, Gaza, for showing me their work in the refugee camps around Gaza and Rafah.
34. See note 25; Leroy Johnson to Henry Byroade, 23 November 1953, NA 784A. 02/11–2353.

35. Intelligence memo. no. 122, 14 January 1949, Truman, NSC, CIA File (Special Evaluations Box 2), HSTL.
36. McGhee, *Envoy to the Middle World*, pp. 205–12; W. R. Louis, *The British Empire in the Middle East 1945–1951* (Oxford, 1984) pp. 583–90.
37. M. Heikal, *Nasser The Cairo Documents* (London, 1971) p. 42.
38. Caffery to State Department, 20 August 1952, *FRUS* 1952–1954, vol. IX pt. 2, pp. 1851–2.
39. Bruce to Caffery, 26 August 1952, NA 611. 74/8–2152.
40. Information from a former CIA officer; M. Copeland, *The Game of Nations* (New York, 1969); W. C. Eveland, *Ropes of Sand* (New York, 1980).
41. S. A. Ambrose, *Eisenhower The President* (New York, 1984) p. 387.
42. J. K. Javits, *Javits* (Boston, 1981) p. 180.
43. Heikal, *Nasser*, pp. 48–9; Memorandum of Conversation, 12 May 1953, *FRUS* 1952–1954, vol. IX pt. 1, pp. 19–25.
44. Memorandum of Conversation, 14 May 1953, *FRUS* 1952–1954, vol. IX pt. 1, pp. 36–40.
45. Tyler to Dulles, 10 July 1953, NA 784A. 02/7–1053; Dulles to Silver, 13 July 1953, NA 784A. 02/7–1353.
46. Dulles to Tel Aviv, 24 July 1953, NA 784A. 02/7–2453; Sharett to Dulles, 27 July 1953, NA 784A. 13/7–2753; Russell, Tel Aviv, to Dulles, 17 August 1953, NA 784A. 02/8–1753.
47. Russell to Department of State, 28 September 1953, *FRUS* 1952–1954, vol. IX pt. 1, pp. 1329–30.
48. Memorandum of Conversation, 25 September 1953, *FRUS* 1952–1954, vol. IX pt. 1, pp. 1320–5.
49. Acting Secretary of State to Truman, 30 June 1952, *FRUS* 1952–1954, vol. IX pt. 1, pp. 953–9.
50. Department of State Position Paper, 5 May 1953, *FRUS* 1952–1954, vol. IX pt. 1, pp. 1188–99.
51. USARMA to DEPTAR, 16 August 1953, NA DA IN 297409.
52. Seelye, Amman, to Department of State, 15 October 1953, *FRUS* 1952–1954, vol. IX pt. 1, pp. 1358–9.
53. Department of State Press Release, 18 October 1953, Secretary of State's News Conference, 20 October 1953, *FRUS* 1952–1954, vol. IX pt. 1, 1367 and 1369–71.
54. Memorandum of Conversation, 26 October 1953, *FRUS* 1952–1954, vol. IX pt. 1, pp. 1384–7; Javits, *Javits*, p. 181; I. L. Kenen, *Israel's Defense Line* (Buffalo, 1981) pp. 103–5.
55. Department of State Press Release, 28 October 1953, *FRUS* 1951–1954, vol. IX pt. 1, 1390–91.
56. Byroade to Dulles, 7 April 1954, *FRUS* 1952–1954, vol. IX pt. 1, pp. 1502–5.
57. Tyler to Department of State, 17 April 1954, *FRUS* 1952–1954, vol. IX pt. 1, pp. 1518–20.
58. Memorandum of Conversation with President Eisenhower, 19 April 1954, *FRUS* 1952–1954, vol. IX pt. 1, pp. 1528–9; Byroade 'The Middle East in Perspective', 9 April 1954, *DSB*, vol. XXX, no. 774,

and 'Facing Realities in the Arab–Israeli Dispute', 1 May 1954, *DSB*, vol. XXV, no. 776.

59. Caffery to Dulles, 22 November 1954, NA 784A. 5274/11–2264.
60. Memorandum of Conversation, 30 November 1954, NA 674. 84A/11–3054; Memorandum of Conversation, 9 December 1954, NA 674. 84A/12–954.
61. M. Heikal, *Cutting the Lion's Tail* (London, 1986) pp. 78–82.
62. Information from a former CIA officer; Heikal, *Cutting the Lion's Tail*, pp. 88–92.
63. Heikal, *Cutting the Lion's Tail*, pp. 101–08.
64. Dwight D. Eisenhower, *Waging Peace* (New York, 1965) pp. 30–3.
65. Anthony Eden, *Full Circle* (London, 1960) p. 65.
66. Eisenhower, *Waging Peace*, pp. 664–5.
67. Eisenhower, *Waging Peace*, pp. 666–7; Eden, *Full Circle*, pp. 463–7.
68. A. Nutting, *No End of a Lesson* (London, 1967) pp. 66–71.
69. M. Dayan, *Story of my Life* (London, 1976) pp. 196–249.
70. S. Lloyd, *Suez 1956* (London, 1978) pp. 90–9; Nutting, *No End of a Lesson*, pp. 90–9; Dayan, *Story of my Life*, pp. 227–48.
71. Eisenhower, *Waging Peace*, p. 56; M. Dayan, *Diary of the Sinai Campaign* (London, 1966) pp. 68 and 74.
72. Information from a senior Israeli officer; Lloyd, *Suez 1956*, p. 193; Dayan, *Story of my Life*, p. 207.
73. Eisenhower, *Waging Peace*, p. 84.
74. Lloyd, *Suez 1956*, pp. 209 and 211; H. Finer, *Dulles Over Suez* (Chicago, 1964) pp. 428–9.
75. Eden, *Full Circle*, p, 458.
76. Eisenhower, *Waging Peace*, p. 98.
77. Eisenhower, *Waging Peace*, pp. 178–83; Message to Congress, 5 January 1957, Department of State Publication 6505.
78. Eisenhower, *Waging Peace*, pp. 185–6.
79. Private information; Kenen, *Israel's Defense Line*, p. 133–7; Radio and Television Address by President Eisenhower, 20 February 1957, Department of State Publication 6505.
80. Eisenhower, *Waging Peace*, p. 189; Abba Eban, *An Autobiography* (New York, 1977) pp. 244–58; G. Meir, *My Life* (London, 1975) p. 254; B. Urquart, *A Life in Peace and War* (London, 1987) pp. 135–8.
81. Eban, *Autobiography*, p. 233.

CHAPTER 4: THE TRANSFORMATION OF AMERICA'S MIDDLE EAST POLICY

1. Private information.
2. Private information; for the opposite viewpoint see B. Urquart, *A Life in Peace and War* (London, 1987) pp. 209–16.
3. Private information.
4. Private information; W. Quandt, *Decade of Decisions* (Berkeley and Los Angeles, 1977) pp. 39–43.

5. US Policy in the Near East Crisis, May 23 1967–April 23 1969, Department of State Publication 8269.
6. Private information.
7. Abba Eban, *An Autobiography* (New York, 1977) pp. 328–38.
8. Eban, *Autobiography*, pp. 339 and 348.
9. Eban, *Autobiography*, pp. 348–64; Quandt, *Decade of Decisions*, pp. 46–54.
10. See Summary of World Broadcasts, ME/2478/A/14.
11. Private information; Quandt, *Decade of Decisions*, pp. 54–9.
12. Private information.
13. Private information; James M. Ennes, *Assault on the Liberty* (New York, 1979) deals at length with the affair and its aftermath.
14. I. L. Kenen, *Israel's Defense Line* (Buffalo, 1981) p. 204.
15. Eban, *Autobiography*, pp. 425–6 and 436.
16. 'Principles for Peace in the Middle East', President Johnson, 19 June 1967, *DSB*, vol. LVII, no. 1463.
17. See Summary of World Broadcasts, ME/2559/A/1–3.
18. Lord Caradon, Arthur J. Goldberg, Mohamed H. El-Zayyat and Abba Eban, *U.N. Security Council Resolution 242: A Case Study in Diplomatic Ambiguity* (Washington, 1981) pp. 26–7.
19. Ibid., *passim*; UNO doc S/RES/242 (1967).
20. For Eban's worries over these events see his *Autobiography*, p. 438.
21. Kenen, *Israel's Defense Line*, pp. 218–20; Quandt, *Decade of Decisions*, pp. 66–7.
22. M. Skale, 'Jews, Ethnics and the American City', *Commentary*, April 1972.
23. E. Raab, 'The Deadly Innocences of American Jews', *Commentary*, December 1970; N. Glazer, 'The Exposed American Jew', *Commentary*, June 1975.
24. Statement of Thomas A. Dine before the Subcommittee on Europe and the Middle East of the Committee on Foreign Affairs, Foreign Assistance Legislation for Fiscal years 1984–85 (Part 3), p. 221.
25. In addition to the account by its founder, I. L. Kenen, in *Israel's Defense Line*, AIPAC's work has been analysed in E. Tivnan, *The Lobby* (New York, 1987) and criticised in P. Findley, *They Dare to Speak Out* (Westport, 1985).
26. Charles Mc. Mathias, Jr, 'Ethnic Groups and Foreign Policy', *Foreign Affairs*, Spring 1981.
27. Findley, *They Dare to Speak Out* p. 32.
28. For a useful discussion see *The Tower Commission Report* (New York, 1987) pp. 6–11.
29. Kissinger is best studied through his magisterial memoirs, *The White House Years* (New York, 1979) and *Years of Upheaval* (New York, 1982). See also M. and B. Kalb, *Kissinger* (Boston, 1974).
30. Kissinger, *White House Years*, p. 360.
31. Kissinger, *White House Years*, p. 373.
32. M. Riad, *The Struggle for Peace in the Middle East* (London, 1981) pp. 110–11.
33. *NYT*, 14 December 1969.

34. Richard Nixon, *RN* (New York, 1978) pp. 478–9; Kissinger, *White House Years*, pp. 373–7.
35. William Rogers, 'A Lasting Peace in the Middle East: An American View', 9 December 1969, *DSB*, vol. LXII, no. 1593.
36. *NYT*, 21 December 1969.
37. *NYT*, 11 December 1969.
38. Eban, *Autobiography*, p. 464.
39. *NYT*, 11 December 1969.
40. See M. Benvenisti, *Jerusalem The Torn City* (Jerusalem, 1976) pp. 243–4.
41. Quoted in *NYT*, 11 December 1969.
42. *NYT*, 12 December 1969.
43. Kenen, *Israel's Defense Line*, pp. 237–9.
44. Kissinger, *White House Years*, p. 376.

CHAPTER 5: CRISIS MANAGEMENT: NIXON, KISSINGER AND THE 1973 WAR

1. H. Kissinger, *The White House Years* (New York, 1979) pp. 1292–300.
2. Richard Nixon, *RN* (New York, 1978) pp. 915–23.
3. G. Meir, *My Life* (London, 1975) pp. 355–8.
4. H. Kissinger, *Years of Upheaval* (New York, 1982) pp. 465–7; Abba Eban, *An Autobiography* (New York, 1977) pp. 500–1; M. Golan, *The Secret Conversations of Henry Kissinger*, (New York, 1976) pp. 33–9.
5. Meir, *My Life*, pp. 358–9; M. Dayan, *Story of my Life* (London, 1976) pp. 463–5.
6. Kissinger, *Years of Upheaval*, pp. 450–5.
7. Kissinger, *Years of Upheaval*, pp. 460.
8. Sadat's Address to the People's Assembly, 16 October 1973, Summary of World Broadcasts, ME/4427/A/7–9.
9. Kissinger, *Years of Upheaval*, pp. 475–6 and 481–2.
10. Nixon, *RN*, p. 922; Kissinger, *Years of Upheaval*, pp. 491–6.
11. Dayan, *Story of my Life*, pp. 518–19.
12. E. N. Luttwak and W. Laqueur, 'Kissinger and the Yom Kippur War', *Commentary*, September 1974.
13. Nixon, *RN*, pp. 924–7; Kissinger, *Years of Upheaval*, pp. 507–15; Anwar el-Sadat, *In Search of Identity* (New York, 1977) pp. 256–60.
14. Statement of the Ministerial Council of OAPEC, 17 October 1973, Summary of World Broadcasts, ME/4428/A/1–2.
15. Private information.
16. Sadat, *In Search of Identity*, pp. 261–4.
17. Kissinger, *Years of Upheaval*, pp. 538–41; Golan, *Secret Conversations*, pp. 70–2.
18. Sadat, *In Search of Identity*, pp. 258–9; M. Heikal, *The Road to Ramadan* (London, 1976) pp. 231–8.
19. Kissinger, *Years of Upheaval*, pp. 545–55; UNO, UN doc. PR/75/29(1973).
20. G. Meir, *My Life*, p. 370.

21. Golan, *Secret Conversations*, pp. 82–7; Kissinger, *Years of Upheaval*, pp. 560–8; Abba Eban, *An Autobiography* (New York, 1977) pp. 531–3.
22. Kissinger, *Years of Upheaval*, p. 569; Golan, *Secret Conversations*, p. 86.
23. Kissinger, *Years of Upheaval*, p. 573.
24. Nixon, *RN*, p. 938.
25. Nixon, *RN*, pp. 937–42; Kissinger, *Years of Upheaval*, pp. 545–613.
26. Kissinger, *Years of Upheaval*, pp. 608–11; Golan, *Secret Conversations*, p. 88; T. Draper, 'The United States and Israel. Tilt in the Middle East?', *Commentary*, April 1975.

CHAPTER 6: STEP BY STEP

1. H. Kissinger, *Years of Upheaval* (New York, 1982) pp. 615–16.
2. Kissinger, *Years of Upheaval*, pp. 628–9.
3. Kissinger, *Years of Upheaval*, pp. 636–46.
4. Kissinger, *Years of Upheaval*, pp. 656–66.
5. Kissinger, *Years of Upheaval*, pp. 747–92; M. Golan, *The Secret Conversations of Henry Kissinger* (New York, 1976) p. 127.
6. Kissinger, *Years of Upheaval*, pp. 792–8; Abba Eban, *An Autobiography* (New York, 1977) pp. 547–55.
7. Kissinger, *Years of Upheaval*, pp. 799–805; Golan, *Secret Conversations*, pp. 146–7.
8. Kissinger, *Years of Upheaval*, pp. 809–53; E. R. E. Sheehan, *The Arabs, Israelis and Kissinger* (New York, 1976) pp. 109–12; Golan, *Secret Conversations*, pp. 158–71.
9. Sheehan, *The Arabs, Israelis and Kissinger*, pp. 111–12; Golan, *Secret Conversations*, pp. 168–9.
10. Kissinger, *Years of Upheaval*, pp. 1032–110; Golan, *Secret Conversations*, pp. 179–212; Sheehan, *The Arabs, Israelis and Kissinger*, pp. 116–28.
11. I am grateful to villagers of the Golan Heights for showing me some of the difficulties they have faced as a result of the disengagement agreement.
12. Kissinger, *Years of Upheaval*, pp. 1138–40; Golan, *Secret Conversations*, p. 217–20.
13. Richard Nixon, *RN* (New York, 1978) pp. 1010–18; Kissinger, *Years of Upheaval*, pp. 1123–42; Golan, *Secret Conversations*, pp. 221–7.
14. Golan, *Secret Conversations*, pp. 221–7.
15. R. Nixon, *No More Vietnams* (London, 1985) p. 185–94.
16. *NYT*, 20 March 1975.
17. Resolution 3236 (XXIX), 22 November 1974, UNO, doc. BR/74/55(1974).
18. *NYT*, 8 March 1975.
19. Golan, *Secret Conversations*, pp. 217–18.
20. Y. Rabin, *Memoirs* (Boston, 1979) p. 249.
21. Golan, *Secret Conversations*, p. 229.
22. *NYT*, 9 March 1975.

23. Golan, *Secret Conversations*, pp. 229–35.
24. *NYT*, 20 March 1975.
25. *NYT*, 24 April 1975; Rabin, *Memoirs*, p. 256.
26. *NYT*, 23 March 1975; Sheehan, *The Arabs, Israelis and Kissinger*, pp. 160–2.
27. *NYT*, 28 March 1975.
28. *NYT*, 1 April 1975.
29. *NYT*, 25 April 1975.
30. *NYT*, 2 April 1975.
31. *NYT*, 22, 25 and 27 April 1975.
32. *NYT*, 6 and 7 May 1975.
33. *NYT*, 2 and 3 May 1975.
34. *NYT*, 21 April 1975.
35. See the findings of L. Harris, 'Oil or Israel', *NYT*, 6 April 1975.
36. *NYT*, 1 April 1975.
37. *NYT*, 29 April 1975.
38. *NYT*, 27 April 1975.
39. *NYT*, 22 and 23 May 1975; W. Quandt, *Decade of Decisions* (Berkeley and Los Angeles, 1977) pp. 270–1.
40. Golan, *Secret Conversations*, p. 246.
41. *NYT*, 18 August 1975.
42. *NYT*, 20 August 1975.
43. For the text of the agreement see Department of State, Selected Documents No. 4. US Policy in the Middle East: November 1974–February 1976, and *NYT*, 2 September 1975. The accompanying Memoranda of Agreement may be found in *NYT*, 17 and 18 September 1975.
44. Ismail Fahmy, *Negotiating for Peace in the Middle East* (London, 1983) p. 168.

CHAPTER 7: CARTER: THE SEARCH FOR PEACE

1. Jimmy Carter, *The Blood of Abraham* (Boston, 1985) pp. 21–31: Jimmy Carter, *Keeping Faith: Memoirs of a President* (New York, 1982); *NYT*, 30 October 1977 and 15 January 1978.
2. G. W. Ball, *Diplomacy for a Crowded World* (London, 1976) p. 149.
3. For the impact of the Brookings report *Toward Peace in the Middle East*, see Z. Brzezinski, *Power and Principle* (New York, 1983). Vance's role is recounted in his *Hard Choices* (New York, 1983). William B. Quandt, *Camp David. Peacemaking and Politics* (Washington, 1986) stands in a class by itself as a blend of inside knowledge and scholarly analysis. H. H. Saunders, *The Other Walls* (Washington, 1985) reflects the degree of professionalism at the administration's disposal.
4. Carter, *Keeping Faith*, p. 277.
5. Vance, *Hard Choices*, pp. 167–8.
6. Ibid., *NYT*, 11 February 1977.

7. Carter, *Keeping Faith*, pp. 279–81; Brzezinski, *Power and Principle*, pp. 90–1; Y. Rabin, *Memoirs* (Boston, 1979) pp. 292–300; *NYT*, 10 March 1977.
8. Brzezinski, *Power and Principle*, p. 91; Quandt, *Camp David*, p. 48; *NYT*, 18 March 1977.
9. Carter, *Keeping Faith*, pp. 282–4; Brzezinski, *Power and Principle*, p. 93; *NYT*, 9 April 1977.
10. Private information.
11. Quandt, *Camp David*, p. 84; Carter, *Keeping Faith*, p. 290–1; Brzezinski, *Power and Principle*, pp. 99–101; Vance, *Hard Choices* pp. 18–84.
12. Vance, *Hard Choices*, pp. 184–90.
13. M. Dayan, *Breakthrough* (London, 1981) pp. 26–54 and 87–8; Carter, *Keeping Faith*, pp. 294–5; Quandt, *Camp David*, p. 139; see also Ismail Fahmy, *Negotiating for Peace in the Middle East* (London, 1983) for a hostile account of Sadat's move.
14. Carter, *Keeping Faith*, pp. 294–5; Vance, *Hard Choices*, pp. 194–5; Brzezinski, *Power and Principle*, p. 111; *NYT*, 17 November 1977.
15. *NYT*, 29 November 1977.
16. Brzezinski, *Power and Principle*, pp. 115–200; Carter, *Keeping Faith*, pp. 299–300; Vance, *Hard Choices*, pp. 198–200; Quandt, *Camp David*, pp. 155–8.
17. Vance, *Hard Choices*, p. 201; Quandt, *Camp David*, pp. 160–1; *NYT*, 5 and 6 January 1978.
18. Quandt, *Camp David*, pp. 162–76; Brzezinski, *Power and Principle*, pp. 240–4.
19. Carter, *Blood of Abraham*, pp. 96–7 and *Keeping Faith*, pp. 310–11; *NYT*, 16, 17 and 18 March 1978.
20. Carter, *Keeping Faith*, pp. 311–13; Brzezinski, *Power and Principle*, pp. 246–7; *NYT*, 24 March 1978.
21. Carter, *Keeping Faith*, p. 313; *NYT*, 20 October 1977.
22. Quandt, *Camp David*, p. 204.
23. Carter, *Keeping Faith*, pp. 391–3; Brzezinski, *Power and Principle*, pp. 246–7; *NYT*, 24 March 1978.
24. Carter, *Keeping Faith*, pp. 396–7.
25. M. I. Kamel, *The Camp David Accords* (London, 1986) pp. 363–9.
26. Private information.
27. Quandt, *Camp David*, pp. 247–51; Carter, *Keeping Faith*, p. 397; Vance, *Hard Choices*, p. 228; Dayan, *Breakthrough*, pp. 186–8.
28. E. W. Said, *The Question of Palestine* (New York, 1979) p. 192; also private discussions.
29. Vance, *Hard Choices*, pp. 229–31.
30. Carter, *Keeping Faith*, p. 413; Brzezinski, *Power and Principle*, p. 276; Quandt, *Camp David*, pp. 28–81.
31. Vance, *Hard Choices*, pp. 241–2; Brzezinski, *Power and Principle*, pp. 277–8; Quandt, *Camp David*, pp. 286–9.
32. Quandt, *Camp David*, pp. 291–2.
33. Carter, *Keeping Faith*, pp. 412–16; Brzezinski, *Power and Principle*, p. 279; Quandt, *Camp David*, pp. 298–302.

34.   Dayan, *Breakthrough*, pp. 275–7; Vance, *Hard Choices*, pp. 249–50.
35.   See Dayan, *Breakthrough*, Appendix 3, pp. 356–8.

CHAPTER 8: REAGAN, ISRAEL AND LEBANON

1.   AIPAC position papers; J. S. Peck, *The Reagan Administration and the Palestinian Question* (Washington, 1984) is useful for the administration's attitudes and policies.
2.   Alexander M. Haig Jr, *Caveat* (London, 1984) pp. 183–4.
3.   E. Tivnan, *The Lobby* (New York, 1987) pp. 135–61; private information.
4.   *NYT*, 5 and 6 June 1982.
5.   The best analysis of Israel's aims in the invasion of Lebanon may be found in S. Feldman and H. Rechnitz-Kijner, *Deception, Consensus and War: Israel in Lebanon* (Tel Aviv, 1984) pp. 10–24.
6.   *NYT*, 17 May 1982.
7.   *NYT*, 5 March 1982.
8.   *DSB*, July 1982, vol. 82, no. 2064; Haig, *Caveat*, pp. 317–35; Z. Schiff and E. Ya'ari, *Israel's Lebanon War* (New York, 1984) pp. 71–7.
9.   *NYT*, 10 June 1982.
10.   *NYT*, 8 June 1982.
11.   Haig, *Caveat*, pp. 38–9; *DSB*, September 1982, vol. 82, no. 2066.
12.   *NYT*, 14 June 1982.
13.   *NYT*, 30 June 1982.
14.   *NYT*, 21 June 1982.
15.   Haig, *Caveat*, pp. 341–2.
16.   *NYT*, 10 June 1982.
17.   *NYT*, 14 June 1982.
18.   *NYT*, 17 June 1982.
19.   *NYT*, 22 June 1982; Haig, *Caveat*, p. 344.
20.   *NYT*, 23 June 1982.
21.   *NYT*, 29 June 1982; Haig, *Caveat*, p. 344.
22.   *NYT*, 4, 5 and 6 July 1982.
23.   *NYT*, 1 July 1982.
24.   *NYT*, 7 July 1982.
25.   Ibid.
26.   *NYT*, 14 July 1982.
27.   Ibid.
28.   *NYT*, 11 July 1982.
29.   Schiff and Ya'ari, *Israel's Lebanon War*, p. 201.
30.   *NYT*, 11 July 1982.
31.   *NYT*, 2 August 1982.
32.   *NYT*, 3 August 1982; *DSB*, September 1982, vol. 82, no. 2066.
33.   *NYT*, 5 and 6 August 1982.
34.   *NYT*, 7 August 1982.
35.   *NYT*, 10 August 1982; Schiff and Ya'ari, *Israel's Lebanon War*, pp. 223–4.

36. *NYT*, 12, 13 and 29 August 1982; *DSB*, September 1982, vol. 82, no. 2066.
37. *NYT*, 13 August 1982; Schiff and Ya'ari, *Israel's Lebanon War*, pp. 225–6.
38. *NYT*, 14 August 1982.
39. *NYT*, 11 and 14 August 1982.
40. *DSB*, September 1982, vol. 82, no. 2066.
41. Schiff and Ya'ari, *Israel's Lebanon War*, pp. 233–6.
42. *Jerusalem Post*, 5 September 1982.
43. *Jerusalem Post*, 2 September 1982.
44. See note 40.
45. *Jerusalem Post*, 3 September 1982.
46. *NYT*, 7 and 9 September 1982.
47. *NYT*, 11, 12 and 24 September 1982; Jimmy Carter, *The Blood of Abraham* (Boston, 1985) p. 146.
48. *NYT*, 18 September 1982.
49. *NYT*, 24 September 1982.
50. *NYT*, 23 September 1982.
51. *NYT*, 30 September 1982; *DSB*, November 1982, vol. 82, no. 2068.
52. *NYT*, 6, 9, 10 and 11 April 1983; A. Hart, *Arafat* (London, 1984) p. 394.
53. *NYT*, 19–20 April 1983; B. Woodward, *Veil: The Secret Wars of the CIA 1981–1987* (New York, 1987) pp. 244–5.
54. *NYT*, 1 and 7 May 1983.
55. *NYT*, 10 May 1983.
56. Private information.
57. *NYT*, 8 February 1984.

CONCLUSION

1. Jimmy Carter, *Keeping Faith: Memoirs of a President* (New York, 1982).
2. See Hanna Siniora, 'An Analysis of the Current Revolt', *Journal of Palestine Studies*, vol. XVII, no. 3, Spring 1988.
3. Private information; J. W. McDonald Jr and D. B. Bendahmane (eds), *Conflict Resolution: Track Two Diplomacy* (Foreign Service Institute, Department of State, 1987); see also H. H. Saunders, *The Other Walls* (Washington, 1985).

Index